FEELING AND CLASSICAL PHILOLOGY

Nineteenth-century German classical philology underpins many structures of the modern humanities. In this book, Constanze Güthenke shows how a language of love and a longing for closeness with a personified antiquity have lastingly shaped modern professional reading habits, notions of biography, and the self-image of scholars and teachers. She argues that a discourse of love was instrumental in expressing the challenges of specialization and individual formation (*Bildung*), and in particular for the key importance of a Platonic scene of learning and instruction for imagining the modern scholar. The book is based on detailed readings of programmatic texts from, among others, Wolf, Schleiermacher, Boeckh, and Thiersch, to Dilthey, Wilamowitz, and Nietzsche. It makes a case for revising established narratives, but also for finding new value in imagining distance and an absence of nostalgic longing for antiquity.

CONSTANZE GÜTHENKE is Professor of Greek Literature at the University of Oxford and E. P. Warren Praelector in Classics at Corpus Christi College. Her main research interests lie in the field of antiquity after antiquity and in questions of the disciplinary shape of Classics and the history of scholarship. Her publications include *Placing Modern Greece: The Dynamics of Romantic Hellenism* (2008). She is a founding member of the Postclassicisms Collective (www.postclassicisms.org), and she is currently editor-in-chief of the *Classical Receptions Journal.*

CLASSICS AFTER ANTIQUITY

Editors
ALASTAIR BLANSHARD
University of Queensland
SHANE BUTLER
Johns Hopkins University
EMILY GREENWOOD
Yale University

Classics after Antiquity presents innovative contributions in the field of Classical Reception Studies. Each volume explores the methods and motives of those who, coming after and going after antiquity, have entered into a contest with and for the legacies of the ancient world. The series aims to unsettle, to provoke debate, and to stimulate a re-evaluation of assumptions about the relationship between Greek and Roman classical pasts and modern histories.

FEELING AND CLASSICAL PHILOLOGY

Knowing Antiquity in German Scholarship, 1770–1920

CONSTANZE GÜTHENKE

University of Oxford

CAMBRIDGE
UNIVERSITY PRESS

CAMBRIDGE
UNIVERSITY PRESS

University Printing House, Cambridge CB2 8BS, United Kingdom

One Liberty Plaza, 20th Floor, New York, NY 10006, USA

477 Williamstown Road, Port Melbourne, VIC 3207, Australia

314–321, 3rd Floor, Plot 3, Splendor Forum, Jasola District Centre,
New Delhi – 110025, India

79 Anson Road, #06–04/06, Singapore 079906

Cambridge University Press is part of the University of Cambridge.

It furthers the University's mission by disseminating knowledge in the pursuit of
education, learning, and research at the highest international levels of excellence.

www.cambridge.org
Information on this title: www.cambridge.org/9781107104235
DOI: 10.1017/9781316219331

First published 2020

Printed in the United Kingdom by TJ International Ltd. Padstow Cornwall

A catalogue record for this publication is available from the British Library.

ISBN 978-1-107-10423-5 Hardback

For my Princeton colleagues, regardless of distance

Contents

Contents

Series Editors' Preface

What would it be like to devote one's life to the study of an object and not feel anything towards it? Is that *humanly* (with all that word implies) possible? Does being in the world inevitably involve commitments of feeling towards it? Once one acknowledges this 'compulsion to feel', it becomes necessary for the critic to ask a number of questions: in what ways do we feel towards an object of study? How do those feelings construct (both in limiting and in freeing) that object? What discourses do those feelings facilitate? What transferences of emotion do they authorize? What disavowals attend those feelings? Do those feelings have a history? And what legacy do those feelings establish for those who come after? Importantly, it invites us to imagine alternative ways of relating to objects and to consider the levels of energy and self-mastery such alternatives demand.

In this book, Constanze Güthenke faces up to these questions by inviting us to revisit a terrain of intense emotion, German philological scholarship in the long nineteenth century. In doing so, she takes us back to the origins of our discipline and shows us how insensible we have been to the passions that animated it. Rather than presenting just the dry, dusty, overly rational, mechanistic scholarship of conventional stereotypes, she shows us a world riven by desires and projections of fantasy. The language of metaphor continually betrays authors who imagine themselves in an interpersonal relationship with antiquity. Crucially, it is a relationship in which the lover imagines the beloved as whole and perfect, a vision that it is literally written into being, assembled from the scraps and fragments of antiquity in such a manner that no gaps are left, no seams exposed. The fallout from this relationship is felt in diverse ways. We see it most obviously in the various forms of biography (antique, scholarly, self-fashioned) that emerge in this period and which still dominate the discipline, as well as only partially suppressed anxieties about the material absences in the survival of classical antiquity and the impossibility of reciprocity between scholars and the inanimate objects of their desire.

This book situates these emotions within the broader intellectual movements that had been sweeping Europe, showing how they emerged from the confluence of strands of thinking that have been developing for centuries. Economic, political, social, theological, and educational structures aligned to bring philology and its adherents into existence. None of the great father-figures of philology proved immune to the lure of recreating a seemingly intact and personified antiquity with which to commune. Readers will encounter in this work many familiar figures – Wilamowitz, Wolf, Schleiermacher, Schlegel, Boeckh, and Nietzsche – all made unfamiliar by the critical lens that Güthenke adopts. Also discussed within this work are a number of figures who deserve to be much better known in the Anglophone world of Classics. Her discussion of the work of Johann Georg Hamann firmly establishes his position as a figure with whom anybody who wishes to understand the history of our discipline needs to engage. As Güthenke shows, Hamann's 'wild, often formally experimental, parodic, and highly allusive writings' pre-empted many of the key discussions that would come to dominate the field of philology.

One of the most compelling aspects of this book is the way it examines epistemological structures of longing. Here Plato and his concomitant erotics of pedagogy played an important role. Güthenke shows how philology returns again and again to the figures of Socrates and Alcibiades. Pygmalion may have been an aspirational figure for his ability to bring dead stone to life, but it was through the figure of Alcibiades that the serious thinking about the practices and ethics of education was done. It is here that contemporary readers will find the politics of this work most urgent. The models established in the nineteenth century still hold tremendous sway today. The legacy of a foundational academic culture in which scholarship was construed as a fundamentally erotic process and the classroom as a space for amatory exploration has consequences. This is especially the case when the model you are wrestling with is Socrates and Alcibiades. There are dozens of ways of rehearsing this relationship – and as this book shows, German philology tried out most of them – but the least likely way is as a meeting of equals. This erotics is almost always hierarchical. It requires all to participate in a shared regime of yearning.

This book is a startling work of intellectual history that exposes classical philology's metaphorical unconscious and, in the process, strikes at the heart of contemporary debates about the embodiment of knowledge, and the place of affect, emotions, and the regulation of desire within the academy. At the same time, it makes an important contribution to reimagining models for classical scholarship and pedagogy. In giving us a study that clarifies the intellectual genealogy and governing metaphors of the discipline, Constanze Güthenke also offers us a powerful provocation for the future as we negotiate the disintegration of the classical canon as fixed corpus and the plural and divergent forms of knowledge that follow in its wake.

ALASTAIR BLANSHARD
SHANE BUTLER
EMILY GREENWOOD
Editors, Classics after Antiquity

Preface

At a time when scholars are being challenged to rethink questions of institutional hierarchies and the structures that may enable the exploitation of inequality and asymmetry, there is urgency in scrutinizing what it means to belong to an academic community and all that this entails in terms of ethics, identity, and sensibility. To call out imbalanced personal relations in institutions of learning may at first look extrinsic to actual scholarship; but when it comes to how human emotions and human behaviour are at work in academic life, it matters how we express scholarly affects and how a language of desire functions in what we do and what we write.

This book offers an exploration of German academic practice and academic prose in the long nineteenth century through the lens of a language of love and intimacy. German academic prose is now largely remembered mostly for its dryness and technicality, and not for its rhetorical flourishes. This book aims not only to recover this forgotten language in a critical mode but also to trace the way in which this language of love continues to be active and how it has shaped scholarly discourse in the Anglophone world as well, both in Classics and in the humanities more broadly that rely on the institutional structures and institutional memory of philology. These metaphors, for all their mutability, are ingrained and persistent.

The 'erotics of pedagogy', the fact that teaching and learning situations generate their own complex forms of intimacy, is currently invoked more than usual on a wide spectrum of both affirmative and critical modes, and the discussion can draw on a range of voices: from George Steiner's hieratic *Lessons of the Masters* (2003) and its praise of the emotionally charged teaching relationship, to Yung In Chae's punchy online editorial 'A Myth on Campus: No, Education Is Not Erotic' (*Eidolon* 2018); and from Mary Beard, who in a *Times Literary Supplement* review of *The Dictionary of British Classicists* (2005) raised the history of harassment, but also reflected more unapologetically on the erotics of teaching, to

Leo Bersani and Adam Phillips' consideration of an 'impersonal narcissism' in their collaborative essay *Intimacies* (2008). It is important to acknowledge that the work of the mind is also work done by real people interacting with each other, creating its own intimacies, affects, and projections; but it is also worth discussing to what extent the language in which we acknowledge that fact has its own genealogy of tropes. What this book hopes to give is a historical perspective that shows how deeply integral to the developing discourse of Classics as a discipline this rhetoric has been, often relying on ancient tropes and underpinning modern ones. At the same time, this study does not aim to recover feeling as a component of institutional structures in order to endorse it in a new light. I offer some form of 'clarification' of such tropes as *eros*, feeling, and individuality and seek to identify how persistently interwoven they have been with disciplinary thinking, for better or worse.

In Classics, we continue to operate to a considerable extent within a tradition of imagining antiquity as if it were an individual writ large, making it a reflection of our own individuality. A case in point is the expectation of exclusivity, which underpins the familiar worry that if one studies more than one thing, let alone more than one antiquity, then this risks a lack of either commitment or thorough care for the separate objects of study; it persists in the tradition of making scholars' biographies and their 'lives and works' the central parameter of an internal historical view of the discipline; it is still visible in anxiety over the loss of a strong sense of individual authorship and style, ancient or modern; and it comes through in the continuing emphasis on and valuation of the vocational imperatives of passion and commitment. One can be extremely critical of one's subject matter, it is assumed, but one cannot be passionate about one's profession and academic work without also being passionate about the *content* of study. There is nothing wrong with commitment – but is commitment best glossed as the desire to come as close as possible to the subject matter at hand and to know it intimately and exclusively? The ultimate provocation in Classics would presumably be not to love one's subject, or to do so only provisionally, strategically, and intermittently.

The language of longing has remained durable in giving expression to scholarly attention that is, after all, predicated on a lack of reciprocity. If understanding a historically distant world and its objects is what we do, then absence, incomplete knowledge, and lack of reciprocity have been fundamental to this labour. The rhetoric of interpretive desire, of wanting to know the other as fully as possible, has served well to compensate for this one-sidedness. This book shows that such a language, linked to a contemporary discourse of love and the continuing relevance of a Platonic language of aspiration and pedagogy, allowed the rise of a new, professional discipline throughout the long nineteenth century. Whether we look up to an erotics of pedagogy, or down on its continuing use as a trope, I hope that a historical analysis of its component parts can help us to ask more pointedly whether there are also alternative ways and images to harness the potential of a language of intimacy, of closeness as much as of distance, and to think through ongoing change in non-nostalgic and non-exclusive ways.

Acknowledgements

This is a book that sets out to critique the image of the individual scholar studying a personified past. For that reason, I am all the more aware that this project has been animated by a range of scholarly environments and scholarly feelings, by colleagues, collaborations, friendships, and, indeed, love. This book is the result of movement, some of it gradual, some of it sudden, some intentional and some serendipitous. This includes movement between disciplines, disciplinary and national cultures, and stages of professional and personal life, quite aside from a very large number of flights, transatlantic and trans-European.

In many ways, it began with a manoeuvre to turn questions about my disciplinary environment and its practices and rhetoric into a main research project. It was written across a dozen years during which I came to inhabit fully the profile of a classicist. Initially trained in Classics, with doctoral work in the study of Modern Languages and Literature in the UK, I was hired by a Classics department in the United States. At Princeton, I settled back into being a professional classicist in a country and within an institutional structure that were both new to me. With a joint appointment in Hellenic Studies, and with a strong humanities community around me, I felt encouraged and enabled to come to look at my own disciplinary situation obliquely and not to take habits for granted, while still working within that same discipline every day. The book was finished in Oxford, where the trajectories and customs again differ and follow very much their own rhythm. There, and especially so at Corpus Christi College, I have had the great good fortune to be part of a Classics community of colleagues and of students who take pride in asking questions about why and how classicists do what they do.

The joint thinking and writing with my colleagues on the Postclassicisms project over the last few years has allowed me to push the boat out even further than I would have thought when I started the project. It's been an education, and it's been fun, too. Colleagues in many locales have discussed parts of this project with me over the years in, among other places, Princeton, Chicago, Boston, Cambridge, Oxford, London, Paris, Berlin, Athens, and Geneva. Thank you especially to Yelena Baraz, Daniel Barbu, Joshua Billings, Alastair Blanshard, Wiebke Denecke, Jaś Elsner, Kristin Gjesdal, Simon Goldhill, Tony Grafton, Barbara Graziosi, Katherine Harloe, Stephen Harrison, Brooke Holmes, Joshua Katz, Colin King, Tom Laqueur, Miriam Leonard, John Ma, Glenn Most, Hindy Najman, Damien Nelis, Thomas Poiss, Jim Porter, Josephine Quinn, Stefan Rebenich, Chris Stray, Jim Tatum, Anna Uhlig, Mathura Umachandran, Phiroze Vasunia, Tim Whitmarsh, Leah Whittington, and Froma Zeitlin.

I would like to acknowledge the financial and institutional resources afforded by a John Maclean Jr. Presidential University Preceptorship at Princeton; a Research Associateship at King's College, Cambridge; a stint as Professeure Invitée of the Maison d'Histoire at the University of Geneva; an invitation to the Kosmos summer school on Globalized Classics at the Humboldt University of Berlin; and an award from the REF Strategic Support Fund given by Oxford University, which allowed me to finish the manuscript.

A much earlier version of Chapter 1 was published as 'The Potter's Daughter's Sons: German Classical Scholarship and the Language of Love circa 1800', *Representations* 109.1 (2010), pp. 122–47; select materials in Chapter 4 appeared in '"Enthusiasm Dwells Only in Specialization": Classical Philology and Disciplinarity in Nineteenth-Century Germany', in B. Elman and S. Pollock (eds.), *World Philology* (Harvard University Press, 2014), pp. 304–38; and some materials in Chapters 5 and 6 were previously published in 'Emotion und Empathie in der Interpretationspraxis der Klassischen Philologie um 1900', in A. Albrecht and O. Krämer (eds.), *Theorien, Methoden und Praktiken des Interpretierens* (Freiburg, 2015), pp. 145–58; '"Lives" as Parameter: The Privileging of Ancient Lives As a Category of Research around 1900', in R. Fletcher and J. Hanink (eds.), *Creative Lives: New Approaches to Ancient Intellectual Biography* (Cambridge University Press, 2016), pp. 29–48; and 'After Exemplarity: A Map of Plutarchan Scholarship', in P. Mack and J. North (eds.), *The Afterlife of Plutarch*, *BICS Supplement* (2018), 179–91. All materials have been significantly revised and rewritten.

Joshua Billings, Jaś Elsner, Kristin Gjesdal, Simon Goldhill, Katherine Harloe, Miriam Leonard, Hindy Najman, Christopher Stray, and Anna Uhlig all read complete versions of the manuscript and gave generous and helpful comments. Thank you for your insights and for your friendship.

I owe a big debt of gratitude to the series editors of *Classics after Antiquity*, Alastair Blanshard, Emily Greenwood, and Shane Butler. I could not have asked for better and more careful and sympathetic editors. They also kept reminding me that short sentences and substantial thought can go very well together. Quite right. Michael Sharp and his editorial team at Cambridge University Press have steered the project not just with professional skill and experience but with patience and good sense.

Gavin Salam and Lucien Salam, our son, gave me love and time and trusted me to see the book through, including its very long tail end (and without the lake in Geneva, the tail end would likely have been even longer). Having a child confirmed to me that trying to understand someone is as challenging as it is amazing. Above all, it is always completely provisional. I thank you both, with all my heart.

Introduction
Feeling and Philology

'Where a thing can be ascertained and proved, and the instances counted, I go to the German; where it is a question of feeling, no.' Thus Gilbert Murray's verdict on the relative merits of German and British classical scholarship, in an account of German 'Kultur' for the general reader, to which Murray contributed a section on the study of the ancient world, that is to say to the field that was in 1915 arguably still tantamount to 'German scholarship' *tout court*.[1] 'Germans do not write Greek verses,' he continues, 'they write books on Greek "Metrik". They aim more at knowing; we at feeling and understanding.'[2] Murray readily acknowledges that German scholarship was at one point based on a similar notion of a classical and essentially gentlemanly education as a basis for all future literary, learned, or professional practice, 'but it would seem', he continues, 'that in England, the study of the classics has conserved to a greater extent this general and foundational character; in Germany it was either dropped or became professional'.[3] Murray's analysis exemplifies two standard narratives that still animate the perception of German classical scholarship: that it amounts to the advocacy and ultimate victory of rational method, scienticity, and data collection over imagination, fluency, style, and good taste; and that the concept of *Bildung*, of the education and formation of the cultural self that marked German idealist humanism and classicism of the late eighteenth and early nineteenth centuries, fell away and gave way to a sterile dominance of institutionalized historicist tedium – well-meaning, compendious, hyper-specialized, authoritative to the point of authoritarian, and essentially a victim of its own success.

The aim of this book is likewise twofold: to offer a historical and textual analysis of the organizing imagery and metaphors of classical scholarship; and to encourage sensitivity to the way those metaphors continue to have

[1] G. Murray, 'German Scholarship', *Quarterly Review* 223 (1915), pp. 330–9, here p. 333.
[2] *Ibid.*, p. 333.   [3] *Ibid.*, p. 334.

an afterlife in the practices of Classics as a discipline. I seek to show that the
energies and structures of 'feeling' were an instrumental part of the self-
perception of German classical scholarship and its programmatic thinking
in the long nineteenth century. As a central, organizing trope of scholarship, the parameters, scenes, and metaphors of the individual and its
Bildung or self-formation, and of the feeling or desire directed at antiquity
exerted influence well beyond Murray. Accordingly, in addition to offering
a broadly historical investigation, this book insists that the use of
a language and rhetoric of feeling and of desire had strong continuities in
the hermeneutic and disciplinary profile of Classics, in the way classical
scholars conceived – and conceive – of what they were doing and what they
were looking for. Classical scholarship is deeply preoccupied with parts and
wholes. This it shares with other branches of knowledge during the rise of
disciplines in the long nineteenth century. But for a field whose objects are
so obviously and for the most part partial and fragmented, it is striking how
much this field has built its world on an image of wholeness, and on the
dream – or fantasy – of being able to put fragments together to see, once
more, a complete outline. Wholeness requires imagination and representation, and the central claim of this book is that German scholarship
articulated its relationship with the classical, and especially the classical
Greek past, as a quasi-personal relationship with a personified entity,
a relationship as if with another individual. This relationship was reflected
in a language of a longed-for and yet sublimated proximity and a related
language of empathy and experience, a language that, at the same time,
acknowledged anxiety about the fact that complete comprehension was
impossible and had to remain out of reach. If classical scholarship imagined
the ancient past as a living being, invested with the characteristics and life
story of a human figure, this made the figure of the modern scholar its
counterpart. The object of study is the other through which a scholarly 'I'
can be circumscribed. This 'I' may not be strongly expressed – German
academic discourse famously avoids the first person, though I will show
that this is also not always the case – but the notion of individuality at stake
in the knowledge of antiquity underpinned a large part of disciplinary self-
reflection.

Such language is not self-evident; neither is it universal or placed outside
history. Instead, it has modelled interpretive strategies within the field in
particular ways in different historical moments. It is, therefore, appropriate
to leverage a historical analysis to ask how the tropes identified in this study
shed light on the context of a discipline (Classics) that has always had
a strong self-historicizing imperative. Still, this is not a book that wants to

excavate and make visible again the 'feeling' at work in German classical philology so as to affirm its libidinal, experiential structures and potential. The aim here is not to conjure up the personal voice of that scholarship. My objective is, ultimately, not so much to recover as to disrupt a discourse of closeness, feeling, and longing that has underpinned philological interpretation and what we expect from it. Also, I want to suggest ways in which this language and its classical scenes are open to being rethought in ways that de-emphasize, or reconfigure the epistemological desires they continue to project; in short, to advocate a rethinking of what it means to maintain distance. This book attempts to excavate some of the history and structures of a language of desire and longing for a personified antiquity; at the same time, it tries to resist the expectation that this is the language we should choose as a matter of fact to validate and continue to use for building our self-understanding as classical scholars, now that we have unearthed it. As a historical study, this is an investigation of the language and epistemological mechanisms of attachment, and it relies both on the theories of a 'discourse of love' and on a form of *Begriffsgeschichte*, a history of concepts, to deliver this analysis. As an exploration of the 'metaphors we live by', to borrow Lakoff and Johnson's phrase, and of the metaphors we research by, it is a suggestion to keep worrying the templates of closeness and distance we have at our disposal and to keep considering their implications.[4]

The Meanings of One-Sidedness

What characterizes the nineteenth century as a whole, certainly in the German context but arguably well beyond it, is the strong interaction of several strands that combine in the production of knowledge, both in classical scholarship and in cognate fields. Those strands are, in very abbreviated form (and covered in much greater detail below): organicism as a guiding metaphor; the importance of individuality, that is to say the individual proposed as a privileged creator of meaning; *Bildung* (the

---

[4] In its desire to uncover historical structures of the rhetoric of philology and suggest modifications of it going forward, this project finds some affinities with a recent study by Yii-Jan Lin, *The Erotic Life of Manuscripts: New Testament Textual Criticism and the Biological Sciences* (Oxford University Press, 2016), which came to my attention as this present book was almost finished. Lin, who understands the 'erotic' to indicate the aspects of gift-giving, circulation, and exchange in the study and constitution of manuscripts, sets out to examine the biological, genealogical, and racial language that marked Biblical textual scholarship and suggests, ultimately, that taking those metaphors seriously should also encourage us to give fresh and critical thought to integrating alternative concepts of the biological sciences now, such as hybridity, the cyborg, or the rhizome.

formation of the self), conceived both as cultural goal and as historical process; biography and autobiography as the narrative form thought best to capture the developmental aspect of *Bildung* and individuality; disciplinarization and institutionalization, that is, the formulation of an agreed set of scholarly expectations and methods and their inclusion within an institutional framework; and, finally, Romantic notions of sentiment and sensibility as sources of knowledge above and beyond rational understanding.

The emergence of classical scholarship as a discipline connects to the rise of the secular university as well as the research university in the eighteenth and nineteenth centuries. The profile of the professional scholar, who is also a professional teacher, is hard to imagine without the top-down support of political administrations – especially the Prussian state – for a model of education that put the individual subject and its training or *Bildung* at centre stage. The 'seminar' had been a site of teacher training but increasingly was also one of research activity. Since the mid-eighteenth century, it had moved from pedagogy and theology to include philology as a free-standing unit. Across the many German states that made up the political and institutional landscape, knowledge of classical antiquity was channelled into an increasingly institutionalized discipline: this signalled a move from knowing ancient things through older forms of transmission, imitation, and erudition towards a newer *Altertumswissenschaft*, or scientific knowledge of antiquity, in the process shifting the monopoly of interpretation away from theology and jurisprudence. Philology, meaning classical philology, was not so much 'invented' at the time as it emerged from a relatively neglected life as an auxiliary branch of knowledge to achieve increased autonomy and to become the main, privileged provider of education for civil servants and other professionals.[5]

The programmatic awareness of historical distance, at the same time, rendered the object of interpretation both other and related to the self-reflexive individual who studied it. Around 1800, classical scholarship's model of itself was informed by the broader contemporary, Romantic

---

[5] R. S. Leventhal, 'The Emergence of Philological Discourse in the German States, 1770–1810', *Isis* 77 (1986), pp. 243–60 is still an excellent overview; as is A. Grafton, 'Polyhistor into Philolog', *History of Universities* 3 (1983), pp. 159–92; also D. Kopp and Nikolaus Wegmann, '"Die deutsche Philologie, die Schule und die Klassische Philologie". Zur Karriere einer Wissenschaft um 1800', in J. Fohrmann and W. Voßkamp (eds.), *Sonderheft der deutschen Vierteljahrsschrift für Literaturwissenschaft und Geistesgeschichte zur Wissenschaftsgeschichte der deutschen Literaturwissenschaft*, 61 (1987), pp. 123*–51*. For an excellent critical narrative of the 'invention' of philology, especially in the figure of F. A. Wolf, see K. Harloe, *Winckelmann and the Invention of Antiquity. History and Aesthetics in the Age of Altertumswissenschaft* (Oxford University Press, 2013).

language of sentimental *Bildung*, of communication between individuals, and of the cultivation of particular emotional attachments. It is at this juncture that figurations of antiquity, specifically the tendency to imagine the ancient past as a quasi-human figure vis-à-vis its observer, influence conceptions of modernity. Scholarship is both informed by and helps to shape this process. The neohumanism of Humboldt's generation focused on the individual and their *Bildung*, a preoccupation that is echoed in the self-understanding of the developing discipline of classical scholarship: both the broader neohumanism and its institutional articulation elaborate a vision of antiquity as a coherent, organic self, a quasi-person and singular personality in its own right. Koselleck, in his work on the modern understanding of history as 'temporalized', has argued that the eighteenth century saw, in its semantic usage, a shift from 'histories' to 'History' with a capital H, part of a general phenomenon of such 'singularizations': histories and History, freedoms or liberties and Freedom, and so on. One could also include here a shift (though he does not do so himself) from 'the ancients' in the plural towards a newly prevalent use of a single 'Antiquity' as the favoured term.[6] It was this Antiquity as an organic body, though, that ideally reflected the modern individual, linking both through the notion of *Bildung*. And so, the metaphor of development was projected onto antiquity and hence 'legible'; the very act of identifying it, and thus of 'understanding' antiquity, itself then helped to constitute and define the modern individual in their own act of formation as well as, by extension, the pursuit of modern scholarship.

Throughout the nineteenth century, classical scholarship achieved and held on to its dominant position as a discipline that modelled interpretive behaviour, historical-philological method, and scientific standards of expertise and practice in view of comprehending cultures past and present.[7] This simultaneous investment in expert specialization and in comprehensive, complete understanding of a whole out of its numerous,

---

[6] R. Koselleck, '*Historia Magistra Vitae*: Über die Auflösung des Topos im Horizont neuzeitlich bewegter Geschichte', in H. Braun and M. Riedel (eds.), *Natur und Geschichte: Karl Löwith zum 70. Geburtstag* (Stuttgart, 1967), pp. 196–219; on the move from antiquities to Antiquity, see also Harloe, *Winckelmann and the Invention of Antiquity*.

[7] For the rise and professionalization of classical philology, see the still instructive F. Paulsen, *Geschichte des Gelehrten Unterrichts auf den Deutschen Schulen und Universitäten vom Ausgang des Mittelalters bis zur Gegenwart. Mit besonderer Rücksichtnahme auf den klassischen Unterricht* (Leipzig: Veit, 1885); L. O'Boyle, 'Klassische Bildung und soziale Struktur in Deutschland zwischen 1800 und 1848', *Historische Zeitschrift* 207 (1967), 584–608; R. S. Turner, 'Historicism, Kritik, and the Prussian Professorate, 1790–1840', in M. Bollack, T. Lindken, and H. Wisman (eds.), *Philologie und Hermeneutik im 19. Jahrhundert II* (Göttingen: Vandenhoeck & Ruprecht, 1983), pp. 450–77; Grafton, 'Philolog'; A. J. La Vopa, 'Specialists against Specialization: Hellenism as a Professional

scattered fragments came with the acknowledgement that a certain one-sidedness (*Einseitigkeit*) was maybe the biggest asset and the biggest risk of the disciplined knowledge of antiquity: the one-sidedness that signals focus, expert knowledge, and quality, but also the one-sidedness that emphasized scientific method and technical practices to the exclusion of the non-rational, non-teachable, not easily grasped elements of feeling, insight, talent, tact, or intuitive experience. The anxiety over this kind of one-sidedness, as I argue, matched the worry over a different kind of one-sidedness or asymmetry: namely that implied in the fundamentally non-reciprocal relationship with the past when the past is imagined as a human individual. It is this 'one-sidedness' that comes to the fore in the insistent return to figures and constellations that address the issue of a lack of reciprocity. Some of these figures and scenes are ancient templates that are repeatedly read in the light of contemporary formulations of interpersonal relationships and the paradigm of love as key to understanding the other, an other that always possibly remains unavailable, elusive, and beyond comprehension. In this way, the search for complete, perfect knowledge becomes correlated to a process of epistemological longing and an erotics of knowledge. This nexus can, on the one hand, map onto the concerns of the role of feeling in the precarious knowledge of self and other in late eighteenth-century notions of *Bildung*; but it can, on the other hand, also model the scholarly striving for completeness and comprehensiveness as forms of comprehension, and at the same time buffer worries over one-sidedness as a lack of feeling and a lopsided prioritizing of science. It can, therefore, communicate with the challenges of idealism as much as those of historicism, connecting with a discourse of *Bildung* as much as of scientific specialization. Feeling, or *Gefühl*, was from the mid-eighteenth century onwards already a term that was associated with mental and intellectual activity as much as with

Ideology in German Classical Studies', in G. Cocks and K. Jarausch (eds.), *German Professions: 1800–1950* (Oxford University Press, 1990), pp. 27–45; T. Ziolkowski, *German Romanticism and Its Institutions* (Princeton University Press, 1990), ch. 5, 'The University: Model of the Mind', pp. 218–308; S. Marchand, *Down from Olympus: Archaeology and Philhellenism in Germany, 1750–1970* (Princeton University Press, 1996); W. Clark, *Academic Charisma and the Origins of the Research University* (Chicago University Press, 2006); C. Güthenke, '"Enthusiasm Dwells Only in Specialization". Classical Philology and Disciplinarity in Nineteenth-Century Germany', in B. Elman and S. Pollock (eds.), *World Philology* (Harvard University Press, 2014), pp. 304–38; J. Turner, *Philology: The Forgotten Origins of the Modern Research University* (Princeton University Press, 2014); C. Wellmon, *Organizing Enlightenment: Information Overload and the Invention of the Modern Research University* (Baltimore: Johns Hopkins University Press, 2015), esp. chapters 8 ('Berlin, Humboldt, and the Research University') and 9 ('The Disciplinary Self and the Virtues of the Philologist').

senses and perception.[8] Given this component of rationality, and its own closeness to intellectual processes, *Gefühl* was already marked as an instrument and, at the same time, an effect of *Bildung*. The rhetoric of attachment to a personified antiquity as the object of study, and of longing for it, helped to define but also to reaffirm and to offset the constitutive tensions of the *Wissenschaft* in *Altertumswissenschaft*.

Pygmalion and Alcibiades

One such figure who is frequently invoked in discussions of late eighteenth-century cultural classicism is Pygmalion. Pygmalion encapsulates the vivid appreciation of art, sensuality, and materiality, but also offers the chance to address the risks of solipsism, self-centeredness, and 'errors of reading'. There are some insights to be taken from Pygmalion, but it is rather a second figure who turns out to play a more decisive role in this study: that of Plato's Alcibiades and his relationship to the pedagogical and erotic model of knowledge that emerges in the Platonic dialogues. If Pygmalion can signal an error of reading, then Alcibiades can help to reflect on the errors of philological reading and on the possibilities that arise from those errors.

The myth of Pygmalion making the crafted sculpture of a beloved woman come to life is itself a personification of the act of personification, a figure of *prosopopoeia*: the address of and the giving human voice to what is out of reach, absent, dead, or inanimate. Personification can have wide rhetorical and epistemological use, as a means of understanding and giving expression to the engagement with what defies or exceeds present, human encounter. In the context of discussing the modern novel, the literary critic J. Hillis Miller offered a powerful reading of Pygmalion as the figure who exposes precisely the vulnerability and the structural pitfalls of almost any act of personification, its simultaneously stabilizing and destabilizing effect, especially when personification relies on desire as a factor in making that which is absent come alive.[9] Miller treats Pygmalion's act of

---

[8] U. Frevert, 'Gefühle definieren: Begriffe und Debatten aus drei Jahrhunderten', in U. Frevert (ed.), *Gefühlswissen: eine lexikalische Spurensuche der Moderne* (Frankfurt am Main: Campus, 2011), pp. 9–39; republished as 'Defining Emotions: Concepts and Debates over Three Centuries', in U. Frevert (ed.), *Emotional Lexicons: Continuity and Change in the Vocabulary of Feeling* (Oxford University Press 2014), pp. 1–31.

[9] J. H. Miller, *Versions of Pygmalion* (Harvard University Press, 1990). For a more recent account of the question about inherent illusion that the figure of Pygmalion raises, see V. I. Stoichita, *The Pygmalion Effect: From Ovid to Hitchcock* (Chicago University Press, 2008), which expands the inquiry well beyond the literary medium.

prosopopoeia, as described by Ovid (*Met.* 10.243–97), as the starting point for all later Pygmalionesque figures, given that repeated metamorphosis is essentially about the concatenation of literalized metaphors. For Miller, Ovid's stories in general suggest the power of aberrant figurative language (insofar as tropes are turned into realities and wishes become fulfilled, revealing their more fearful elements in the process); they give narrative shape to the logic that any such materialization of desire and wish fulfillment is never completely paid off as the stories inevitably reach over into the textual body of always another tale.

Pygmalion, though, is particularly resonant when it comes to the strategies of personifying antiquity that are at work in classical scholarship. For one thing, in Ovid's version, he is not just bringing to life a statue, but a statue of Galatea specifically, not an anonymous figure, but a figuration of, and the realization of a figure from Greek mythology and Greek literature.[10] From Ovid's perspective, Pygmalion is already himself engaged with the reception of antiquity, and with the challenge of making earlier textualities come alive – and so, Ovid may already have bequeathed later readers, reading through Pygmalion, a model for thinking about the paradoxes and category errors of coming and being close to a Greek past. In addition, the Pygmalion story overturns a central supposition of metamorphosis. Galatea, the statue that comes to life through Pygmalion's desire, is not so much an other, caught in the in-between-life-and-death state of metamorphosis that marks her as irreducibly separate, as she is already intimately connected to the self: Pygmalion crafted her in the first place out of his imagination. Miller is keen to address the uneasy fact that Pygmalion, in his autoerotic undertaking, appears unexpectedly successful in his act of transforming a statue into a living human being, and that he ostensibly escapes the retribution inherent in metamorphoses, with no disaster befalling anyone. Within the Ovidian chain of tales, the punishment is merely delayed to the grandson and great-granddaughter of Pygmalion and Galatea, Cinyras and Myrrha, and their tale of incest which follows directly upon that of Pygmalion (*Met.* 10.298–355). Their child, born out of the trunk of a myrrh tree, is Adonis, for whom, in turn, the goddess Venus falls, exposing herself to the human pain of loss. This, for Miller, is an even stronger indicator that the category mistake implied in Pygmalion's act of personification does, after all, have consequences and

---

[10] Ovid does not name her as Galatea, though the subsequent artistic tradition did. Galatea may well be a generic name, but the Galatea familiar from Theocritus's *Idyll* 11 was certainly a meaningful Hellenistic reference point within Ovid's literary and cultural environment.

points directly to what is at stake in all acts of personification: namely, the experience of human loss, amplified when, in the case of Aphrodite, it is visited upon a goddess whose defining feature is desire.

For Miller, Pygmalion's knowing illusion is symptomatic of a fundamental 'error in reading' that occurs in the act of personification, of 'treat[ing] something dead as if it were alive', an error that is essential to all those literalized allegories and 'that can be exposed by another act of reading. Whether this knowledge can be gained without repeating the error that the knowledge warns against remains to be seen.'[11] This suggests that acts of critical reading and rereading, in short, acts of philological practice, are tangled up in the deceptive stability inherent in the figure of *prosopopoeia*, of an ongoing substitution that keeps being repeated in an ambivalent cycle of comfort and disillusionment: a suggestion that is also a prompt to ask where the blind spots are in the figurative language with which classical scholarship has operated. *Prosopopoeia* operates by addressing the distant and unknown, a feature that makes it a fruitful concept in analysing representations of the distant, unavailable past and thus goes straight to a central challenge for scholarship and its self-conception. This is not to propose, along the lines of Miller, a poetological, deconstructive reading of scholarly writing; instead, it is to draw attention to the structural fallibility, or illusion, of personification and make such awareness part of a historical examination of the framework of nineteenth-century classical scholarship and its discourses.

One of the fundamental challenges of understanding antiquity through an act of personification is the essential lack of reciprocity that is captured in this act of substitution. As this book will argue, classical scholarship, in response, would draw on Platonic scenes and a Platonic language of understanding and of desire, *eros*, as a means of producing knowledge, to offer a solution, or at least a way of containing and articulating those challenges. One figure develops a particular profile for the affirmative use of such aspirational scenes of knowledge and instruction: that of Alcibiades, especially as he is described in Plato's *Symposium*. The *Symposium*, discussed in detail below, is a dialogue about articulating the praise of *eros* and about harnessing the power of desire to reach knowledge and, in the process, transcend the human object of desire. In addition, it is also a dialogue that explicitly raises questions about the unreliability of communication and of its

---

[11] Miller, *Versions of Pygmalion*, p. 11.

incomplete memory. Alcibiades is the Athenian 'golden boy', the object of desire who, in the dialogue, turns out to have his own story to tell about desire of and for the philosopher, the failures of desire, and the failures of teaching and pedagogy. Compared to Pygmalion, Alcibiades may be a less obvious reference point; and even compared to Socrates or Plato, within the sphere of classical scholarship, he may at first sight rather fly under the radar, disavowed as much as he is invoked. But he, too, has traction as a figure to consider the disturbances, or illusions, of reciprocal relationships in the context of longing for knowledge of an other. Unlike that of Pygmalion, the narrative of Alcibiades introduces a pedagogical frame, highlighting a scene of instruction that makes him eminently appealing for disciplinary concerns. Institutionally and ideologically, the study of antiquity was considered the manifestation of an educational as much as a hermeneutic task.[12]

Plato's *Symposium* is a text that dramatizes particularly well the incompleteness of understanding and of desire. Showing a group of Athenian worthies gathered to celebrate for a second time the poet Agathon's victory at the dramatic festivals, the scene of the 'after-party' sees them engaged in a game of offering praise speeches to the god Eros. The sequence of speeches culminates in Socrates's account of the teachings he received from the priestess Diotima, but the scene is interrupted by the arrival of Alcibiades, drunk, keen to join the company and the game, and offering what is essentially a speech in praise of Socrates as an embodiment of Eros. The dialogue as a whole is framed as a multiply nested, mediated account of the symposium years after the fact, a story passed on from one disciple to another, keen to recreate an image of the living Socrates and his previous company, thus exemplifying and underlining the incompleteness of full access. In turn, it offers a model of knowledge that is calqued from a language of *eros* and erotic desire, and that suggests a process of sublimation and abstraction that proceeds from the attraction to specific instances of beauty towards the true knowledge of Beauty itself and of other Forms.

---

[12] Like Pygmalion, Alcibiades was of interest also to late eighteenth-century visual culture, which focuses on capturing Alcibiades's moral education and Socrates's attempts to dissuade him from a life of pleasure. For a discussion of some of the traditions in painting, from the seventeenth well into the nineteenth century, see G. Most's afterword 'Classicism, Modernism, Postclassicism', in A. Leonard and L. Norman (eds.), *Classicisms* (Chicago: Smart Museum of Art, 2017), pp. 129–35. Most uses the visual treatments to reflect on the potential of Alcibiades for a disturbance of classicism's affective aporias, as well as Alcibiades's own, an approach that resonates with the emphasis on Alcibiades suggested in my argument here.

Alcibiades is a desirable yet flawed figure who irrupts into a gathering of experts. Through his own account, he contrasts the future-oriented longing for knowledge with the backward-looking memory of desire for and of Socrates. In the process, he also confuses and overturns expectations of reciprocity, directionality, and attraction. Alcibiades, recounting his own wooing of Socrates and thus a significant and painful moment of disconnect from human reciprocity, is the embodied failure of learning and of a failure of teaching, yet also of its possibilities. Proudly, he admits to his failed seduction and flawed reasoning, but equally proudly he matches his critical insight with a continuing misreading of Socrates's approach. His drunken, gate-crashing entry and his praise speech of Socrates that follows already underline asymmetry and one-sidedness. Within the narrative, he responds to Socrates's preceding speech about the ascent of knowledge through *eros* that necessarily transcends human reciprocity – even though he responds to it unwittingly, for he had not yet arrived to hear it. His very presence touches all the neuralgic points about the precariousness of understanding. It does so within a dialogue that itself evokes the present tense of conviviality, of direct speech and response, but which is framed as a complex and imperfect recollection, and so it also highlights the scholar's predicament in any dialogue with the past, as an affective, philological, and/or transformational object of knowledge and of education.

Feeling and Metaphor

Arguably, by emphasizing rhetorical structures and organizing my analysis around recurring figures and tropes such as those just mentioned, this study is itself one-sided. Many of the texts examined here are, effectively, paratexts: programmatic writings, introductions, and lectures; or scholarly texts that have, in one way or another, been considered unusual. A good case in point is the argument often put to me while writing about Wilamowitz, that one text or another of his was 'late', 'not representative', or 'not much read these days'. And yet, how many texts can fit into this rather crowded category before it overflows? Those exclusionary mechanisms themselves reflect the standardizing and compartmentalizing tendencies of a discipline, the lasting decisions about what counts and what does not count as scholarship proper. Introductions, public lectures, and letters are an integral part of scholarly work and scholarly knowledge, not a lesser frame. Just so, this study is based on the assumption that imagery, metaphors, and language describing affective relationships are themselves not paratextual or ornamental, but have been relevant across time and continue to be efficacious.

A substantial amount of work in both historical scholarship and scholarship in the history of science in the last two decades has argued for the active role that both figures of speech generally, and emotional speech in particular, play in social interaction and in interpretation.[13] In the 1970s, the philosopher of history Reinhart Koselleck already argued for a method of *Begriffsgeschichte*, the historical study of concepts and images as 'factors' rather than only 'indicators' of a changing social and historical reality. More recent histories of emotion have more generally put renewed emphasis on historically conditioned emotions as agents rather than reflections of historical context and change.[14] Like metaphors, emotional expressions are features of discourse that have a feedback effect on perception, on cognition, on linguistic representation, and thereby on the organization of knowledge, which makes them particularly significant when examining the language of academic research.

This is, then, not about psychological processes or expressions, but about the hermeneutic consequences of how, in the case of classical scholarship, ancient texts and materials have been read and understood, and how the articulation of hermeneutic expectations has shaped disciplinary reading practices and self-perceptions of the modern, disciplined scholar. The history of science has for a good while already been examining emotions and passions not in a psychological mode, but as 'agents integral to scientific practice', putting, as a consequence, increasing pressure on the historical notions of objectivity and, by extension, the binary with subjectivity.[15] If modes of attention, to which claims about objectivity and feeling belong, are historically constituted, then forms of attention to the past are equally included.

---

[13] The most recent comprehensive survey is J. Plamper, *The History of Emotions: An Introduction* (Oxford University Press, 2015).

[14] R. Koselleck, 'Einleitung', in O. Brunner, W. Kunze, and R. Koselleck (eds.), *Geschichtliche Grundbegriffe. Historisches Lexikon zur zur politisch-sozialen Sprache in Deutschland* (Stuttgart: Klett, 1972), pp. xiii–xxvii, here p. xiv; W. Reddy, *The Navigation of Feeling: A Framework for the Study of Emotion* (Cambridge University Press, 2001), speaks of emotives in analogy to performatives, effecting and marking change, as cognitive habits and dynamic tools that have self-altering effects.

[15] P. White, 'Introduction', special issue The Emotional Economy of Science, *Isis* 100.4 (2009), 792–7; L. Daston and K. Park, *Wonders and the Order of Nature, 1150–1750* (Boston, MA: MIT Press, 1998); L. Daston and P. Galison, *Objectivity* (Boston, MA: MIT Press, 2007); specifically on the potential for the study of the humanities and philology, L. Daston and G. Most, 'History of Science and History of Philologies', *Isis* 106.2 (2015), 378–90.

It is not that scholars of classical and philological scholarship have been unaware of the role of passions, though the discussion has largely, and maybe unsurprisingly, been framed in the Freudian and poststructuralist language of desire, not least in light of Freud's own indebtedness to the texts and language of antiquity and his use of classical knowledge in the development of his theories of the psyche.[16] Even so, the critical language of desire tends to focus on power relations, whether in critically denouncing the scholar's desirous gaze, or in a no less critical but also celebratory vision of philology's renewed empowering potential. Hans Ulrich Gumbrecht, for example, makes an eloquent and strong case for the manifold overlaps between the powers of philology and the structures of desire that inhere in its practices, such as commenting, editing, or teaching. At the same time, his analysis upholds a strong and admiring sense of the aura and charisma of the teaching situation.[17] What has been missing, as a complementary perspective, is an effort to historicize the 'knowledge equals desire' formula itself and to examine carefully how historically specific notions of love, feeling, attachment, and desire have been activated within interpretive and critical practices of scholarship.[18]

The claim that a language of emotion has historical agency also finds support from a less historically oriented corner, that of the theory of metaphor. When George Lakoff and Mark Johnson published their seminal *Metaphors We Live By* in 1980, the tendency in philosophy had been to examine metaphor as ornament or paraphrase rather than as something with a cognitive function. Their re-evaluation of metaphor as itself structuring experience helps to link the active role of articulated feeling with the strategies of personification.

Literary and historical studies of emotion in the eighteenth and nineteenth centuries stress the concern with the sometimes unpredictable feedback effect of emotional expression, and Lakoff and Johnson likewise

---

[16] S. C. Humphreys, 'Classics and Colonialism: Towards an Erotics of the Discipline', in G. Most (ed.), *Disciplining Classics – Altertumswissenschaft als Beruf* (Göttingen: Vandenhoeck & Ruprecht, 2002), pp. 207–51, with further bibliography; H. U. Gumbrecht, *The Powers of Philology: Dynamics of Textual Scholarship* (Urbana, IL: University of Illinois Press); on Freud's antiquity, R. Armstrong, *A Compulsion for Antiquity: Freud and the Ancient World* (Ithaca, NY: Cornell University Press, 2005); for the poststructuralist investment in antiquity that is also a reflection of critical psychoanalytic approaches, see M. Leonard, *Athens in Paris: Ancient Greece and the Political in Post-War French Thought* (Oxford University Press, 2005).

[17] Gumbrecht, *Powers of Philology*.

[18] A good example of applying this approach to an examination of the study of (English) literature is offered in D. Lynch, *Loving Literature: A Cultural History* (Harvard University Press, 2015), which argues for the affection for books as an index of an eighteenth- and nineteenth-century cultural history and politics of the self.

use the notion of a feedback loop to describe the workings of metaphor.[19] Metaphors, however conventional they are or strike us, help to understand concepts or aspects through 'experiencing one kind of thing in terms of another', thus structuring language, thought, actions, and values through the influence they have on categorization, in the form of an 'imaginative rationality'.[20] Such metaphorical structuring involves patterns of highlighting and of hiding, which allows the coexistence of conventional and novel metaphors whenever less obvious areas of a conventional image are activated.[21] This offers a handle on some of the dominant conventional metaphors that permeate nineteenth-century scholarship, for example, the ubiquitous organic imagery. Without having to claim that every instance of organic imagery is an intentionally meaningful metaphor, Lakoff and Johnson's account can make room for deliberately used figurative speech while not losing a critical hook on conventional metaphor either.

For Johnson and Lakoff, personification may be among the most obvious ontological metaphors, 'allow[ing] us to comprehend a wide variety of experiences with nonhuman entities in terms of human motivations, characteristics, and activities'.[22] To contain abstract entities in the imagination of the human figure helps to understand them. This is not so different from Mary Douglas's famous anthropological definition of the body as 'a model which stands for any bounded system', even while 'the functions of its different parts and their relations afford a source of symbols for other complex structures'.[23] The use of the human figure as an image to articulate and interrogate an abstract concept such as the past is therefore always potentially creating meaning for other structures that are by way of this imagery seen as related – for example, in the mutual entailment of concepts of the self, of history, of education and formation, or of the position of the scholar. Their insistence on the feedback effect which

[19] G. Lakoff and M. Johnson, *Metaphors We Live By* (University of Chicago Press, 1980), p. 142; for the eighteenth and nineteenth centuries, see, for example, N. Wegmann, *Diskurse der Empfindsamkeit. Zur Geschichte eines Gefühls in der Literatur des 18. Jahrhunderts* (Stuttgart: Metzler, 1988); Reddy, *Navigation of Feeling*; A. Pinch, *Strange Fits of Passion. Epistemologies of Emotion, Hume to Austen* (Palo Alto, CA: Stanford University Press, 2006); Lynch, *Loving Literature*.
[20] Lakoff and Johnson, *Metaphors*, pp. 5, 193. Lakoff and Johnson developed their theory of metaphor with a view to a particular account of experientialism, which makes their larger agenda and their view on metaphor by no means indefensible; for a contextualization of their work, see E. Camp, 'Metaphor in the Mind: The Cognition of Metaphor', *Philosophy Compass* 1.2 (2006), 154–70.
[21] The example they give is the metaphor of a theory as a 'building' with a basis and a superstructure, in which the 'unused' parts of corridors, rooms, or chimneys were suddenly invoked; Lakoff and Johnson, *Metaphors*, pp. 52–4.
[22] Lakoff and Johnson, *Metaphors*, pp. 33–4.
[23] M. Douglas, *Purity and Danger: An Analysis of Concepts of Pollution and Taboo* (London, New York: Routledge, 2002 [1966]), p. 3.

rhetorical imagery exerts on conceptualization and on interpretation has found some application to the discourses of archaeology.[24] There is every reason, though, to extend the view to philological, textual practices. Keeping such an account of metaphor side by side with the historical analysis of emotion and insights from literary and sociological studies allows us to highlight several things together: the structuring role of emotional imagery, its historical specificity, but also the interaction of emotional discourse and textual production – reflected in the often anxious preoccupation with texts as active mediators of individual sentiment and individual knowledge.

Philology and Historical Distance

If personification is, in Lakoff and Johnson's words, an obvious ontological metaphor, then it is just as justifiable to claim that to imagine the past as a present figure may be *prima facie* nothing new. The tradition of imagining a book as a friend or of treating texts and authors as peers goes back at least as far as Petrarch, and his first-person letters addressed to Homer, Cicero, and Virgil, in book 24 of his *Epistolae Familiares*. Kathy Eden has persuasively shown that such an investment in intimate reading and writing looked in two directions: backwards towards the concepts of familiarity and decorum in ancient rhetoric, and forwards towards Early Modern articulations of the individual and, ultimately, to reading practices we still adopt as our own.[25] To bring Eden's insights forward in time means to underline the continuities of how the intimate relationship with a text established itself as an expected, yet a historically configured and not self-evident practice of the humanities.[26]

At the same time, moving the perspective to the period of institutional self-definition and the rise of the professional scholar, a shift happened that was one of degree, about interiorization and the language through which desire for intimate understanding was formulated, while simultaneously accounting for distance. Not the least important feature of that shift was that it is no longer the individual texts or authors that are the objects made present, brought into the present as *exempla*, but individual

---

[24] C. Y. Tilley, *Metaphor and Material Culture* (Oxford: Blackwell, 1999); R. Joyce, *The Languages of Archaeology: Dialogue, Narrative, and Writing* (Oxford: Blackwell, 2002).

[25] K. Eden, *The Renaissance Rediscovery of Intimacy* (Chicago University Press, 2010).

[26] Eden herself speculates that the line of tradition she identifies could be extended beyond the Early Modern period as far as the hermeneutics of Hans Georg Gadamer; Eden, *Rediscovery of Intimacy*, pp. 4–9.

personifications that are meant to give access to the nature of a larger entity, such as a culture or nation altogether, an entity that is becoming defined and delineated in the shape of the human other, expected to be complete. There was no longer an 'I' calling upon Virgil or Homer in the first person, as there was for Petrarch; instead now an individual subject was postulated, theorized, and observed, standing in close relation to an ancient object, author, or nation that is imagined as another individual writ large. It is not only that the metaphor of a 'body of knowledge', or for that matter a 'body of works' gains increased currency from the eighteenth century, but it is a body that is expected to have a life narrative, a definable character, and its own historical depth.[27]

To gauge that other body, a measure of historical distance is needed, or needs to be overcome. As Mark Salber Phillips has argued, historical understanding is generally keyed to specific and historically changeable notions of distance, making it a central axis in the analysis of historical writing. The construction of historical distance is a significant part of historical representation, and it serves as a signature of sorts for historical practice.[28] Phillips encourages his readers to de-familiarize common-sense ideas of historical distance as a stable prerequisite for historical comprehension and instead take on board the pliability of those ideas and their ability to be integrated into the images of the past they produce. Phillips's claim that historical distance is created or uncreated largely by way of a 'historical vocabulary soaked in metaphors of presence or proximity' bears out the idea that metaphors in scholarly writing have a feedback effect on perception and scholarly interpretation, and it exemplifies an approach that is sensitive to historically specific expressions of emotion, and to disciplinary frames and expectations of scholarship.[29] If his findings are valid for historiographical texts (his focus is on European, and especially British, historiography of the eighteenth to the twentieth centuries), there is no reason they cannot also offer insights for the work of philology and *Altertumswissenschaft*.

In this study, I treat *Altertumswissenschaft* as a disciplinary project rather than as a conglomerate – or, as some of the nineteenth-century scholars would call it, an 'aggregate' – in terms of its programmatic nature and its objective of creating knowledge about the ancient past as an organic whole.

---

[27] For the 'body of knowledge', see N. Zemon Davis, 'History's Two Bodies', *American Historical Review* 93 (1988), 1–30.

[28] M. S. Phillips, *On Historical Distance* (New Haven, CT: Yale University Press, 2015).

[29] The quotation comes from an earlier piece outlining his research, M. S. Phillips, 'Distance and Historical Representation', *History Workshop Journal* 57.1 (2004), 123–41, here p. 132.

It is easy enough, when looking at some of the contemporary accounts of its remit and method, to view *Altertumswissenschaft* as a grid of areas and sub-disciplines (Chapter 4 in particular will discuss some of those programmes). But it is just as important to recognize the drive towards overarching coherence and the search, often anxious, for the possibility of overall understanding that is reflected in those drafts of the new discipline. If I use *Altertumswissenschaft* and philology as almost interchangeable terms, this is not meant to overlook the wide range of disciplinary fields within the study of antiquity that indeed inhabit their own microclimates. Nor is it meant to shortchange the fundamental discussion over the relationship between the historical and philological sciences, especially in the later nineteenth century. Most of the scholars whose writings I address and think with in this study sought to identify a specific but fairly capacious notion of philology;[30] more importantly, all areas of a science of antiquity essentially relied on a template of textual understanding as the default for gaining and formulating knowledge, and they relied on the acknowledgement of historical distance and development as an inevitable feature and precondition for any such comprehension.

It is symptomatic that Friedrich Ritschl, professor of Classics at Bonn (and now mostly famous as Friedrich Nietzsche's teacher and supporter), looks back over philological studies as they 'have been tended among the most cultivated nations of Europe since the fourteenth century, with a love that has overall not been interrupted'.[31] In supplying the justification and definition that he sees necessary for the modern period, Ritschl considers the relationship between philology as, in his understanding, the domain of the real reproduction of texts, and history as the domain of the ideal reproduction of the past. He does so by imagining quite literally a relationship between them, using terms that exemplify the semantics of romantic love and its hermeneutic challenges: a personified Philology increasingly 'strives towards its marriage with History' wherein its future lies; and yet, 'as long as humans are humans, this marriage will not be truly consummated, and their activities will remain relatively separate'.[32]

---

[30] Turner, *Philology*, on the perception of philology as either mere linguistics or text criticism.

[31] F. Ritschl, 'Ueber die neueste Entwicklung der Philologie', in C. Wachsmuth (ed.), *Kleine Philologische Schriften* (Leipzig: Teubner 1866), vol. v, pp. 1–18, here p. 1, a lecture originally delivered to the Philomathische Gesellschaft of Breslau in 1833.

[32] Ritschl, 'Zur Methode des philologischen Studiums (Bruchstücke und Aphorismen)', *Kleine Philologische Schriften*, pp. 19–32, here p. 25. Ritschl may well have in mind here the imagery of Martianus Capella's fifth-century CE allegory *De nuptiis Philologiae et Mercurii*, with Mercury standing in for profitable intellectual pursuits; the phrasing, however, resonates in a mid-nineteenth-century context just as much.

Philology is set up at the intersection of historical study and that of textual evidence, both of which are understood to be the articulation of individual experience. Ritschl's statements come from a public lecture given in front of a learned society. They were reprinted almost immediately as the entry for the lemma 'Philology' in the *Brockhaus*, the standard encyclopedia of the German language of the nineteenth century.

A final comment is necessary on the relationship between Greek and Roman materials within this understanding of a science of antiquity. In the wake of institutionalization, the separation into Greek and Latin as two related yet distinct parts of the study of the ancient world became more pronounced, too, at the same time when antiquity, with its analogous term Middle Ages, became a free-standing period designator. It is possible to make a case for the specific place Greece holds in the classical imagination, as a period linked to youth, beauty, and educability, and as a period whose own preoccupation is considered to be with the formation of the individual; this is largely the argument on which this present study rests. That said, it should certainly also be possible to examine the imagery of historical distance and of scholarly passion in the case of the Roman world more specifically, even if that lies outside the stated framework of the study at hand.[33] For that reason, I will continue to speak about classical scholarship rather than Greek scholarship only, even though I will argue throughout that the feedback loop of the discipline's imagery onto the interpretation of Greek texts and culture was a particularly strong one.

Chapter Outline

I identify three interlinked sets of strategies that were in play for activating antiquity: personification as its main rhetorical figure; the biographical as its narrative extension; and emotion or feeling, themselves historically shaped in their expression, as the language in which to formulate the aspirations and precariousness of understanding and interpretation.

The first chapter concentrates on the period around 1800, laying the groundwork by examining the concepts of sentimentality, the code of

---

[33] Unlike the study of Hellenism and its institutional manifestations, there is, certainly for the German side, a notable dearth of studies on the dynamic and cultural history of Latin scholarship within Classics. Important starting points are in P. L. Schmidt, 'Zwischen Anpassungsdruck und Autonomiestreben: die deutsche Latinistik vom Beginn bis in die 20er Jahre des 20. Jahrhunderts', in H. Flashar (ed.), *Altertumswissenschaft in den 20er Jahren. Neue Fragen und Impulse* (Stuttgart: Franz Steiner Verlag, 1995), pp. 115–82, and A. Holzer, *Rehabilitationen Roms: Die römische Antike in der deutschen Kultur zwischen Winckelmann und Niebuhr* (Heidelberg: Winter, 2013).

Romantic love, *Bildung*, interpretation, and the appeal of Greek antiquity as an analogue to the history and formation of the self. Beginning from Winckelmann's erotic classicism, it draws on the writings of Friedrich August Wolf, Friedrich Schleiermacher, Friedrich Schlegel, Wilhelm von Humboldt, and Johann Georg Herder, together with insights from recent literary, historical, and sociological work on the discursive codification of emotions and of closeness in that period.

The second and third chapters turn to the specific examples of Plato and of Socratic teaching as a template used for formulating an approach to the study of antiquity. Compared to an earlier interest in mainly Socrates (rather than Plato) as a mostly ambivalent figure, I trace a new understanding of Plato as the ostensibly unified author of systematic works centrally concerned with educational progress. My main example, after a look at the Socratic *Memorabilia* of J. G. Hamann (1759), is the influential translation project of the Platonic dialogues by Friedrich Schleiermacher and its relation to his own hermeneutics.

The fourth chapter follows the ramifications of this investment in a Platonizing imagination of learning and knowledge into the discipline of philology, showing how such a template interacted with the tensions inherent in philology as a practice. If it is the case that the demands of an increasingly specialized scientific philology and the expectation of a fully personal and individualized formation of the self (*Bildung*) were increasingly drifting apart, I want to show that philology in its self-descriptions still tried to keep those poles together, *especially* through maintaining a rhetoric of philological feeling.

The fifth chapter considers the narrative overlap of disciplinary filiation and the biographical. It does so through readings of Carl Justi's biography of Winckelmann and Wilhelm Dilthey's biographical work on Schleiermacher. Both were begun in the 1870s, within a web of hermeneutic thinking about the biographical that characterized the *Geisteswissenschaften* and that reflected back into the study of ancient biographical materials, too, and rendered scholars and their subject matter coextensive.

The sixth chapter examines, against this background, the claims to biographical possibilities as a key to modern scholarship itself, such as those raised by Wilamowitz in his works on Plato, Plutarch, Greek lyric, tragedy, and Pindar. By juxtaposing Nietzsche's own work on ancient biography, I allow the similarities of the concerns raised, rather than the difference in answers, to come to the fore.

The epilogue offers a reflection on detachment not as a form of progression from immersive feeling to critical distance but instead as an opportunity to consider forms and images of attention that resist the rhetoric of a transformative longing for comprehension and comprehensiveness. It also offers some suggestions for reframing the classical scenes of instruction and of understanding that have been part of such a language.

In classical scholarship there has been a marked consciousness of the field's own history, often enough expressed in prosopographical terms.[34] The biographical and personal have had a solid part in how the discipline looks at itself, and its historiography, even if the parameters are changing, has remained indebted to biographical models of one kind or another to an ostensibly self-evident degree.[35] 'Histories of fields are told as histories of the self', as Seth Lerer has put it in a perceptive study of philological error and narratives of personal displacement: 'Recounting the history of the field effectively justifies the field; anecdotalizing the experience of its experts is the means by which one makes oneself an expert.'[36] What this study hopes to do is in part to explain how this persistent model is deeply imbricated in a disciplinary habitus and rhetoric, answering to and in turn affirming specific needs and expectations about the role of individual personality and its relation to *Wissenschaft*. If a good number of the readings in this study are themselves arranged around specific scholars, this is not to return, disingenuously, to that same strategy. Instead, it is to ask pointedly how the (self-)representation of scholars within a discipline affects the development of the discipline, as well as the content of the discipline and the ancient objects it studies.

Gilbert Murray, in the peroration of his portrait of German scholarship, offered his own taxonomy of contemporary scholars: 'In England there is more humanity, more interest in life, more common sense, and, as an almost inevitable consequence, less one-sided devotion and less industry. Browning's grammarian would be more at home in Germany. He would be decorated and made a "Geheimrath".'[37] And yet it is exactly the combination of one-sidedness and of devotion and the rhetoric it generated that let German scholarship imagine a relationship with antiquity in which feeling was inseparable from philology.

---

[34] R. Herzog, 'On the Relation of Disciplinary Development and Historical Self-presentation – the Case of Classical Philology since the End of the Eighteenth Century', in L. Graham, W. Lepenies, and P. Weingart (eds.), *Functions and Uses of Disciplinary Histories* (1983), pp. 281–90.

[35] See Mary Beard's review of the *Dictionary of British Classicists*, on issues and pitfalls of interpreting personality as part of a history of classical scholarship; 'Nil nisi bonum', *Times Literary Supplement* April 15, 2005, pp. 3–4.

[36] S. Lerer, *Error and the Academic Self. The Scholarly Imagination, Medieval to Modern* (New York University Press, 2002), p. 9.

[37] Murray, 'German Scholarship', p. 339.

CHAPTER I

The Potter's Daughter
Longing, Bildung, and the Self

Winckelmann's Beloved: The Longing of Philhellenism

Johann Joachim Winckelmann's *History of the Art of Antiquity* (1764) was influential for the development of art history, and foundational for the discipline of *Altertumswissenschaft* as a whole. With his twin emphasis on charting the historical development of style while highlighting aesthetic experience as a component of scholarly expertise, Winckelmann lent himself as an appropriate founding figure of classical scholarship, elevated as its *heros ktistes*, to use Katherine Harloe's words.[1] In part, the continuing fascination of Winckelmann, and of his classicism, arose from the narrative of his own biography: humble origins, learned isolation, exposure to classical art works at the court of Saxony, conversion to Catholicism to attain a position in Rome, and his early death in Trieste after a stabbing that was the result of a robbery as much as it carried implications of a homosexual crime of passion, adding to the lore accruing around Winckelmann.[2] At the same time, his 'Greeks', at least at the moment of the fifth-century height of Athenian art, were representative and literal embodiments of the confluence of a gently temperate South, political freedom, and a celebration of beauty, producing artworks that the scholar approached with care and desire as much as they, ostensibly, expressed such affects.

By the same token, and precisely because of Winckelmann's 'heroic' status as a historian of Greek art, he could also be increasingly superseded as *Wissenschaft* tried to shed what it perceived as its antiquarian eggshells.

---

[1] K. Harloe, *Winckelmann*, esp. pp. 1–25, here p. 7. On Winckelmann and art history, see Alex Potts, *Flesh and the Ideal: Winckelmann and the Origins of Art History* (New Haven, CT: Yale University Press, 1994).

[2] On the biographical traditions of Winckelmann that set in immediately after his death, see Chapter 5.

For the increasingly disciplined, institutionalized, professionalized sphere of classical scholarship, Winckelmann was, in retrospect, the model of a scholar not (yet) professionalized, the outsider whose interpretations were soon overtaken by the progress of scientific historical (or rather historicist) and archaeological research. And yet, he continued to be a presence in terms of maintaining a vision of aesthetic impact.[3]

The *History* closes with a remarkable visualization of what it means to investigate the cultural remains of a past age:

> I have in this history of art already gone far beyond its bounds; and while in observing its decline I almost feel like someone who, when describing the history of his fatherland, has to touch on its destruction, which he himself has experienced, all the same I could not restrain myself from gazing after the fate of works of art as far as my eye could see. Just as a woman in love (*Liebste*), standing on the shore of the ocean, seeking out with tear-filled eyes her departing lover (*Liebhaber*) whom she has no hope of ever seeing again, thinks she can glimpse in the distant sail the image of her beloved (*Geliebten*); we, like the woman in love (*Geliebte*), have remaining to us, so to speak, only the silhouette (*Schattenriss*) of our desires (*Wünsche*): but this makes the desire (*Sehnsucht*) for the objects we have lost ever more ardent, and we examine the copies of the original masterpieces with greater attention than we would have done were we to be in full possession of them.[4]

This extraordinary passage, speaking in someone else's voice, describes what 'we' do when we approach the history of antiquity – in fact, Winckelmann here puts emphasis on the creation of a 'we' as he subtly

[3] Again, Harloe makes a strong case for this double status. On the simultaneous praise and disdain for Winckelmann, especially in the late nineteenth century, and on Winckelmann's impact on classical, especially archaeological, scholarship as well as his continued use for cultural criticism and the production of culture more generally, see E. S. Sünderhauf, *Griechensehnsucht und Kulturkritik. Die deutsche Rezeption von Winckelmanns Antikenideal 1840–1945* (Berlin: Akademie, 2004). See also a forthcoming special issue of the *Zeitschrift für Ästhetik und Allgemeine Kunstwissenschaft* on Winckelmann around 1900, ed. C. Keller and Ch. Schmälzle.

[4] 'Ich bin in der Geschichte der Kunst schon über ihre Grenzen gegangen, und ungeachtet mir bei Betrachtung des Untergangs derselben fast zu Muthe gewesen ist, wie demjenigen, der in Beschreibung der Geschichte seines Vaterlandes die Zerstörung desselben, die er selbst erlebt hat, berühren müsste, so konnte ich mich dennoch nicht enthalten, dem Schicksale der Werke der Kunst, so weit mein Auge ging, nachzusehen. So wie eine Liebste an dem Ufer des Meeres ihren abfahrenden Liebhaber, ohne Hoffnung ihn wieder zu sehen, mit beträhnten Augen verfolgt und selbst in dem entfernten Segel das Bild des Geliebten zu sehen glaubt. Wir haben, wie die Geliebte, gleichsam nur einen Schattenriss von dem Vorwurfe unsrer Wünsche übrig; aber desto grössere Sehnsucht nach dem Verlornen erweckt derselbe, und wir betrachten die Copien der Urbilder mit grösserer Aufmerksamkeit, als wie wir in dem völligen Besitze von diesen nicht würden gethan haben.' J. J. Winckelmann, *Geschichte der Kunst des Alterthums*, Schriften und Nachlaß, IV.1, ed. M. Kunze (Mainz: von Zabern, 2002), p. 838; the translation of that passage is adapted from that of Potts, *Flesh and the Ideal*, p. 49.

shifts from singular to plural, from 'I' to 'we' in this passage, a 'we' that, despite its identity as part of a group of modern viewers, retains some of its origin in the personal experience of the beloved left behind. By making us the marked, empathetic observer of someone else's act of longing and observation, Winckelmann creates a founding scene for imagining the study of antiquity. It is a scene that quite literally configures the object of study as the human figure of an absent other; a scene with a complex affective economy built on the interaction of distance and closeness; and a scene whose second-order observation, mediated in Winckelmann's felt comparison of his first-person 'I' to the beloved on the shore, and then compared to all of us, creates its own disavowals. It raises the question of what kind of self-observation is entailed, what kind of relationship is created in the act of 'feeling like' and 'being like' that imagined beloved looking out.

This closing passage of Winckelmann's *History* has been rewarding material for a number of recent readings that see larger significance in Winckelmann's choice of image. Winckelmann's text continues to be a reference point for the historiography of art history, and this scene has lent itself as a key in the discussion of how the twin gestures of historicism and aesthetic response relate, have related, or should relate in the under-standing of art and the practice of art history.[5] The splitting off into the voice of the male historian and into the female lover gazing out after a no-longer-visible male beloved may well map onto the split between the objective historian and the connoisseur spectator whose roles and relation to each other were consciously negotiated in both art theory and historio-graphy of the eighteenth century.[6] On this reading, the persona of the female lover in analogy to (yet not in identity with) the author of the present history writ large makes visible, and maybe elides the tension between systematic history and aesthetic engagement. Yet why the veiled, nested description of longing? Alex Potts has interpreted this passage as a 'ventriloquizing' of female desire 'so that his male readers can imagine without inhibition an intense eroticized longing for the ideal manhood conjured up by the Greek ideal';[7] in fact, this has led to a wider argument for Winckelmann giving the erotic a new epistemological function,

[5] Potts, *Flesh and the Ideal*, 48–50; W. Davis, 'Winckelmann Divided: Mourning the Death of Art History', in idem (ed.), *Gay and Lesbian Studies in Art History* (Binghamton, NY: SUNY Press, 1994), pp. 141–59.
[6] Davis, 'Winckelmann Divided'; K. Parker, 'Winckelmann, Historical Difference, and the Problem of the Boy', *Eighteenth Century Studies* 25.4 (1992), 523–44.
[7] Potts, *Flesh and the Ideal*, p. 49.

turning the desire for something considered beautiful and hence valuable into an instrument of historical criticism and, in addition, articulating this criticism in the language of a newly developing and decidedly homoerotic configuration.[8] Can we, though, add to Winckelmann's epistemological structure of desire another layer that points beyond the important emphasis on the homoerotic and its social and cultural implications, towards the question of how and why the relationship of the observer or scholar with antiquity is in its representation bound up in a language, often ventriloquized, to use Alex Pott's term again, of feeling and longing for that which has sailed out of reach? My point is not the logic of homoerotic desire specifically, which I am setting aside here.[9] Rather, I ask why the imagery of interpersonal affection, its disavowals, and its disturbances is predicated on acts of personifying ancient Greece and is so effective not just in the special (though far-reaching) case of Winckelmann but also more widely in the scholarly discourse establishing itself in and after Winckelmann's time.

The motif of the lover left on land suggests classical precedence, and Winckelmann's figure aligns with a whole range of characters: Penelope, whose cunning can match that of her departing lover; Ariadne, deserted on an island shore by Theseus; or Dido, left at Carthage by Aeneas.[10] Joshua Billings has suggested a genealogical web of deserted female figures on the shore that stretches from Winckelmann back through early opera and forward to such icons of classicism as Goethe's Iphigenia.[11] Winckelmann's assertion, that 'we, like the woman in love, have remaining to us, so to speak, only the shadowy outline of our desires' suggests that yet

[8] See especially W. Davis, 'Winckelmann's "Homosexual" Teleologies', in Natalie B. Kampen (ed.), *Sexuality in Ancient Art* (Cambridge University Press, 1996), pp. 262–76; Potts, *Flesh and the Ideal*, pp. 47–50, 201–16. For the literary articulation of sexual ethics and orientation in relation to the knowledge of antiquity, see also P. Derks, *Die Heilige Schande der Päderastie. Homosexualität und Öffentlichkeit in der deutschen Literatur, 1750–1850* (Berlin: Rosa Winkel, 1990); S. Richter, 'Winckelmann's Progeny: Homosocial Networking in the Eighteenth Century', in A. Kuzniar (ed.), *Outing Goethe & His Age* (Palo Alto, CA: Stanford University Press, 1996), pp. 44–6; for an extension of those issues into the late nineteenth and early twentieth centuries, see A. Blanshard, 'Hellenic Fantasies: Aesthetics and Desire in John Addington Symond's *A Problem in Greek Ethics*', *Dialogos* 7 (2000), 99–123, and D. Orrells, *Classical Culture and Modern Masculinity* (Oxford University Press, 2011).
[9] This is not to say that same-sex desire and the language of 'queering' isn't fruitful and highly appropriate for getting a new and well-theorized handle on the history of disciplinary expectations and practices. It is, and this is an exciting growth area in the study of Classics. See, for example, aside from Orrells, *Classical Culture and Modern Masculinity*, S. Matzner, 'Queer Unhistoricism: Scholars, Metalepsis, and Interventions of the Unruly Past', in S. Butler (ed.), *Deep Classics: Rethinking Classical Reception* (Bloomsbury Academic: London, 2016), pp. 179–201; S. Butler, 'The Youth of Antiquity: reception, homosexuality, alterity', *Classical Receptions Journal*, 11.4 (2019), 373–406.
[10] Davis, 'Winckelmann Divided', pp. 151f.; Potts, *Flesh and the Ideal*, p. 49.
[11] J. Billings, 'The Sigh of Philhellenism', in Butler (ed.), *Deep Classics*, pp. 49–65.

another female persona is part of this overdetermined set-up: that of the daughter of a Corinthian potter whom some ancient sources credited with the invention of sculptural art. Chief reference to her comes from Pliny the Elder's *Natural History* and his account of the origins, development, and techniques of the visual arts:

> On painting we have now said enough, and more than enough; but it will be only proper to append some accounts of the plastic art. Butades, a potter of Sicyon, was the first who invented, at Corinth, the art of modelling portraits in the earth which he used in his trade. It was through his daughter that he made the discovery; who, being deeply in love with a young man about to depart on a long journey, traced the profile of his face, as thrown upon the wall by the light of the lamp. Upon seeing this, her father filled in the outline, by compressing clay upon the surface, and so made a face in relief, which he then hardened by fire along with other articles of pottery. This model, it is said, was preserved in the Nymphaeum at Corinth, until the destruction of that city by Mummius (XXXV.151; tr. Rackham).

Motivated by love, discovering a skill, and stimulating the development of this skill in her father's craft, she represents for Pliny a prehistory of sorts all of her own, placed as she is in the text where she precedes the discussion of the great male artists of antiquity. Pliny's account of ancient art had been a staple of writing on artistic practice and theory since the seventeenth century, and Winckelmann, too, discusses Pliny in various places throughout his *History*.[12] The girl herself, often named Butades or Dibutades after her father, became a popular subject of paintings and of poetry in her own right during the second half of the eighteenth century, not least because of the significance of line, contour, and silhouette, some of the terms associated with her actions, in contemporary visual arts and their theory. (A line drawing of her by George Romney is shown on the cover of this book.)[13]

---

[12] Pliny's account appears in Franciscus Junius, *De Pictura Veterum* (1637), a standard text for ancient sources before Winckelmann; see E. Décultot, *Johann Joachim Winckelmann. Enquête sur la genèse de l'histoire de l'art* (Paris, 2000), pp. 42, 84, 101, 204–6; Potts, *Flesh and the Ideal*, pp. 72–4, 89–91.

[13] F. Muecke, '"Taught by Love": The Origin of Painting Again', *The Art Bulletin* 81.2 (June 1999), 297–302; also S. King, 'Amelia Opie's "Maid of Corinth" and the Origins of Art', *Eighteenth-Century Studies* 37.4 (2004), 629–51; on the increasing frequency of the motif between 1760 and 1830, and Dibutades as a legitimating figure of female artists, see R. Rosenblum, 'The Origin of Painting: A Problem in the Iconography of Romantic Classicism', *Art Bulletin* 39 (1957), 279–90. For a revisionist reading, see V. Schmidt-Linsenhoff, 'Dibutadis. Die weibliche Kindheit der Zeichenkunst', *Kritische Berichte* 4 (1996), 7–20; see also the discussion of Dibutades's art in V. I. Stoichita, *A Brief History of the Shadow* (London, 1997), pp. 14–20, and the essayistic reflections on her in M. Bettini, *The Portrait of the Lover* (Berkeley: University of California Press, 1999), pp. 7–17. On the significance of the 'contour' in aesthetic theory and art writing, including Pliny, Junius, and Winckelmann, see C. Kurbjuhn, *Kontur. Geschichte einer ästhetischen Denkfigur* (Berlin:

Adding Dibutades's own shadow to a discussion of Winckelmann's female lover underscores her more active role. In Pliny, she may not be an artist to the same degree as her more famous, and named, male successors of antiquity, and it is still her father who creates the actual artisanal product; but her original role in developing the outline, quite literally, of an artistic form gives Winckelmann's figure greater agency than that suggested by the model of the deserted lover, especially with a view to the 'split' between connoisseur and historian that he so subtly seeks to negotiate in this passage.[14] The contour of the human figure, and especially the silhouette of a portrait, is a form of managing absence: it reduces what is not present or not fully representable to an essential outline. That this has particular traction with regard to the lost forms of antiquity is reflected in the exclamation that Andreas Heinrich Schott records having heard, in the preface to his 1783 treatise on the teaching of Homer in schools: 'Where then does he live, this dear man? Why has he remained incognito for so long a time? A propos, would you not know how to procure me a silhouette of him?' – a quotation that in turn is quoted by Friedrich Nietzsche in his inaugural lecture of 1869, 'Homer and Classical Philology', this time apropos Friedrich August Wolf's achievement to have wrested away the hard-to-grasp figure of Homer from an unhelpfully diffuse category of an unlocalizable 'natural genius'.[15] The creation of a silhouette, itself an art form that was popular in Schott's time, is a promise as much as an acknowledgement of the impossibility of capturing a portrait fully.

The gaze out to sea is an act Winckelmann also links elsewhere with the active, epistemological charge of practising the history of art,[16] and thus Winckelmann's beloved, far from passively left behind, is herself a figure of knowledge. Her role as a proto-historian of art tallies well with Harloe's gesture to put back into focus the first comparison with which Winckelmann opens this passage: 'I almost feel like someone who, when

---

de Gruyter, 2014). For the contour as a specifically erotic marker, see J. Endres, 'Diderot, Hogarth, and the Aesthetics of Depilation', *Eighteenth-Century Studies* 38.1 (2004), 17–38. Of the studies of Winckelmann's closing paragraph or of Dibutades, neither mentions the other, with the exception of Barbara Stafford, who refers to Winckelmann and the potter's daughter in the same breath, yet without specifying the end of the *History of the Art of Antiquity*; B. M. Stafford, 'Beauty of the Invisible: Winckelmann and the Aesthetics of Imperceptibility', *Zeitschrift für Kunstgeschichte* 43.1 (1980), 65–78, here p. 77.

[14] Schmidt-Linsenhoff, 'Dibutades', 13–16.

[15] F. Nietzsche, 'Homer und die klassische Philologie (1869)', in NWKG 2.1 (1982), pp. 247–69, here p. 268; the unmarked reference ('a learned man of excellence') is to A. H. Schott, *Über das Studium des Homers in niederen und höheren Schulen* (Leipzig: Crusius, 1783), pp. 3–4.

[16] Stafford, 'Beauty of the Invisible', esp. 67–69; Potts, *Flesh and the Ideal*, p. 2.

describing the history of his fatherland, has to touch on its destruction, which he himself has experienced', he declares, and Harloe has persuasively argued that this scene deliberately evokes the persona of Pausanias, whose second-century CE *Periegesis*, or *Description of Greece*, serves as another template for Winckelmann deliberating what is essentially the intersection of antiquarianism, aesthetics, and historiography.[17]

Winckelmann's female *figura*, then, nested doubly in the voice of the male historian, opens the view beyond (or rather, across from) the visual arts and ancient artefacts and their history to the interpretation of antiquity in other branches of learning. As I said above, the relationship of classical scholarship with Winckelmann as a founding figure is a highly ambivalent one, marked by attraction and repulsion, admiration and keeping at arm's length. Likewise, Winckelmann's foundational scene on the shore is significant for its economy of distance, closeness, and loss as imagined and embodied through the human figure, or rather through the two human figures, a present and an absent one, marked as connected by love. It is when the persona of Pausanias the historian overlooking the ruins of the past *and* the configuration of an interpersonal, exclusive relationship marked by emotional investment come together, as they do in Winckelmann's scene, that a powerful set of expectations emerges which, as I argue in this book, continues to structure the self-representation, self-justification, and figurative language of classical scholarship and inflect the articulation of *Wissenschaft* in the developing field of classical philology and the professionalized study of antiquity as an autonomous discipline, well into the nineteenth century and beyond. The philologist and archaeologist Ernst Curtius, for example, thus describes in 1857 the attitude of his former mentor K. O. Müller: 'Just as Müller positions himself at the beginning of a first publication on the coast of Attica, in order to survey the sea of Aegina, just so he felt a need to put himself (*sich versetzen*) with a vivid soul right into antiquity, to understand it as a whole and to penetrate it (*es als ein Ganzes aufzufassen und zu durchdringen*), investing it everywhere with life.'[18] His starkly figurative language breaks down

---

[17] K. Harloe, 'Pausanias as Historian in Winckelmann's *History*', *Classical Receptions Journal* 2.2 (2010), 174–96.

[18] E. Curtius, 'Das Mittleramt der Philologie' (1857), in *Göttinger Festreden* (Berlin: Hertz, 1964), pp. 23–51, here pp. 31–2, 49. An element of nostalgia and *prosopopoeia* is not absent, either: Müller's untimely death on a research trip in Greece in 1840, to which Curtius had been witness, had quickly made him a figure of disciplinary memorialization in his own right.

the boundaries between textual, spatial, and affective stance, and ostensibly integrates scientific practice with life-giving, empathetic feeling.

If a language of interpersonal relationships, guided by a discursive code of love and feeling (exemplified below in this chapter), structures the imagination of antiquity and of the study of antiquity alike, this hermeneutic challenge, the understanding of another, contains a significant and often conscious element of the impossibility of the undertaking. Joshua Billings has rightly drawn attention to the fact that Winckelmann's closing section of the *History* adds one further image, that of the historians' 'we' as those who risk exposure to their own imagination, which covers a void, even though it profitably eggs us on:[19]

> We often act like people who claim to have met ghosts (*die Gespenster kennen wollen*), and believe they see them where there is nothing: the name 'antiquity' has become a prejudice, but even this prejudice is not without use. One always ought to imagine that one will find much, so that one seeks much, in order to catch sight of something.[20]

The spectre of illusion, of understanding reduced to an act of the imagination, is a possibility, and this is an anxiety about understanding and its incompleteness that courses through eighteenth-century hermeneutics, as we will see. What is important about Winckelmann's scene and about the fashioning of antiquity as the beloved other is that such incompleteness is figured precisely through the human form, and through giving expression, and meaning, to this cognitive dissonance by way of imagining what is lost in terms of who is other. For those who claim to have seen ghosts, there needs to be an argument made for the usefulness of their prejudice; for those who are like the woman in love, the striving is ostensibly more self-evident, integrated as it is into ancient precedent and a story of its own, and cushioned by the recent presence of the beloved who is, in Winckelmann's text, after all not simply lost but still suspended in the act of leaving (*der abfahrende Geliebte*), just barely out of reach. Figuring that which needs understanding as a human individual creates temporality, character, development, relationality, and emotion, and it thus feeds directly into (and back from) the concepts and expectations of historicity, formation, and aesthetics that were central components of the humanist vision of knowing classical antiquity and of the *Bildungsideal* that fundamentally

---

[19] Billings, 'Sigh of Philhellenism', p. 56.   [20] Winckelmann, *Geschichte,* p. 838.

shaped the development of Classics as a discipline with its proper institutional features.

'Torso of a Memorial': Sculpture and Empathy

Winckelmann was not alone in recognizing that the figure of the potter's daughter as witness of the past combines the lover with the historian, so to speak. Johann Gottfried Herder, a keen reader of Winckelmann's works, offers another good example of a scholar eliding the task of the historian with his aesthetic and emotional experience apropos the absent human figure who is the object of attention. Herder's important early essay on the Enlightenment philosopher Thomas Abbt (1768), a memorial portrayal and really an obituary, presents itself not only as valuable in and of itself, but also as an analogy, a kind of script, for the work of the scholar. Beyond the specific portrayal of Abbt, the text is an explicit reflection on how to represent the character, individuality, and life story of an absent other – the first of its two parts is in fact entitled 'Introduction, which speaks of the art of giving an image of another's soul (*die Seele des andern abzubilden*)'.[21] Abbt (1738–66) had been Herder's predecessor at the Bückeburg ducal court, where Herder served as pastor and preacher. His early death, before he reached the age of thirty, makes Herder's written memorial associate even more closely the youthful statuesque beauty that is also at the core of Winckelmann's reflections – whom Herder would go on to memorialize in similar form in his later essay 'Denkmal Johann Winckelmanns' (1777).[22] Herder's memorial profile of Abbt is a commentary on the relation between scholarly thinking, general 'human' thought, and the consideration of a human life, a commentary on a recently dead man that encourages Herder to assume the voice of a numismatist and antiquarian:

> Abbt has portrayed himself, but only as an author; so I am considering only one side of his mind, the scholarly thinking, without undertaking to sketch his human thinking. I know that both sides explain each other, as in the case of coins the obverse and reverse image do.[23]

---

[21] J. G. Herder, 'Über Thomas Abbts Schriften' (1768), in B. Suphan (ed.), *Sämmtliche Werke*, 33 vols. (Berlin: Weidmann, 1877–1913), ii, pp. 249–94, here p. 257. On Herder's reading of Abbt as himself a thinker concerned with sympathetic interpretation of the other, see K. Gjesdal, *Herder's Hermeneutics: History, Poetry, Enlightenment* (Cambridge University Press, 2017), pp. 110–18.

[22] See Harloe, *Winckelmann*, pp. 213–22, on Herder's essay.

[23] Herder, 'Abbt', p. 260; the English translation is, with some modifications, that of Michael N. Forster's selection of the essay in his J. G. Herder, *Philosophical Writings* (Cambridge University Press, 2002), pp. 167–77, p. 170; on Herder's engagement with Winckelmann on the cognitive and aesthetic question of understanding antiquity, see Harloe, *Winckelmann*, pp. 205–43.

Oscillating between the visual and the written, between the numismatic likeness and the narrated life, Herder asks in the same essay:

> What is not required of a biographer, who wants to present a true image of his author, neither beautified, nor distorted, nor unresembling, and to put it in its rightful place among the rank and file of great minds? As Rousseau knew the son of his imagination, the wonderful Emile, both before his birth and in the marriage bed, the biographer, too, would have to have accompanied his friend through all the scenes of his life and to have become the intimate of his secrets; and yet he would have to be able to observe him as a stranger and like a leisurely spectator in order to follow every moment with attention. He would have to judge without bias like a judge of the dead; and yet – does it not also require a small amount of love-struck enthusiasm (*verliebte Schwärmerei*) to imprint one's subject sufficiently into one's imagination so as to sketch his image afterwards, as though out of one's head?[24]

Throughout, Herder uses the terms 'biographer' and 'historiographer' quite interchangeably, and, like Winckelmann, he is aware that either role is built on a subtle oscillation between affective closeness and distance. It is distance that reveals beauty and truth at the intersection of the historian's and the artist's work, and it is ostensibly only by way of an affective engagement that both can be realized together. The creation of biography is linked, with a nod to Rousseau, to the creation of a fictional character, albeit one who is the main figure in a novel of education, and whose progress is the concern of his author, Rousseau, just as the act of biographizing reflects back on Herder. The distance implied in the imaginative act is mirrored in the practice of portraying: the imprinting of the imagination is followed by the (biographical) sketch – and it is worth remembering that this is the sketch of a man Herder had never actually met in person. The notion of mental or imagined contact with the human figure and of its imprinting is one Herder uses and develops regularly throughout his writings, especially in his discussions of the role of touch, and of sculpture in comparison to painting: an argument that upgrades this non-visual form of knowledge, yet puts all the epistemological weight on the imagination and reflexivity of the touching subject, making the actual act of touching one that in the moment of closeness also requires a necessary distance.

Even though Pygmalion is not mentioned by name, the reflections on the link between enlivening and the statuesque nature of the object of

---

[24] Herder, 'Abbt', p. 260.

viewing and longing chime well with Pygmalion's figure and with Herder's recurring interest in the myth.[25] Pygmalion, increasingly popular in the eighteenth century, was a figure not only reflecting artistic autonomy and the creative process, but more importantly a figure that could offer models of reading and of communication between text and reader, that is, between a work and its observer, a communication often explicitly linked to the workings of love and empathy or *Einfühlung*, a term that literally contains an element of feeling as touch (*fühlen*).[26]

Herder was an avid reader of Winckelmann and could find echoed in his work Pygmalion's potential to capture some of the contemporary debate regarding historical, intellectual, and sensual comprehension through the human figure. Already at the beginning of his *Thoughts on the Imitation of Greek Works of Art* (1755), Winckelmann took up the old personifying gesture of becoming familiar with ancient works of art 'as if with one's friend' in order to appreciate them as much as ancient authors;[27] it is the observer's knowledge, and that means scholarly knowledge and expertise, that necessarily supplements the subject matter at hand and gives it life and a shape. This is the joint work of scholarly knowledge and erotics; as if that was not enough, it is a joint work that is also projected back into antiquity. Thus, in his *History of the Art of Antiquity* Winckelmann suggests that '[t]he great Greek artists – who viewed themselves as new creators, so to speak, though they worked less for the mind than for the senses – sought to overcome the hard objectivity of matter and, if it had been possible, to animate (*begeistern*) it. Their noble efforts to achieve this even in the earlier periods of art gave rise to

---

[25] On Herder's logic of touch, especially in relation to Winckelmann, see I. Mülder-Bach, 'Eine "neue Logik für den Liebhaber". Herders Theorie der Plastik', in H.-J. Schings (ed.), *Der Ganze Mensch. Anthropologie und Literatur im 18. Jahrhundert. DFG-Symposium 1992* (Stuttgart: Metzler, 1994), pp. 341–70; 'Ferngefühle. Poesie und Plastik in Herder's Ästhetik', in T. Borsche (ed.), *Herder im Spiegel der Zeiten. Verwerfungen der Rezeptionsgeschichte und Chancen einer Relektüre* (Munich: Fink, 2006), pp. 264–77; also her monograph *Im Zeichen Pygmalions. Das Modell der Statue und die Entdeckung der "Darstellung" im 18. Jahrhundert* (Munich: Fink, 1998); D. von Mücke, 'Pygmalion's Dream in Herder's Aesthetics, or Male Narcissism as the Model for *Bildung*', *Studies in Eighteenth-Century Culture* 19 (1989), 349–65. R. Bayley, 'Herder's Sculptural Thinking', *Parallax* 17.2 (2011), 71–83, includes a perceptive look ahead to the narrowing of vision when what is quite a broad Herderian concept of *Bildung*-through-contact is translated into the German research university after 1810.

[26] Mülder-Bach, *Im Zeichen Pygmalions*, p. 8.

[27] Winckelmann, *Gedanken über die Nachahmung der Griechischen Werke in der Malerei und Bildhauerkunst* (1755), chapter 2; for an excellent discussion of the ecphrastic energy at play in Winckelmann's prose, and the extent to which it is indebted to ancient ways of describing art works, such as Philostratus or Lucian, see K. Harloe, 'Allusion and Ekphrasis in Winckelmann's Paris Description of the Apollo Belvedere', *The Cambridge Classical Journal* 53 (2007), 229–52.

the fable of Pygmalion's statue.'[28] Pygmalion's desire assumes the form of a transhistorical human and artistic affect, though one that aims at sublimation rather than simply materialization. Winckelmann prefaces the sentence just quoted with a Platonic-sounding comment on the human 'innate inclination toward and desire to rise above matter into the mental realm of concepts, and its true satisfaction is the production of new and refined ideas'.[29]

If, to return to Herder's reflections on Thomas Abbt's portrait, the intimacy afforded by fiction is unavailable, there is, he suggests, at least a dream scenario of the biographer's satisfaction, in which a figure, oscillating between Winckelmannian statuesque beauty and the warmth of life, imparts knowledge:

> First of all, I should show the proper manner of my author and remark on the original contours of his mind: a difficult business, even if a useful one. These moments are few and difficult to catch, when the soul lays itself bare (*da sich die Seele entkleidet*), to present itself to us like a beautiful woman in enchanting nakedness; so that we sidle up to someone else's way of thinking (*dass wir uns an die Denkart des andern anschmiegen*), and learn wisdom as if through a kiss.[30]

Like Winckelmann, Herder's narrator is historian and a lover at the same time. But Herder's thought, deliberately or not, also echoes Plato's *Symposium* and the question of how physical closeness may or may not relate to insight and knowledge. When Socrates sits down next to his beautiful host Agathon, he wishes – thus underlining its impossibility – that wisdom and knowledge could be transmitted through closeness, like water flowing from vessel to vessel (*Symp.* 175d). Alcibiades, much later, reprises the scene when he wants to see and sit next to Agathon, just before his speech in which he describes his past failure to elicit a physical response from his beloved Socrates while lying close to him (*Symp.* 212d).

To achieve wisdom through proximity, as Herder concedes, happens only in rare moments, if at all, because the biographer's position is exactly that of foreignness. And as with Winckelmann, ancient precedent is never far from Herder's outline; a little further on, he evokes another model of capturing a life through such a measure of 'love-struck enthusiasm':

[28] Winckelmann, *Geschichte*, p. 262 ; the translation is that of H. F. Mallgrave in J. J. Winckelmann, *History of the Art of Antiquity*, introduction by A. Potts (Los Angeles: Getty Research Institute, 2006), p. 199.

[29] Ibid., p. 262 (trans. p. 199).   [30] Herder, 'Abbt', p. 262.

I have thus indicated some main lines of Abbt's character – perhaps lines like those drawn by that Corinthian girl around the shadow of her sleeping lover, lines in which she thought she saw his image because her imagination (*Einbildungskraft*) filled up the outline, even though an alien observer saw nothing.[31]

Here is Dibutades again. Just as she, faced with the departure of her lover, traces his shadowy outline on a wall, so Herder traces that of Abbt, and Winckelmann that of ancient art. Notice that Herder mentions another element to the triangulation: the figure of an alien observer who saw nothing, pointing to the anxiety that there may be nothing to see. But unlike Winckelmann's 'we' who are like those claiming to have seen ghosts where there is nothing, here, subtly, Herder suggests the uninitiated, those who operate outside the exclusivity of vision that marks the scholar's eye. Even so, his own vision will remain incomplete, too, though possibly deliberately incomplete. Just as the outline may have a limited meaning only, especially to the uninvolved eye, the act of biography results in a monument *manqué*: '[Abbt's] writings are a small fragment', Herder readily admits, 'a small but that much more valuable relic, of his mind. And if now I want to erect for Abbt a memorial statue out of his writings, how could I call it anything but a mutilated torso?'[32] 'Torso of a memorial', erected out of a corpus of writing, is in fact the full subtitle of Herder's attempt to bring Abbt back to life. And yet, by 1768, the observation, through senses and mind, of the mutilated torso as both indicating past beauty and imparting present knowledge is the precise sign of being a modern human being – a modern human being with a critical sensibility for the works of antiquity.[33]

Bildung as the Formation of the Self

Herder's textual and cultural knowledge of antiquity is not coincidental to his argument, neither here nor in his other more explicitly historiographical writings; while he is no classical scholar in the professional sense, it is the conception of modernity by way of *Bildung* that connects his work to

---

[31] Ibid., p. 290.　　[32] Ibid., p. 262.

[33] Of course, to use visual imagery and anecdotes to describe rhetorical, stylistic, or hermeneutic manoeuvres is itself not a modern phenomenon, but one that has considerable ancient precedent – thus making it another example of distinctly modern practices recycling tropes of understanding that are gleaned from ancient materials. On ancient rhetorical theorists' use of visual anecdotes, see J. Elsner, 'Introduction', in J. Elsner and M. Meyer (eds.), *Art and Rhetoric in Roman Culture* (Cambridge University Press, 2014), pp. 1–34.

the realm of classical knowledge as a discipline. For this imagination of the
modern subject, the concept of *Bildung* was essential, and it was *Bildung*
that linked the various forms of cultural classicism and preoccupation with
antiquity with the imperative of pedagogy – and its institutional consequences. It was the concept of *Bildung* that to a large extent structured the
language of classical scholarship, in terms of subject matter as much as of
self-justification. The *Bildung* of the scholar as a modern individual, and
the *Bildung* of antiquity as a whole and of its own individuals, functioned
as mirror concepts. By argument from analogy, *Bildung* linked the individual, or particular, and the universal, and, as one critic has put it apropos
this new concept of individuality in the late eighteenth century, 'individuality can only be articulated in terms of development' (*Individualität ist
nur formulierbar als Entwicklung*).[34] This individual development is structurally related to historical development, both in terms of the individual
history of a human character and in terms of serving as a mutual analogy
with the history of larger units conceptualized as individuals, such as entire
nations, languages, or cultures. Dorothea von Mücke speaks, apropos
Herder, of *Bildung* as a 'neohumanist sublimation script' that reaches full
traction in the last decades of the eighteenth century when 'both language
and the subject are invested with an organic depth and an individual
history in terms of an entelechial development'.[35] Herder, like
Winckelmann, was indeed one of the great 'visualizers' of this new historicism, and both relied heavily on the model of the human body and the
human life cycle to make their point.[36]

   To conceive of the past as an organism or to use the metaphor of the life
cycle may not have been a new phenomenon, nor is this a strategy restricted
to imagining and representing Greece as opposed to other cultures of the
past.[37] Ancient, classical Greece, however, was thought to have a history

---

[34] F. Jannidis, '"Individuum est ineffabile". Zur Veränderung der Individualitätssemantik im 18.
    Jahrhundert und ihrer Auswirkung auf die Figurenkonzeption im Roman', *Aufklärung* 9.2 (1996),
    pp. 77–110, here p. 83.
[35] This comes apropos Herder's attention to Pygmalion and Narcissus, both classic figures of longing
    for human form; von Mücke, 'Pygmalion's Dream', p. 351.
[36] Herder defines history as a 'geography of times and peoples put in motion'; 'Von der
    Annehmlichkeit, Nützlichkeit und Notwendigkeit der Geographie', *SWS*, xxx, p. 102.
[37] The life-cycle metaphor has proven popular from Aristotle through the Hellenistic age to Pliny, the
    Renaissance, and Winckelmann, among others, and it has had a continuing impact on modern
    historiography; cf. A. Momigliano, *The Classical Foundations of Modern Historiography* (University
    of California Press, 1990), chapter 4. For the prevalence of organic imagery as part of German
    Hellenism and Classicism, and its particular use as a key for describing and constructing cultural
    autonomy, see also B. Vick, 'Greek Origins and Organic Metaphors: Ideals of Cultural Autonomy
    in Neohumanist Germany from Winckelmann to Curtius', *Journal of the History of Ideas* 63.3

that seemed to exemplify this developmental structure (and in Chapter 3 I will examine in more detail how arguments for the exceptionality of the life of Greek culture were invoked). If human reason characteristically perceives historicity and makes sense of history, then history, in turn, conforms and bears witness to the development of human reason.[38]

For Herder, Greece was the cultural stage analogous to the age of maturing, beautiful *youth*, the period of 'youth and bridal bloom', of 'the dream of the young man and the fancy tales of the maiden'.[39] Ancient Greece, in particular, had a history in which, at least for a brief, privileged (classical, fifth-century BCE, Athenian) moment, human reason and beautiful self-realization seemed to come together in perfect harmony, balance, and, hence, freedom.[40] Both Winckelmann and Herder are adamant that Greece is also one of the prime examples of a culture or nation containing the entire circle of *Bildung* – its growth, maturity, and decline – in its history, enabling the reader to comprehend and thus advance the progress of history.[41]

If Greece represented the entire circle of *Bildung* in its history, it thus emerged as a *changeable* and transformative culture (as opposed to other static Eastern ones), which in turn perfectly matched the expectations of pedagogy as development. In short, Greece itself represented a culture of development, and *Bildung*, as a program of self-transformation or self-direction, therefore aligned itself smoothly with the study or understanding of antiquity, as effectively both its content and its end result.

A quotation from Friedrich Ast's later university textbook *Outline of Philology* (1808) – the term he uses for 'outline' is *Grundriss*, not *Schattenriss* (silhouette), but the image of the line drawing remains in this architectural metaphor, too – shows how philology, *Bildung*, and operative images of life, liveliness, and individual personality coalesce in what was a standard

---

(2002), pp. 483–500. That narratives of the self or of culture according to an organic and temporal, biographical model may be a dominant but again not necessarily an undisputed or self-evident notion is provocatively challenged by Galen Strawson, who offers a strong refutation of self-perception in terms of narrative biographical sequence, as ostensibly natural and uncontroversial; 'Against Narrativity', *Ratio* 17(4) (2004), pp. 428–52.

[38] On the historicizing of reason, see Y. Yovel, *Kant and the Philosophy of History* (Cambridge, MA: Harvard University Press, 1980), pp. 3ff.

[39] *Auch eine Philosophie der Geschichte der Menschheit, SWS*, v, pp. 495, 497.

[40] That this postulating of a cultural flourishing in a moment of freedom has significant political implications is clear, though not the main trajectory of my argument here.

[41] Herder makes use of the full etymological range of the term; R. Vierhaus, 'Bildung', in O. Brunner et al. (eds.), *Geschichtliche Grundbegriffe: historisches Lexikon zur politisch-sozialen Sprache in Deutschland* (Stuttgart: Metzler, 1972–97), vol. i, pp. 508–51; also R. Koselleck, 'Zur anthropologischen und semantischen Struktur der Bildung', in R. Koselleck (ed.), *Bildungsbürgertum im 19. Jahrhundert*, 4 vols. (Stuttgart: Klett-Cotta, 1985–92), vol. ii, pp. 11–46.

example of classical philology's self-presentation. Philology is the study of the spirit (*Geist*) suffusing the inner and outer life of the classical world and its textual sources, and true philology harmonizes the study of material, or essence, and form: 'In this unity Being and Form are sublimated into a true Essence; the latter comes alive (*wird Leben*), and the former takes (human) shape (*Gestalt*), both together become an intricately formed and cultivated life, as an expression of spirit.'[42] Given the balance of those elements in the ancient world, Ast concludes that, as opposed to a dead learnedness and mechanical knowledge, philology's true objective is 'to reach a true and lifelike intuition (*Anschauung*) and understanding (*Erkenntnis*) of classical antiquity, which is, as the ancient world, the paradigm of genuine *Bildung*'.[43] What is more, he argues, 'in Germany it was the three heroes of our artistic and scientific *Bildung*, Winckelmann, Lessing, and Herder, who recognized and reconceived once more of antiquity as it really was; by their own example they showed how a mind nourished by classical antiquity partakes of true *Bildung*, when the spirit of antiquity, as beautiful and living form, and as pure and genuine sense, weds itself to modern *Bildung* (*dass sich der antike Geist als schöne, lebendige Form, als reiner gediegener Sinn mit der modernen Bildung vermählet*)'.[44] This not only attaches the personalities of specific scholars to the affective imperative to study and to intuit antiquity as a living being; it also indicates that the work of non-institutional figures of the previous generation, such as Winckelmann and Herder, continued to be a reference point for the developing discipline, now inscribed in its own quasi-biography.

With *Bildung* being about the development of the individual, antiquity in turn became personified. To describe the character of antiquity was to recount its life story, and to understand its *Wesen* (essence, character, or being). The scholar, diplomat, and administrator Wilhelm von Humboldt, who would in 1809 be tasked with developing the plan for the newly established Prussian research university in Berlin that would (much) later bear his name, makes this form of understanding antiquity quite literally the goal in his programmatic essay *On the Study of Antiquity, and of Greek Antiquity in Particular* (1793):

> The study of a nation offers all the advantages which history has in general, namely to increase our knowledge of human beings by examples of actions and events, to sharpen our power of judgment, and to improve and raise our character. Yet it does more. In trying not only to unravel the thread of successive events, but rather to explore the condition and the state of the

---

[42] F. Ast, *Grundriss der Philologie* (Landshut: Krüll, 1808), p. 3.   [43] Ibid., p. 6.   [44] Ibid., p. 5.

nation altogether, this kind of study gives us a *biography*, as it were [italics Humboldt].[45]

Humboldt's mirroring of *Bildung* and biography was symptomatic, and this study argues that Classics as a discipline is lastingly indebted to this biographical, developmental, narrative model both as a scholarly method and for articulating its own self-understanding. Just as antiquity, in particular Greek antiquity, came to be understood through the model of an organic whole with the characteristics and properties of an individual, scholarly research was articulated as a quasi-personal and also affective relationship with antiquity – in short, as an attempt to understand what is past in terms of someone who is other than oneself.

Bildung and Love

How much of that other, though, could be known? Present or absent, past or present, understanding individuality, one's own as much as another's, emerged as a defining challenge of the age. There, again, the languages of *Bildung* and of feeling and especially of love overlap. Talk of love became a code to help think through and articulate the self in relation to others, and by around 1800, love, like *Bildung*, involved reflection of and reflection on autonomy and self-referentiality. Love thus came to function as a prominent topos of culture altogether.[46] If love, as a literary and non-literary preoccupation of the late eighteenth and the nineteenth centuries, is the field of debate where nature and culture cross, then it is the writing off which *Bildung*, as another such cross between nature and culture, could be read. Goethe's Wilhelm Meister, in the novel that, according to Friedrich Schlegel, was one of the three milestones of the Romantic age, claims to know one thing for sure on his path to education, namely that 'I am *gebildet* enough to love and to grieve.'[47] The mention of grief in the

---

[45] 'Das Studium einer Nation gewährt schlechterdings alle diejenigen Vortheile, welche die Geschichte überhaupt darbietet, indem dieselbe durch Beispiele von Handlungen und Begebenheiten die Menschenkenntniss erweitert, die Beurtheilungskraft schärft, den Charakter erhöht und verbessert; aber es thut noch mehr. Indem es nicht sowohl dem Faden auf einander folgender Begebenheiten nachspürt, als vielmehr den Zustand und die gänzliche Lage der Nation zu erforschen versucht, liefert es gleichsam eine *Biographie* derselben'; 'Über das Studium des Alterthums, und des Griechischen insbesondre', in A. Leitzmann (ed.), *Gesammelte Schriften* (Berlin: de Gruyter, 1968), vol. I, pp. 255–81, p. 257.

[46] G. Neumann, 'Lektüren der Liebe', in H. Meier and G. Neumann (eds.), *Über die Liebe. Ein Symposion* (Munich: Fink, 2001), pp. 9–79, p. 10.

[47] G. Neumann, '"Ich bin gebildet genug, um zu lieben und zu trauern." Die Erziehung zur Liebe in Goethe's *Wilhelm Meister*', in T. Heydenreich (ed.), *Liebesroman – Liebe im Roman. Eine Erlanger Ringvorlesung* (Erlangen: Universitätsbund Erlangen-Nürnberg, 1987), pp. 41–82.

context of both love and *Bildung* triangulates the elements of understanding related to sentiment and feeling with the aspect of loss and the past; it expresses, in one short sentence, the encroachment of conscious distance and the passionate navigation of impossible closeness onto the concept of individual formation.

Likewise, Friedrich Schleiermacher, theoretician of hermeneutics, theologian, philosopher, and future comprehensive translator of Plato's dialogues into German (on whom more in the following chapters), develops an ethics of individuality that posits love as a central motor to guarantee contact with what is other than the self, provoking and furthering self-awareness and self-knowledge in turn. In his *Soliloquies* (*Monologen*) – originally of 1800, a strangely confessional systematic account of individualization as the highest good, which he affectionately addresses to an unnamed 'You' – he makes *Bildung* and love actually conditional upon one another: 'No *Bildung* without love, and without one's own proper *Bildung* no perfection in love; one complementing the other both grow inseparably together (*Keine Bildung ohne Liebe, und ohne eigne Bildung keine Vollendung in der Liebe; eins das Andere ergänzend, wächst beides unzertrennlich fort*). I find united in myself the two great conditions for morality! I have made both sense (*Sinn*) and love my own, and both continue to develop, a testimony that life is fresh and healthy and that my proper *Bildung* is to grow stronger yet.'[48]

Schleiermacher may not have been a classicist in the institutional sense, but his impact on the programmatic outlook of institutionalized philology has been considerable. Given the generative potential of love as a cultural term (for framing *Bildung*, the individual subject, and its place in society), it is a language that not only expresses but also shapes the expectation of what the relationship with an other, or, in the case of scholarship, the object of that study, can be and can achieve. This language lends itself particularly well to expressing the challenge and paradoxes that arise vis-à-vis the recognition of historical difference. Romantic love integrates the fact of the other's separateness as part of the self-understanding prompted by love. By analogy, the scholar who employs such a rhetoric of love can make meaningful and communicable, up to a point, the alternation of proximity and distance that is conceivable as both personal and historical; and it opens the possibility also of addressing the lack of availability and reciprocity that is always implied in encountering the past.

[48] 'Monologen', in *Friedrich Schleiermacher. Kritische Gesamtausgabe*, I.12, ed. G. Meckenstock (Berlin: de Gruyter, 1995), pp. 323–93, here p. 350. The work was published anonymously in 1800, under Schleiermacher's name in 1810, and subsequently reprinted twice more, with additions, until 1829.

Such a language had effectively since mid-century begun to sweep through a range of interconnected fields of social, scientific, and artistic expression: rhetoric, aesthetics, physiology and biology, education, and literature. Aside from offering a way of describing objects at hand (art works, the human organism), it generated a recognizable model for orientation and communication, and parameters for 'disciplining' the self-perception of the subject and its relation with others in society.[49] I follow here the sociologist Niklas Luhmann's theorization of love as – like *Bildung* or, for that matter, science – a 'code', that is to say not as the emotion itself, but as a historically variable discursive language that enables communication and minimizes lack of understanding. Luhmann's 'code of love' describes a language and a set of expectations that essentially cushions the challenges encountered in what he sees as an increasingly functionally differentiated society, in which the individual emerged not only as a parameter of thought but as a new site of making freer social choices, including marriage and forms of sociability, and where the choice of career, too, opened up beyond earlier social restrictions, and a new range of professions became possible (including, incidentally, new careers in education, knowledge, and scholarship).[50] In an environment in which social relations become increasingly less predictable, feeling and love, as focused on the other, offered a promise of creating a language in which those anxieties surrounding the individual as a basic parameter could be framed.

Luhmann postulates a historical narrative that takes him from the idealization of medieval love through the code of paradox in the seventeenth and eighteenth centuries, on to the heightened reflection of autonomy and self-referentiality that occurs around 1800 in the paradigm of romantic love. What made modern subjectivity 'romantic', in terms of period designation, was the assumption that each individual perceives the world separately, that individuals are subject to change and development,

---

[49] I rely on the very useful full exploration of this discursive phenomenon, its origins and its corollaries, in N. Wegmann, *Diskurse der Empfindsamkeit. Zur Geschichte eines Gefühls in der Literatur des 18. Jahrhunderts* (Stuttgart: Metzler, 1988).

[50] '[L]iterary, idealizing and mythifying representations of love do not choose their themes and arguments randomly; rather, they respond to their respective society and its changing tendencies. Even if they appear descriptive they do not necessarily mirror the real conditions of loving, but they solve definable problems, namely to translate the functional needs of a social system into a form that can be passed on. The semantic code of love can therefore in each case give access to the relation between media of communication and social structure and make that relation understandable', N. Luhmann, *Liebe als Passion. Zur Kodierung von Intimität* (Frankfurt am Main: Suhrkamp, 1982), p. 24 (my translation); published in English as *Love as Passion. The Codification of Intimacy*, tr. J. Gaines (Cambridge, MA: Harvard University Press, 1987).

and that engagement with an other, loved one, and his or her world heightens the awareness of one's own singularity, an awareness in which it is precisely the perception of distance from the other that amplifies the experience.[51] The philosophical anthropology of the late eighteenth century with its stress on the world-creating qualities of the subject raises the particularity and singularity of the individual to the level of a universal principle: two souls equal two worlds, mutually bound and exclusively related. Such a code of romantic love thus increases individuality, reflection, and the preservation of the self, and renders love an ostensibly self-justifying code, not unlike the circular logic of *Bildung* (Luhmann here in fact quotes Humboldt).[52]

The awareness of the other's and one's own singularity brings, in turn, the threat of incommunicability, of the possibility that communication is not (fully) possible. At the same time, this language of love helped to integrate the possibility of incomprehension and absence, and it made emotionally marked distance a precondition of selfhood. The anxiety over communicability of emotion and, with it, of the standing of the self is part and parcel of a broader sentimentalism. We can see not only an anxiety over whether and how the self can be expressed but also an anxiety over the power of feeling that can replicate and generate even without a determinate link to a single individual, and in textual form. In other words, it is the act of speaking about love and of articulating feeling that, independent from particular subjects, can generate and maintain feeling.[53] As Herder puts it in an essay of 1797, 'Love and Selfhood' (*Liebe und Selbstheit*), the highest degree of delight in the encounter between two individuals is not their physical union, but rather it lies 'in that first happy act of finding each other, in that moment sweet beyond description when both lovers become aware of the fact that they love each other and *when they say so to each other*, surely, sweetly, and in concert, however incomplete and uncontrolled otherwise'.[54]

This is why it is crucial to extend Luhmann's systems-theoretical analysis and to link up its insights with considering the act of reading and of textual production, as well as of textual interpretation and criticism, as

---

[51] Luhmann, *Liebe als Passion*, p. 172. Luhmann uses mainly literary texts from the German, English, and French traditions as his primary material.
[52] Ibid., p. 167, with reference to Humboldt's 'Theorie der Bildung', *Werke*, vol. 1, pp. 234–40.
[53] For a philosophical analysis of the effect whereby speaking of love creates and amplifies affect, see O. Ware, 'Love Speech', *Critical Inquiry* 34.3 (2008), 491–508. Stendhal, in his long essay 'De l'amour' (1822), knows also of that same pattern and describes it in greatly fascinated detail.
[54] Herder, 'Liebe und Selbstheit', *SWS* 15, pp. 304–26, here p. 314, my italics.

a crucial sphere where feeling becomes operative.[55] This agitation over whether and when feelings are one's own is an anxiety over the knowledge inherent in feeling. If those feelings can be provoked even by texts and textuality without the actual presence of an other, then it is this epistemological angle that makes discussions and reference to feeling relevant in the context of the disciplines of textual and historical scholarship that articulates its relationship with an absent past. If the writer, the reader, and the critic likewise have the power to bring alive the subjects of their writing, reading, and interpretation and to be, in turn, challenged by the dialectic between control and involvement, then it is no coincidence that the motif of Pygmalion should have particularly strong traction in the late eighteenth and the turn of the nineteenth century.

In the same essay on 'Love and Selfhood', Herder comments apropos the articulation of the self that is only possible by way of the other, and *vice versa*: 'The existence of others rests entirely on our own being and consciousness, insofar as they are connected to us through love and longing (*so fern sie durch Liebe und Sehnsucht mit uns verknüpft sind*); were we to lose the latter, we would also be without enjoyment of the former.'[56] Possession of the other may not be fully possible (nor fully desirable), though it keeps us going, just as Winckelmann had claimed that our attention to copies of lost ancient artefacts is much greater than if we were in full possession of them: we must long for the artefacts, conscious that we do not have full possession, but we must have traces of them in copies and thus not lose them entirely either.

The point of including the analytical vocabulary of Luhmann is not to drown textual observations in the terminology of systems theory; rather, it is to make use of the insight that a language of love and interpersonal affection, as a discursive preference, addresses communication and self-positioning in the face of the cognitive challenge of interpretation. If this 'cognitive strain' of trying to include the other's universe into one's own was practised, addressed, and to an extent cushioned through a language of love, then it extended to the cognitive challenge of encountering *historical* difference and distance that was encountered and expressed in the practice of scholarship and the creation of scholarly knowledge. In fact, a discourse

---

[55] This is in line with an objection that has been raised to the sociologically oriented criticism of Luhmann, namely that it underestimates the code-breaking and code-changing functions of discourses, especially as they are expressed in textual form; see, e.g., W. Hinderer, 'Introduction', in W. Hinderer (ed.), *Codierungen von Liebe in der Kunstperiode* (Würzburg: Königshausen und Neumann, 1997), pp. 7–33.

[56] Herder, 'Liebe und Selbstheit', p. 325.

of love, a discourse on textuality, and a discourse on history all overlapped considerably. The historical semantics of love suggested here help to elucidate why so much programmatic writing around 1800 on how to approach antiquity operates openly with a language of emotional attachment that authorizes the undertaking of scholarship and makes it comprehensible. If classical scholarship sets itself up to become the representative pedagogical discipline of the period, then it needs to be able to do the work of 'disciplining' the individual, and it does so in a language that chimes with an available discourse of love and feeling.

If the function of a code is to facilitate communication and accommodate change, then its success in a complex society can be measured in the number of connecting points to other codes. While Luhmann suspects that the romantic code of love in particular may offer fewer such connectors to discourses such as economics or political power than did earlier codes of love, he does point out the affinity of the code of love to that of education; and that, of course, had particular traction in a field that keyed *Bildung* to the understanding of classical antiquity.[57] The anxiety over the self, such as it emerges from contact with others, was an anxiety that infiltrated the self-definition of the reasonably recent category of the professional scholar as well. As the philosopher J. G. Fichte put it in the opening lecture of a popular series, 'On the Definition of the Scholar' (*Über die Bestimmung des Gelehrten*), in 1794, and with a ring of structural linguistics *avant la lettre*, 'The scholar is a scholar only to the extent that he is opposed to other human beings who are not scholars' (*Der Gelehrte ist nur insofern ein Gelehrter, inwiefern er anderen Menschen entgegengesetzt wird, die das nicht sind*).[58] In a later, equally programmatic essay of 1807 on the creation of a new educational institution (namely the future Friedrich-Wilhelm-University in Berlin, whose first rector he became), Fichte will likewise give 'love' a central function in the creation of the 'art of science': 'the principle by which the art of science will rise to its great height is the love of art (*die Liebe zur Kunst*). It is that same love which always has to revitalize the

---

[57] On Luhmann analysing science (*Wissenschaft*) as a social system with its proper code, and its transferability to the special case of classical philology, see I. Gildenhard, '*Philologia Perennis?* Classical Scholarship and Functional Differentiation', in *Out of Arcadia. Classics and Politics in Germany in the Age of Burckhardt, Nietzsche and Wilamowitz*, in I. Gildenhard and M. Ruehl (eds.), *Out of Arcadia. Classics and Politics in Germany in the Age of Burckhardt, Nietzsche and Wilamowitz*. Bulletin of the Institute of Classical Studies Supplement 79 (London: Institute of Classical Studies, 2003), pp. 161–203.

[58] J. G. Fichte, 'Einige Vorlesungen über die Bestimmung des Gelehrten', in R. Lauth and H. Jacob (eds), *Gesamtausgabe der Bayerischen Akademie der Wissenschaften*, vol. I.3: *Werke 1794–1796* (Stuttgart-Bad Cannstatt: Frommann, 1966), pp. 23–68, here p. 27.

formation of artists (*Künstlerbildung*) anew, stimulate it in each particular case, and lead it on the right way.'[59] The identity of the scholar, the *Wissenschaftler*, is articulated in the same nexus of feeling, *Bildung*, and knowledge that emerges vis-à-vis the formation of an other and its recognition. And to the extent that feeling and love were structured around autonomy and the singularity of the individual, there was a parallel claim to be made for the increasing autonomy of scholarship, if it presented itself as an exclusive and justified bond with its object of study.[60]

The Outline of *Wissenschaft*

I want to finish this chapter with a brief look at Friedrich Schlegel as a transitional, or rather as an eccentric figure, not an institutionalized classicist, and as a philosopher, philologist, and poet as experimental in his views as he was and is hard to categorize.[61] Still, he was a writer of programmatic essays on classical scholarship, and his oscillating between the discourses of scholarship, literature, and philosophy underscores the transferability of the language and structure of love. In *On the Study of Greek Poetry* (1795–1797), his stated aim is to reconcile the positions of the *Querelle des anciens et des modernes*, the cultural debate about the validity of ancient texts as models for art and science that had dominated the turn of the preceding century and a good part of the eighteenth. Schlegel, in his preface to the essay, sees his work as

> an attempt to prove that the study of Greek poetry is more than a forgivable fancy (*Liebhaberei*): but that it is, and always will be the necessary duty of all lovers (*Liebhaber*) who want to embrace the beautiful with true love, of all

[59] J. G. Fichte, 'Deduzierter Plan zu einer zu Berlin zu errichtenden höhern Lehranstalt, die in gehöriger Verbindung mit einer Akademie der Wissenschaften stehe' (1807), in W. Weischedel (ed.), *Idee und Wirklichkeit einer Universität: Dokumente zur Geschichte der Friedrich-Wilhelms-Universität zu Berlin* (Berlin: de Gruyter, 1960), pp. 30–105, here p. 44. The essay is now also newly available in English translation as 'A Plan, Deduced from First Principles, for an Institution of Higher Learning to Be Established in Berlin, Connected to and Subordinate to an Academy of Sciences', in L. Menand, P. Reitter, and C. Wellmon (eds.), *The Rise of the Research University: A Sourcebook* (Chicago University Press, 2017), pp. 67–83.

[60] Wellmon captures well the imperative for the scholar to be imagined as both individual and part of a like-minded group, and the 'organic', unity-creating nature of the scholarly perspective: '[Fichte and Schleiermacher] tied the legitimacy of a uniquely scientific knowledge to the character and virtue of the scholar, whose distinguishing feature was a capacity to discern unity and make connections in a modern media environment that seemed fractured and fragmented', *Organizing Enlightenment*, p. 210.

[61] See R. S. Leventhal, *The Disciplines of Interpretation: Lessing, Herder, Schlegel and Hermeneutics in Germany, 1750–1800* (Berlin: de Gruyter, 1994), on Schlegel's notion of hermeneutics and a new philology as it departs from what will establish itself as the mainstream; see also U. Breuer, R. Bunia, and A. Erlinghagen (eds.), *Schlegel und die Philologie* (Paderborn: Schoeningh, 2013).

experts who want to arrive at universal judgments, and of all thinkers who
seek to define once and for all the pure laws of beauty and the eternal nature
of art.[62]

Liebhaberei and *Liebhaber* may initially suggest an 'amateur' approach, one
meaning of the word *Liebhaber*, but it is, incidentally, a term that in
contemporary parlance and dictionaries attached itself first of all to interpersonal relationships, even before attachment to an object or pursuit. *Liebe*
likewise, if dictionary usage is any indication, was in the late eighteenth
century increasingly a designator of interpersonal or object-related affect
before it was, secondarily, a term with a spiritualized, religious meaning.[63] In
other words, Schlegel's use of the term deliberately links 'our' attitude
towards ancient poetry to the imagery of an earthly, personal form of
affective relationship.

The concern close to Schlegel's heart here is the renewal of modern
poetry, and he, like Winckelmann, is simultaneously invested in historical
analysis and in the consideration of contemporary artistic, aesthetic practice.
Like Winckelmann, he recognizes that an incomplete vision is a condition of
modernity and of the modern view on antiquity. Modern poetry, in his
diagnosis, is neither 'satisfying' (*befriedigend*), nor has it found satisfaction
(*Befriedigung*). Instead, it thrives on actually keeping open the rifts left by
Sehnsucht and *Streben*, longing and striving. It cannot achieve completion,
and it lacks the repose brought by completion, a '*complete beauty*, which
would be *whole* and *persistent*; a Juno, which would not turn into a cloud at
the very moment of ecstatic embrace'.[64]

But a Juno will inevitably reveal itself to be a cloud: the reference is to
the mythological figure of Ixion, who desired Hera and whom Zeus tricked
by having him lie with a cloud in the shape of the goddess (as told in, for
example, Pindar, *Pyth.* 2, 21–48). But this Juno also invokes the sculptural
portrait of the *Juno Ludovisi*, which Winckelmann had singled out in his
History as an example of the high style and which in turn had become
a topos of the philosophical and art criticism of Weimar classicism.[65] In

[62] Schlegel, 'Über das Studium der Griechischen Poesie' (1795–97), in E. Behler (ed.), *Kritische
Friedrich-Schlegel-Ausgabe* (*KFSA*), vol. i: *Studien des Klassischen Altertums* (Paderborn:
Schöningh, 1979), pp. 205–367, here p. 207.
[63] E. Kapl-Blume, 'Liebe im Lexikon. Zum Bedeutungswandel des Begriffes "Liebe" in ausgewählten
Lexika des 18. und 19. Jahrhunderts. Ein Forschungsbericht', in L. Jäger (ed.), *Zur Historischen
Semantik des deutschen Gefühlswortschatzes. Aspekte, Probleme und Beispiele seiner lexikographischen
Erfassung* (Aachen: Alano, 1988), pp. 215–46.
[64] Schlegel, 'Über das Studium', p. 217 (his italics).
[65] R.-P. Janz, 'Ansichten der Juno Ludovisi. Winckelmann – Schiller – Goethe', in P.-A. Alt, et al.
(ed.), *Prägnanter Moment. Studien zur deutschen Literatur der Aufklärung und Klassik* (Würzburg:

Schlegel's diction, Ixion's Juno and Winckelmann's admirable statue combine into another classical figure of the impossible and unreachable, another phantom wanted by those who act as if they have seen ghosts.

But Schlegel does not stop at this condition. The literature of the moderns, in order to become truly modern, needs continued contact with and a gradual understanding of the ancients, again a gradual self-realization in empathetic response to an other, and Schlegel is just as willing to imagine such contact in personified form.[66] With reference to the genre of elegy, Schlegel announces, radically: 'She [Elegy] is no longer merely a beautiful antique; she is indigenous (*einheimisch*) and she now lives among us.'[67] But the way, for Schlegel, to achieve such actual cohabitation, to reimagine an understanding of antiquity as successful and present, is to overcome the divide between ancient and modern in the act of criticism, which, as an act of modern reflection, can comprehend historically the gulf that separates the *Bildung* of antiquity and of modernity.[68] The synthesis promised by criticism is also enacted in co-operative, radical symphilosophy, which operates on the horizontal, synchronic plane; this is Schlegel's key term for an extreme, experimental, future-oriented philology and way of knowing marked out as a literal interpersonal project, in which poetry, philosophy, and philology and their practitioners become, quite literally, indistinguishable:

> We could see the start of a new epoch of *Wissenschaften* and arts, if symphilosophy and sympoetry became so universal and so intimate (*innig*) that it would not be a rare occurrence for several complementing natures to come together and create works. One cannot help thinking that two minds truly were and belonged together, like separated halves, and achieved everything only when linked to each other.[69]

Königshausen & Neumann, 2002), pp. 357–72; on Juno-as-cloud as invoked by Kant and countered, with reference to the *Ludovisi*, by Schiller, see J. Tresch, 'Even the Tools Will Be Free: Humboldt's Romantic Technologies', in D. Aubin, C. Bigg, and O. H. Sibum (eds.), *The Heavens on Earth: Observatories and Astronomy in Nineteenth-Century Science and Culture* (Durham, NC: Duke University Press, 2010), pp. 253–85, 263 ff.

[66] C. Armstrong, *Romantic Organicism: From Idealist Origins to Ambivalent Afterlife* (New York: Palgrave Macmillan, 2003), p. 36, uses Schlegel's 1797 essay on the literature of the Greeks and Romans as exemplary of interrelatedness and reciprocity, rather than causality, as one crucial element of the Idealist organicism of the period around 1800.

[67] F. Schlegel, *Elegien aus dem Griechischen* (1798), *KA*, vol. i, pp. 369–86, here p. 370.

[68] See also the useful introduction by Stuart Barnett to his edition and translation of Schlegel's *On the Study of Greek Poetry* (Albany, NY: SUNY Press, 2001).

[69] 'Athenäum-Fragmente', *KFSA*, vol. ii: Charakteristiken und Kritiken I (1796–1801), ed. H. Eichner (Paderborn: Schöningh, 1967), no. 125, pp. 165–255, here p. 185.

Schlegel knows his classical texts and he invokes clearly the language of Plato's *Symposium,* where Aristophanes, in a discussion in praise of Eros, famously tells the myth of how human beings used to be complete, two-bodied creatures, cut apart, and ever since longing and seeking for their lost half (*Symp.* 189d-194e). Schlegel in fact toggles between creating identity on a diachronic and synchronic level, and he identifies the point of leverage where his own radical new science of antiquity goes beyond Winckelmann's diagnostic achievement:

> The systematic Winckelmann, who read all ancients as One Author, saw everything as a whole, and focused all his energy on the Greeks, recognized the fundamental difference between antiquity and modernity and so laid the foundations for a material study of antiquity. Only when the point of reference has become clear from which we can establish the absolute identity of ancient and modern, which was, is or will be, only then will we be able to say that we have found the contour of this science (*der Kontur der Wissenschaft*) and that we can now turn to its methodical execution.[70]

Winckelmann imagined antiquity as one person. In this aphorism, Schlegel leaves open whether the answer is that individuality must be taken even further and disaggregated to such an extent that different 'figures' of antiquity, like the individual genres that already 'live among us', can and must be distinguished, or whether the reference point for identity between the modern and the ancient each imagined as a person needs to be established in a way that exceeds Winckelmann's material, object-based study. In either case, the imagination of antiquity and its texts as human figures stays in place. Schlegel's new science of antiquity itself, like one of Winckelmann's statues, has a contour that is culture-defining as much as it creates methodical standards of science, and that is traced, like that of Dibutades's departing lover, in an act of making culture – and of making scholarship. The poet, he continues, 'if he wants to be an expert and understand his fellow citizens in the realm of art, has to be a philologist as well'.[71] Unlike Winckelmann, Schlegel's ideal poet-scholar-citizen wants to draw the contour not of something that is remote and past, but of something that ought to be fully integrated, and that integrates himself. The outline, the *Kontur,* invites to be filled in.

Schlegel's risky, utopian, and modern philology seeks the Archimedean point from which identity with the other and with the past is possible through the longing process of getting to know antiquity as if it were another human subjectivity – a process that has all the benefits and risks of the act of

---

[70] 'Athenäum-Fragmente', no. 149, pp. 188–9.   [71] 'Athenäum-Fragmente', no. 255, pp. 208–9.

personification: as giving voice to something that cannot speak itself, on the other hand. Like the structure of *prosopopoeia*, of personification as the 'giving of face or of voice', the rhetorical strategy that relies on the absence, or impossibility of voice, of that which is made to speak, just so does the past need to be thoroughly absent in order to be made present. The question remains to what extent the relationship between two human beings conforms to the (scholarly) relationship with something that is irrevocably past – even if its imagination as a living being is exactly what helps negotiate the value of engaging with the past, presented as the promise of a unique, coherent, even if complex and therefore 'legible' whole. A feature of *prosopopoeia* is its simultaneously stabilizing and destabilizing force. To make what is absent speak is in some ways an easy and obvious movement, a gentle manoeuvre and gliding displacement. But it is also 'erroneous', and this ambiguity is particularly marked when *prosopopoeia* is consciously and reflectively employed as a figure of speech. If *prosopopoeia* describes the constant and futile attempt to define absence by revealing essential similarities with the figure that is seen and heard speaking, the tensions of scholarly identity crystallize particularly around the act of personifying the past. The image of the woman looking out after her departing lover suggests an actually experienced earlier presence and immediate knowledge of that lover and in this way glosses over the radically different trajectory of past and present that concerns the historian of antiquity, whose object has not ever actually been present to the scholar.

It is that very cognitive strain that can be articulated in a code of love, a code which values engagement for its own sake with what is not self, postulates and communicates the epistemological and pedagogic pay-off of that engagement, and includes the awareness of its limits. Schlegel operates within this same imagery, but his radical philology also points to the potential of criticism as a shared act between contemporary subjects, emphasizing the mutual, complex implication of self and other *between* those who seek to understand antiquity, a triangulation that scholarship in its institutional development eventually took much less note of. The exclusive, interdependent relationship between the modern subject and the ancient past imagined as a human subject has, for better or worse, continued to take precedence, and classical scholarship has continued to think with Winckelmann rather than with Schlegel.

CHAPTER 2

From the Symposium to the Seminar
Language of Love and Language of Institutions

Friedrich Schlegel considered Diotima's dialogue with Socrates, as told in Plato's *Symposium*, 'one of antiquity's most exquisite remains', and he declared that any reader's only appropriate response to knowledge of this work could and should only be love (*Liebe*), a love that mirrors the teachings about love which Socrates receives from Diotima.[1] The next two chapters trace a line, backwards and forwards, between two poles: on the one hand, the attempts around 1800 to formulate the ambition to know antiquity, attempts implicated in a language of feeling and love; on the other hand, the increasing institutionalization of scholarship that found in a Platonic template a way to express the link between pedagogy, *Bildung*, feeling, and knowledge with regard to antiquity. In this template, the *Symposium* takes on particular plasticity, not least insofar as it models lack and incompleteness as a driving force of scholarly *eros*.

If the eighteenth century has been described as an 'age of Socrates', then one could also argue for a contemporary and subsequent move towards an 'age of Plato' that gathers steam and is reflected in new methods and institutions of knowing antiquity. As Miriam Leonard put it, in analogy with the twentieth century as the 'age of Oedipus', 'Socrates's rediscovery is in part the story of the discovery of classics as a discipline.'[2] Socrates had by the second half of the eighteenth century become a focus of renewed interest across Europe, known through translations, adaptations, and

---

[1] 'Über die Diotima', *KFSA*, ed. Ernst Behler, vol. 1 (Paderborn: Schoeningh, 1979), pp. 70–115, here pp. 71–2; for the close structural connections between Plato's *Symposium* and Schlegel's *Gespräch über die Poesie*, see S. Matuschek, 'Die Macht des Gastmahls. Schlegels *Gespräch über die Poesie* und Platons *Symposion*', in S. Matuschek (ed.), *Wo das philosophische Gespräch ganz in Dichtung übergeht. Platons Symposion und seine Wirkung in der Renaissance, Romantik und Moderne* (Heidelberg: Winter, 2002), pp. 81–96; a similar claim for its importance, but a different reading in detail, is offered by M. Mergenthaler, *Zwischen Eros und Mitteilung. Die Frühromantik im Symposion der "Athenäums-Fragmente"* (Paderborn: Schöningh, 2012).

[2] M. Leonard, *Socrates and the Jews: Hellenism and Hebraism from Moses Mendelssohn to Sigmund Freud* (Chicago University Press, 2012), p. 24.

visual representations. In fact, he was most prominently a figure thought to represent not only a form of practical, and sometimes eccentric, wisdom, but also an authority figure who dramatized sociability, intellectual exchange, and friendship among a circle of the like-minded.[3] Around the turn of the century, the shift of attention towards Plato, as disciple, philosophical thinker, editor, and effectively 'author' of Socrates, mirrors a shift towards the organization of disciplinary methodology and the self-reflection of the professionalized classical scholars. This is a shift from the imagined symposium as institution to the *Symposium* as a text in need of edition and interpretation, and from the sympotic sociability of Socrates and his interlocutors to the seminar as a form of pedagogic communality.

While Socrates had been available as a figure of the eccentric thinker and as moral precept for a long time, his and Plato's profile was shifting. An increasing number of Platonic text editions had been appearing and extended the canon of readily available Platonic texts, both in Germany and in other parts of Europe, especially so in England.[4] The *Symposium*, though, had special status even within that Plato renaissance of the late eighteenth century.[5] Its themes and dramatic framework resonated with sentimental tendencies. The theme of love as a guarantor of immortality, just as in the similarly popular *Phaedo*, chimed with philosophical and theological questions.[6] The Dutch philosopher Frans Hemsterhuis, for example, had set off a fashion for newly considering the character of Diotima – Herder's essay on 'Love as Selfhood' mentioned in the last chapter was in part an explicit response to Hemsterhuis. In addition, the dialogue was generally considered one in which poetry and philosophy were most closely related, taking up an ancient topos already current in Cicero and Quintilian.[7] But Plato's work, as this chapter and the next

---

[3] B. Boehm, *Sokrates im achtzehnten Jahrhundert: Studien zum Werdegang des modernen Persönlichkeitsbewusstseins* (Leipzig: Quelle & Meyer, 1929); B. Auerochs, 'Platon um 1800. Zu seinem Bild bei Stolberg, Wieland, Schlegel und Schleiermacher', in K. Manger (ed.), *Wieland-Studien III 1996* (Biberach: Wieland-Archiv), pp. 161–93; E. Wilson, *The Death of Socrates* (Cambridge, MA: Harvard University Press, 2007), p. 73.

[4] M. Wundt, 'Die Wiederentdeckung Platons im 18. Jahrhundert', *Blätter für deutsche Philosophie* 15 (1941–42), pp. 149–58. A good example is the so-called Bipontina edition, published in Zweibrücken by the *societas Bipontina* (Zweibrücken, 1781–87) in both (Stephanus's) Greek and (Ficino's) Latin, with further bibliography, and an additional catalogue of variants by C. G. Heyne. The first volume reprinted Diogenes Laertius's biography, and D. Tiedemann's *Dialogorum Platonis Argumenta exposita et illustrata* (Biponti: ex typographia societatis, 1786), which gave summaries of the content of all dialogues, was attached to the Bipontina as its last, twelfth volume; for an evolutionary survey of Plato's work, betraying the new interest in his philosophy as systematic, see also the contemporary W. G. Tennemann, *System der Platonischen Philosophie* (Leipzig: Barth, 1792).

[5] Matuschek, 'Die Macht des Gastmahls'; Auerochs, 'Platon um 1800'.

[6] Leonard, *Socrates and the Jews*, pp. 32–49.   [7] Matuschek, 'Die Macht des Gastmahls', p. 83.

suggest, and especially as it concerns the Socrates of the *Symposium*, is also
an intersection for some of the main issues of what it meant to be a classical
philologist. There is the role of philosophical, and by extension scholarly
eros, which variously leaves the modern reader in general and the philologist in particular to identify with a variety of figures: Plato, Socrates, and,
not to forget, Alcibiades. The tendency to articulate the practice and
justification of philology in proximity to strategies of personification,
biographizing, and a narration of the self in turn overlaps with increasing
scholarly attention to Plato as a systematic philosopher, an undertaking
that tries to combine both individuality and biographical integrity.[8]

Wolf's Symposia: Community and Text

If the romantic code of love involves the non-utilitarian (and in that sense
disinterested), self-directed, and self-replenishing reflection of autonomy,
and the desire for knowing the other as fully, as comprehensively, and as
exclusively as possible, then these themes of projected completeness and
a special kind of interestedness, or disinterestedness, also exercised the self-
description of scholarship. In Wolf's *Darstellung der Alterthumswissenschaft*
(orig. 1807), one of the key founding treatises of professionalized classical
scholarship, a similar logic is at play, including the desire to imagine the
object of study in terms of a living human form. While he justifies the
study of any foreign peoples or cultures on the basis of our natural interest
and sympathy (*Theilnahme*) in fellow human beings, it is, first of all, the
richness, quantity, and quality of material that singles out Greek
civilization.[9] The overall aim is to make antiquity in its important relations
and characteristics once more a *belebtes Ganzes*, a unity come alive. Like
love justifying love, the study of ancient languages reveals its dignity and
fruitfulness only when it is 'an end in itself', just as the ancients, Wolf
argues, inquired for the sake of inquiry alone and in this way rose to the
proper height of their civilization.[10] The beneficial and educational effect
of such study, in turn, is expressed with the language of intimacy: 'To read
and to reflect on the works [of the ancients] will steadily rejuvenate our
mind and spirit, not as if they were staged historical characters, but as in
intimacy with those we respect and have grown fond of (*wie die*

---

[8] 'Systematic' is here understood to mean constituting a coherent whole rather than implying that
Plato advocates a clearly delineated philosophical system. On this distinction, see more below.
[9] F. A. Wolf, 'Darstellung der Alterthumswissenschaft', in G. Bernhardy (ed.), *Kleine Schriften in
lateinischer und deutscher Sprache* (Leipzig: Waisenhaus, 1869), vol. ii, pp. 808–95; here p. 822ff.
[10] Ibid., pp. 821, 847, 863.

Vertraulichkeit mit geschätzten und liebgewonnenen Personen). Communicating their attitudes and feelings, they will correct the injuries of education in our deficient time.'[11] As mentioned in the Introduction, the topos of reading figured as intimacy with familiar friends reaches back to antiquity. What was new now was the emphasis on the mutual expression of feeling and on the developmental, transformative benefit of such interaction.

One of the first publications of Wolf was his 1782 edition of Plato's *Symposium*, with a German commentary. This is a good case study for the way the rhetoric of romantic love, in tandem with a focus on the personality of the scholar, is on show not only in his programmatic writings but in his actual scholarship, too. To publish scholarly commentary in German rather than in Latin was not yet a self-evident strategy, though we should bear in mind that the textual culture in which a language of love flourished in the late eighteenth century was marked by the explosion of materials available in the vernacular, thus creating a much expanded, much more diverse readership.[12] It is precisely in this context, when the readership of texts about antiquity changes, that new strategies of communication were required, and new images gained traction. The imagery of intimacy, feeling, and *Bildung* essentially both projected a new inclusivity and at the same time allowed the reader to maintain a sense of exclusivity, in the attention and affinity that matches the scholar of antiquity with his object. Incidentally, the question of the vernacular raises not only the issue of a broader readership, but it also underlines the importance of national languages and national cultures in the discourses of Hellenism. As just mentioned, Wolf maintained an argument from both quantity and quality, whereby ancient Greek culture was much better documented than others. But the strengthened claims to a specifically German national affiliation with the Greek world – with the nation understood as an extension of the individual – also tallied with the new sense of exclusiveness. It is the same exclusive relation between two subjects, propelled as much as threatened by elusiveness, that the codes of romantic love tried to articulate.

Wolf's lasting fame as a classical scholar rested not only on the content of his scholarship but also on the fact that he increasingly cultivated his own persona as that of a visionary scholar.[13] His *Symposium* makes it quite clear

[11] Ibid., p. 878.
[12] See Wegmann, *Diskurse der Empfindsamkeit*, p. 15f. with further bibliography.
[13] See, for example, Anthony Grafton's introduction to F. A. Wolf, *Prolegomena to Homer*, ed. A. Grafton, G. Most, and J. Zetzel (Princeton, 1986); F. Turner, 'The Homeric Question', in B. Powell and I. Morris (eds.), *A New Companion to Homer* (Leiden: Brill, 1999), pp. 123–45.

that the edition presents its author as much as its text. His name on the cover is printed in the same size as that of Plato, and the tag 'in places corrected (*verbessert*) and edited, with critical and interpreting annotations, by ... ' reveals an even stronger sense of personal influence when the original German is considered, where *verbessert* has a secondary meaning of 'improved' rather than simply 'emended' or 'corrected'. The quantity of introductory material, including a preface, an introductory essay, and a detailed summary that altogether amount to almost a hundred pages, adds to Wolf's prominent position.[14]

In Wolf's introduction, Plato's dialogue emerges as the perfect match for an understanding of classical education as both based on and imagined in terms of close interpersonal relationships. The *Symposium*, he suggests, is a novel choice, given the relative neglect of newer editions of Plato, and Wolf uses the opportunity to call for new surveys and summaries of Plato's works in general.[15] Unlike the attempts of earlier scholars, his own contribution is thus 'no longer a bare skeleton, but already closer to a body made up of flesh and bones' (*schon mehr ein mit Fleisch überzogener Körper, als ein blosses dürres Skelett*). This is a deliberately striking image (and one indebted to ancient rhetorical tropes, especially Quintilian) that bestows a certain corporeality on the act of research. Wolf is at pains, though, to emphasize that it is his own choice of image compared with one of his models, Floyer Sydenham's *Plato: A General View of His Dialogues* (1760). As Wolf tells us, Sydenham relied instead on the image of the map (*Charte*) to describe the task of presenting Plato to a new readership.[16]

Plato in general, and the *Symposium* in particular, which can 'do great service to both heart and mind', are singled out for their usefulness for education: 'it was partly because of its flourishing style and its other internal advantages that I considered it most suitable for waking and

---

[14] Quotations here are from the 1782 edition ΠΛΑΤΩΝΟΣ ΣΥΜΠΟΣΙΟΝ. *Platons Gastmahl: ein Dialog* (Leipzig: Schwickert, 1782); Wolf's paraphrase of the dialogue was republished as 'Übersicht des Inhalts von Platons Dialog Das Gastmahl', in the more readily accessible *Kleine Schriften*, vol. 2, pp. 593–620.

[15] Wolf mentions the recent Greek text edition of the *Symposium* by Johann F. Fischer (Leipzig, 1776), and the volume of four Platonic dialogues in translation (*Meno*, *Crito*, and the two *Alcibiades*, though not the *Symposium*), edited by J. E. Biester and translated by Friedrich Gedike (Berlin, 1780). As with his work on Homer, Wolf is very insistent on and confident in the originality of his publications. There was also strategic thinking involved. Wolf's biographer Körte singles out the edition of the *Symposium* as his response to King Frederic the Great's call for more and better Greek and Latin texts, in a conscious attempt to further his career. W. Körte, *Leben und Studien Friedrich August Wolfs, des Philologen* (Essen: Bädeker, 1833), I, pp. 78–9.

[16] Wolf, *Platons Gastmahl*, p. xxiv. Sydenham's text is often dated to 1759 and introduced his translations of Plato.

maintaining in young people an urge to study Plato (*den Trieb zum Studium des Platon zu wecken*). I looked at it with an eye to the young boy, and I followed my design with a view to his needs and desires.'[17] Both the content and the hoped-for effect of the *Symposium* are about educating the young individual and instilling love and friendship in them as, he continues, they enter into social life and its demands – a thought that mirrors Pausanias's speech at *Symp.* 184 c-e, where he argues for the social and educational benefits of the correctly practiced pederastic relationship. The implications of transferring the Greek pederastic model of educational (and in the Greek context also sexual) *eros* to a modern situation were obviously problematic, and Wolf addresses this through a double strategy. In his summary of Pausanias's speech, he is firm that 'love is decent and laudable only when it is based on the lasting beauty of spirit or mind (*dauerhafte Schönheiten des Geistes*), and when it has been provoked by the noble intention to perfect our souls mutually in any area of knowledge (*in irgendeinem Teil der Wissenschaften*) or virtue; whatever its outcome, the intention is the measure of that love's worth, as it is guarded by the Amor of Venus Urania, and as it has the greatest influence on the happiness of human society'.[18] Aside from downplaying the physical aspects, Wolf also tries an argument about historical change to make the presentation more palatable. In a footnote, he adds: 'It is truly remarkable how customs and costumes are able to invert things and matters! In most sections of this speech, especially in the latter half, the reader can mentally replace the [male] lover with a *[female] lover*, and he will have no reason to find fault with Pausanias' argument.'[19]

With a view to the educational benefit of the text, Wolf declares that he has chosen to present his edition in German, to make it more easily accessible and understandable (*leichter verständlich*). At the same time, the challenge of incommunicability that is the obverse of an educational *eros* stays in the picture. Here is how Wolf summarizes Aristophanes's iconic speech in the *Symposium* about the myth of human beings once

---

[17] Wolf, *Platons Gastmahl*, p. vi; it is notable that in the next few decades Plato would indeed advance to being a main author especially with a view to education; his rise to being a 'main author' is reflected in the gradually changing school syllabi around 1800, which increasingly put Plato as the author towards whom other readings lead; see, for the Prussian Gymnasium, S. Kipf, 'Von Arrian bis Xenophon. Der griechische Lektüreplan der Berliner Gymnasien unter dem Einfluss des Neuhumanismus', in B. Seidensticker and F. Mundt (eds.), *Altertumswissenschaft in Berlin um 1800 an Akademie, Schule und Universität* (Hannover: Wehrhahn, 2006) pp. 167–87.

[18] Wolf, *Platons Gastmahl*, p. lxix.

[19] Ibid., p. lxix, Wolf's italics. Wolf is not alone with this combined idealizing and historicist strategy; for similar examples, see Orrells, *Classical Culture and Modern Masculinity*, pp. 52–96.

having been two-bodied spherical creatures, then cut apart and ever since looking for their other half: 'the change in our nature described here is the basis for our eternal longing (*ewiges Sehnen*) to be reunited in one whole, the very longing which we call *love*'.[20] The cut-apart Aristophanic lovers famously cannot articulate what it is they want (*Symp.* 192d), and the speech prompts Socrates to move in his definition of *eros* beyond their and Aristophanes's account. Just so, Wolf in his presentation of the *Symposium* emphasizes the pedagogical importance of communication, intermingled with a speechlessness that is a firm part of Plato's *eros*: something 'ineffable' (*unaussprechliches*), and 'incommunicable' (*nicht mitteilbares*), which is not bodily lust (*körperliche Begierde*), but part of the delight of souls (*beider Seelen Entzücken*).[21]

There is a section in Wolf's introductory essay where he attempts to untangle the question of whether or not Plato is citing and using actual speeches by contemporaries to put in the mouths of his symposiasts. He discusses Sydenham's earlier attempt, 'going even further', to match those speeches with specific lost originals and he concludes the section: 'these are merely the assumptions of a man who has been prompted by love for this, his, author, wanting to penetrate all his beauties (*in alle Schönheiten desselben einzudringen*), and even those which time has covered already with her veil'.[22] Following directly from his reading of Sydenham, those 'assumptions' must be his. Still, the sentence sits uneasily at the end of a longer passage dedicated to Wolf's discussion of Plato's characters, integrated into a continued discussion of his own view ('we') that modifies but does not quite discount Sydenham's reading. In other words, it is unclear what the distance is between 'a man who has been prompted by the love of his author' and Wolf's own persona. Like Herder hoping for wisdom from an *entkleidete Seele*, a soul undressed, Wolf considers the attempt of a scholar to uncover the veil of time from the author figure, from 'his' Plato, whom he desires, merging Plato the man and Plato the body of texts. It is no accident that for Wolf the Platonic symposiasts are themselves scholars, whose talk of *episteme* is, every time it appears, glossed and translated as *Wissenschaft*: 'It is decided to let everyone drink according to their pleasure and to spend the time rather with discussions of a scientific (*wissenschaftlicher*) nature.'[23]

If literary culture of the late eighteenth century imagined Plato's academy, glossed on Socratic interaction, as a place of friendship and sociability, academic culture was itself busy redefining the shape and boundaries

[20] Wolf, *Platons Gastmahl*, p. lxxvi.   [21] Ibid., pp. lxxv–vi.   [22] Ibid., p. liv.   [23] Ibid., p. lxv.

of scholarly communality.[24] For the study of the ancient world, the philological seminar (with its own family resemblance to the pedagogical and theological seminar) had become the new and increasingly formalized site of intellectual and social interaction.[25] Wolf, founder of the philological seminar at the university of Halle in 1787 and instigator of the seminar as a central institution of the Prussian education system, may himself have been conscious of the calculated echoes with a sympotic precedent. His students and his biographer Körte certainly were: there are reports of visits to his students' rooms, camaraderie, regular group walks, and academic encouragement and confidence-boosting 'with a cup in hand'.[26] The imagination and enactment of sociability, and an acknowledgement of its sensual aspects, became part of institutional memory and, as soon as they were in place, of institutional nostalgia, too.

'Oh That I Were Alcibiades for One Day and One Night' – Hamann's *Socratic Memorabilia* (1759) and the Failures of Learning

As noted above, Pygmalion was one figure of the eighteenth century that had prominent epistemological traction. He was a figure whose tale could provide a commentary on knowledge and sense perception (in Pygmalion's touch of Galatea and in Galatea's own transition from inanimate to sensate), on creation, and on the workings of signification and hence of textual understanding itself. There is a side of Pygmalion, though, that overlaps with figures from the Platonic repertoire. Those are Socrates, Alcibiades, and Plato himself as embodiments of the striving for knowledge, and, by extension, as figurations of the scholar. In fact, they might be even stronger reference figures compared to Pygmalion when it comes to connecting the desire for wisdom and virtue to the value of antiquity and its study. In the works considered here, the scholar is explored as simultaneously a Socratic *and* an Alcibiades figure, just as Socrates and Alcibiades

---

[24] Auerochs, 'Plato um 1800', describes in detail some of the fictional imaginations of Platonic sentimental sociability, especially in the journal *Der Neue Teutsche Merkur*, as well as in the novels of C. M. Wieland.

[25] Clark, *Academic Charisma*, pp. 141–82; for Göttingen, and with further literature, Harloe, *Winckelmann*, pp. 161–6; for Wolf's seminar in particular, C. Spoerhase and M.-G. Dehrmann, 'Die Idee der Universität. Friedrich August Wolf und die Praxis des Seminars', *Zeitschrift für Ideengeschichte* 5.1 (2011), 105–17.

[26] R. Hanhart, *Erinnerungen an Friedrich August Wolf* (Basle: Wielandt, 1825), p. 10; Körte, *Leben und Studien*, I, p. 127; recounted again in J. Arnoldt, *Friedrich August Wolf in seinem Verhältnis zum Schulwesen* (Braunschweig: Schwetschke, 1861), p. 109. My thanks to Mark-Georg Dehrmann and Carlos Spoerhase for pointing me in this direction.

in the textual tradition cycle through the roles of lover and beloved alike. Eventually, both also connect as a mutually enlightening analogy of Plato, as author, disciple, and scholar all together.

There is a cluster of Platonic dialogues – aside from the *Symposium* also the *Phaedrus*, the *Lysis*, and the two *Alcibiades* dialogues of disputed authorship – that negotiate the link between desire (*eros*), lack, and knowledge in the context of discussing or indeed enacting the affection between a beautiful younger boy and an older male.[27] In addition, the figure of Alcibiades was known from Xenophon's Socratic works, and there was also a tradition that viewed him as a disciple and *eromenos* (the beloved younger partner of a pederastic-pedagogical relationship) of Socrates, especially with a view to Alcibiades's later actions as a charismatic, risk-taking general and scandalous deserter during the Peloponnesian War.[28] The *Alcibiades I* (also known as *Alcibiades maior*), in particular, was in the later Platonic and Neoplatonic tradition considered foundational as an introduction to the *cursus* of Platonic philosophy – and it is the only Platonic, or pseudo-Platonic dialogue that is specifically concerned with self-identity and the development of the self.[29] As a discussion between Socrates and Alcibiades on self-knowledge and how to achieve it, and especially with one of its display passages about the self's mirroring itself in the eye of an other, it had a particularly strong persistence in philosophical texts and compilations.[30] If we add to this the particular currency of Alcibiades's speech from the *Symposium*, which was accessible not only in new editions and translations but had already been made popular through Giordano Bruno and Marsilio Ficino's partial Latin translations of the fifteenth century, the erotic Alcibiades was thus a readily available figure.[31]

---

[27] For a discussion of the 'erotic' dialogues as connected, see E. Belfiore, *Socrates' Daimonic Art: Love for Wisdom in Four Platonic Dialogues* (Cambridge University Press, 2012); for a discussion of the contested authorship of the *Alcibiades I*, see F. Renaud and H. Tarrant, *The Platonic Alcibiades I: The Dialogue and Its Ancient Reception* (Cambridge University Press, 2015).

[28] This is also the tradition that is deliberately worried at in the *Symposium*, where Alcibiades is revealed as the pursuer, not the pursued, of Socrates.

[29] For the reception, see Renaud and Tarrant, *The Platonic Alcibiades*; also M. Johnson and H. Tarrant (eds.), *Alcibiades and the Socratic Lover-Educator* (London: Bloomsbury, 2012).

[30] *Alcibiades I* 133b: Socrates: 'Then if an eye is to see itself, it must look at an eye, and at that area of the eye in which the excellence of the eye happens to occur; which is sight, correct?' Alcibiades: 'Indeed.' Socrates: 'And so, my dear Alcibiades, if the soul is to know itself, it must surely look at a soul, and especially at that area of it in which the excellence of a soul occurs, namely wisdom, and at any other part of a soul which resembles this?' Alcibiades: 'I think so too, Socrates.'

[31] For Bruno and Ficino, see D. Clay, 'The hangover of Plato's Symposium in the Italian Renaissance from Bruno (1435) to Castiglione (1528)', in J. Lesher, D. Nails, and F. Sheffield (eds.), *Plato's Symposium: Issues in Interpretation and Reception* (Washington, DC: Centre for Hellenic Studies), pp. 341–60.

Johann Georg Hamann is a good example of paying polemical attention to the close and tense link between rational, learned inquiry and feeling represented in the case of Socrates and of the Socratic *dramatis personae*. Hamann was a philosopher, Enlightenment (or, arguably, anti-Enlightenment) critic, and thinker, but he was also an outsider to the academic world. He initially undertook studies in theology and law at Königsberg (where he read Kant and also got to know him personally), yet he left without a degree in 1752. He tried his hand at trade, including time spent in England, published a literary journal, and continued to write critical and philosophical works even after he returned to Königsberg and to a bread-earning position as a customs official. His provocative essay *Socratic Memorabilia* (*Sokratische Denkwürdigkeiten*) was published in 1759, a short but dense, punchy polemic against rationalist, pedantic learning (*Gelehrsamkeit*), a *Streitschrift* composed in the name of intuitive religion and of a Socratic, critical method, that he understood to be genuinely open and probing.[32] Hamann is another of the 'eccentric' thinkers who do not fit the mould of the professionalizing, disciplinary spheres of scholarship and the knowledge of antiquity. He is also a thinker who in his wild, often formally experimental, parodic, and highly allusive writings, pre-empted many of the debates that would exercise philology, as a separate discipline, throughout the nineteenth century.[33] He composed this piece, in his own telling, after a religious (re-)conversion experience that had led him to rethink his formerly held rationalist and utilitarian positions as well as his entire life to date, including his studies in theology and law, independent research, a position as tutor, and employment by a trading firm. In his

---

[32] J. G. Hamann, *Sokratische Denkwürdigkeiten*, ed. F. Blanke (Gütersloh: Mohn, 1959); Denis Thouard calls Hermann 'notoriously at odds with the Enlightenment', but sees him as its 'difficult child', critical and probing, rather than hostile; D. Thouard, 'Hamann and the History of Philosophy', in C. R. Ligota and J.-L. Quantin (eds.), *History of Scholarship* (London: Warburg Institute, 2006), pp. 413–31, here p. 415; Leonard, *Socrates and the Jews*, pp. 27–31 discusses the ways in which Hamann plays havoc with the pagan and Christian associations of Socrates as both precursor of Christianity and as its opposite, associations that gained new traction in the context of Enlightenment thought. Hamann's text was published in a second edition twenty-five years later, which suggests that it retained some of its appeal.

[33] Kaspar Renner discusses Hamann's self-curated collection of critical and formally varied essays on poetics, literature, and writing, 'Crusades of the Philologist' (1762), which was widely reviewed and followed in 1763 by a 'Palinode of the Philologist'; K. Renner, '"Kreuzzüge des Philologen": Polemics and Philology in Johann Georg Hermann', in H. Bajohr et al. (eds.), *The Future of Philology* (Newcastle: Cambridge Scholars Publishing, 2014), pp. 120–45. This is a good account of Hamann's polemics and the link between Enlightenment polemics as a path to knowledge and the authority of sacred and/or secular philology. See also V. Hoffmann, *Johann Georg Hamanns Philologie: Hamanns Philologie zwischen enzyklopädischer Mikrologie und Hermeneutik* (Stuttgart: Kohlhammer, 1972).

preface, 'To the Two', he addresses without naming them his former patron, the merchant Christian Berens, and the young Immanuel Kant, the mutual friend whom Berens took along as moral support on a friendly mission to talk sense into Hamann. In this rhetorical firework, a broadside against Enlightenment precepts of rational epistemology launched in the name of intuition and feeling, Hamann reformulates the question of how to do the history of philosophy. He asks what it means to learn, he asks about its how and why, and how to interrogate the role of reason in it.[34] This 'metacritique of the historiography of philosophy', as Thouard calls it, is at the same time an extended reflection on interpretation, its conditionality, and its ambitions.[35] Hamann begins to answer these questions through an account of Socrates, in the style of a series of anecdotes rather than of a rationalist treatise. The method is programmatic, giving a new, subversive edge to the kind of old, antiquarian, and *gelehrte* scholarly habit that he also sets out to criticize, namely the type of biographical summary known since Diogenes Laertius. Hamann's self-proclaimed aim, as he states in a letter of the same year 1759, is to develop a way to write and also to study a 'more vivid history of philosophy', literally one that is 'more alive' (*eine lebendigere Philosophiegeschichte*).[36]

The *Denkwürdigkeiten* is modelled not so much on the Platonic Socrates as on the presentation of the philosopher in Xenophon's *Memorabilia*, a reminder that until the end of the eighteenth century knowledge about Socrates relied predominantly on non-Platonic sources. Hamann himself did most likely not read any of Plato's Socratic works in Greek until quite a while after the publication of his essay.[37] When he announced in a letter that he had read Plato with great 'intimacy' (*Intimität*), having already previously thought 'Platonically', then we should, according to the editor of Hamann's text, understand this as a typically playful statement about his intuitive knowledge as *reactivated* by Plato (a Platonic thought itself) rather than as a factual comment about Plato's direct impact on his, Hamann's, description of

[34] For the place of Hamann's Socrates in the context of the particular German debate over 'What Is Enlightenment?', the title of programmatic works by both Immanuel Kant and Moses Mendelsohn, see Leonard, *Socrates and the Jews*, pp. 27–35.

[35] Thouard, 'Hamann', p. 414.

[36] Letter to J. G. Lindner of August 1759, quoted in F. Blanke, 'Einleitung', in Hamann, *Denkwürdigkeiten*, pp. 11–48, here p. 19, after W. Ziesemer and A. Henkel (eds.), *Johann Georg Hamann: Briefwechsel (Briefe von 1751–1777)*, 3 vols. (Wiesbaden: Harassowitz, 1955–7), vol. I, p. 404.

[37] Blanke, 'Einleitung', pp. 27, 45; Hamann, by his own acknowledgement, reads Plato in 1761, and he adds additional quotations from Plato to his manuscript of the *Denkwürdigkeiten*, with a view to future reprints and editions.

Socrates.[38] Diogenes Laertius's life of Socrates in the *Lives of Eminent Philosophers*, for example, and especially Xenophon were among the default sources relied on since the Renaissance, not least because Xenophon's Greek was easier to read than that of Plato and had a long tradition of being used as a school text in pedagogic instruction. Both authors, Diogenes Laertius and Xenophon, had become more widely known throughout the first half of the eighteenth century.[39] It was from the mid-century, largely as a knock-on effect of the intensified study of Plato in England and France, that the Platonic dialogues (in Greek) became more of a staple in the reception of Socrates, especially with Heyne's reprint of Stephanus's complete Greek text of Plato and Ficino's Neoplatonist-inspired translation in the 1780s, but also with new critical editions and translations only a generation later.[40] Some of the more contemporary sources that Hamann explicitly names for his own work, such as François Charpentier's *La vie de Socrate* (1699) and John Gilbert Cooper's *Life of Socrates* (1749), also testify to a reading practice still heavily indebted to Xenophon.[41]

This new, more vivid history of philosophy begins, in Hamann's characteristically allusive style, with a densely opaque opening salvo.[42] It certainly is vivid, but it also immediately addresses how thin and how instrumental the line is that separates liveliness from lifelessness:

> The history of philosophy has suffered a fate similar to that of the monument of the French minister of state. A great artist showed off his chisel; a monarch, his name the name of an entire century, gave the funding for the memorial and admired the creation of his subject. The Scythian, though, who was travelling for his craft, like Noah or Julian's Galilean, to be the god of his people, this Scythian had a moment of weakness enough to memorialize him for ever. He ran up to the marble, and offered half of his large kingdom to the mute stone if only he would teach him how to rule the other

---

[38] Blanke, 'Einleitung', p. 27, quoting Ziesemer and Henkel, *Briefwechsel*, ii, pp. 117–18.

[39] It is worth noting, though, that Diogenes's account itself can be read in terms of its Platonizing overtones; James Warren has argued that Diogenes effectively creates a genealogical narrative in which Platonic–Hellenistic themes of pedagogy as a specifically Greek achievement play a large role, J. Warren, 'Diogenes Laërtius, Biographer of Philosophy', in J. König and T. Whitmarsh (eds.), *Ordering Knowledge in the Roman Empire* (Cambridge University Press, 2007), pp. 133–49.

[40] Thouard, 'Hamann', p. 417.

[41] Charpentier is a paraphrase of Xenophon with some additional Diogenes Laertius; Thouard notes that Hamann relies on Christian Thomasius translation-adaptation 'against the grain' of Charpentier, emphasizing Socrates as a non-pedantic, practical, popular philosopher; Thouard, 'Hamann', pp. 419–20.

[42] Thouard speaks, appropriately, of his 'Sybilline vocabulary', as well as his 'centos' of 'obscure concision' that distill enormous erudition and, strategically, address questions of understanding; Thouard, 'Hamann', pp. 414–15.

half. Should history ever become mythology with us, this embrace of a lifeless teacher, who works miracles of fulfillment without serving his own interests, will turn into a fairytale resembling the relics of Pygmalion's life. In some unspecified future, a creator of his people will have to be understood in the language of our wit just as poetically as the sculptor of his own wife.[43]

The statue is meant to be that of Cardinal Richelieu. It had been crafted by François Girardon on the order of Louis XIV, who in this way set up a monument to his influential minister of finance.[44] The Scythian refers to the biographical anecdote told of Tsar Peter the Great of Russia, who, before taking up the burden of rulership, travelled through parts of Europe gaining practical experience as a ship builder and mason (hence the reference to that other man from the north, the Scythian Anacharsis, known from Herodotus, who travels the world of the Greeks to gather knowledge about them). Yet how do the anecdote and Pygmalion's fashioning of his sculpted wife cohere? The opening paragraph is essentially an extended comment on epistemology, on knowledge and the art of understanding, ranging from understanding the history of philosophy to history and myth more generally, and Hamann chooses two images, those of Peter and of Pygmalion, that both involve the approach to a statue. Not only does Hamann suggest a greater similarity of myth and history than his rationalist opponents would grant (history might well in the long run have to be understood as poetically as myth), but he also offers a critique of how an understanding of the past is being sought in his own time.

Hamann's sympathies seem clear. The enthusiasm of Tsar Peter to learn from the mute statue is not so far from Hamann's self-professed enthusiastic adoration (*schwärmerische Andacht*) for Socrates, which, he

---

[43] 'Der Geschichte der Philosophie ist es wie der Bildsäule des französischen Staatsministers ergangen. Ein grosser Künstler zeigte seinen Meissel daran; ein Monarch, der Name eines ganzen Jahrhunderts, gab die Unkosten zum Denkmal und bewunderte das Geschöpf seines Unterthanen; der Scythe aber, der auf sein Handwerk reisete, und wie Noah oder der Galiläer des Projektmachers, Julians, ein Zimmermann wurde, um der Gott seines Volkes zu seyn, dieser Scythe begieng eine Schwachheit, deren Andenken ihn allein verewigen könnte. Er lief auf den Marmor zu, both grosmüthig dem stummen Stein die Hälfte seines weiten Reichs an, wenn er ihn lehren wollte, die andere Hälfte zu regieren. Sollte unsere Historie Mythologie werden; so wird diese Umarmung eines leblosen Lehrers, der ohne Eigennutz Wunder der Erfüllung gethan, in ein Mährchen verwandelt seyn, das den Reliquien von Pygmalions Leben ähnlich sehen wird. Ein Schöpfer seines Volkes in der Sprache unseres Witzes wird nach einer undenklichen Zeit eben so poetisch verstanden werden müssen, als ein Bildhauer seines Weibes'; Hamann, *Denkwürdigkeiten*, pp. 80–3.

[44] The identification of the figures as Girardon, Louis XIV, and Peter the Great is Hamann's own, added to his own copy in handwritten notes, a copy that, incidentally, ended up in Herder's possession; Hamann, *Denkwürdigkeiten*, 82.

claims, mirrors that which Plato held for him as his subject.[45] Hamann himself, as much as the Plato he imagines, is not a builder of scientific structures, but his method is formed by the mingling of ideas with sentiments or impressions (*Zusammenfluss von Ideen und Empfindungen*).[46] In the same vein, Hamann's *Denkwürdigkeiten*, inasmuch as in their very name ('the things worth thinking about') they are meant to encourage thought, are not intended to appeal to objective reason, if we believe his preface addressed to the Two, but instead they advocate the 'affect of friendship', which Hamann submits throughout as the most promising way of reading his very own text.[47]

On the other hand, how well have Peter and Pygmalion, the historical figure and the mythical one, and their statues fared? The inspiration offered to the future statesman by a mute Richelieu cast in stone, commissioned and paid for by royal power, cannot hide the essential unresponsiveness of the statue. Pygmalion's intimate activation of dead stone to life, on the other hand, may counteract the failures of history by the promise of myth, and counter the historiography of rationalist philosophy by insisting that knowledge comes from *Empfindungen*. If literally an approach, then the Tsar's intimate coming closer in the embrace of an unresponsive statue is what the history of philosophy currently suffers, even though Hamann's Peter shows that enthusiasm born out of affinity is, arguably, productive. Just as Pygmalion's Galatea is his own creature, all his and no other's, Peter's embrace is that of a statesman by a statesman, and Hamann goes on to add to his story the examples of Caesar's enthusiasm for Alexander, Alexander's for Achilles, and that of Erasmus for Socrates.[48]

By aligning rather than contrasting Tsar Peter and Pygmalion, and by underlining the similarity of their approaches, Hamann appears to suggest a sentimental, an *empfindsam*, way of knowing as a promising complementary alternative to rationalist thought – providing it is consciously acknowledged, just as when myth and history become explicitly read on similar terms. At the same time, the juxtaposition of the uncannily successful Pygmalion and the ironically, maybe blindly enthusiastic modern Tsar also recalls the unease that Miller expressed over Pygmalion's literalized act of *prosopopoeia*: an error in reading, an act of unstable 'reciprocity in which

---

[45] Ibid., p. 76.   [46] Ibid., p. 78.   [47] Ibid., p. 73.
[48] Hamann, *Denkwürdigkeiten*, p. 94; H. Schlüter, *Das Pygmalion-Symbol bei Rousseau, Hamann, Schiller. Drei Studien zur Geistesgeschichte der Goethezeit* (Zurich: Juris, 1968), p. 63. The alignment with Erasmus emphasizes Hamann's portrait of Socrates as an emblem of 'folly's virtue'; theirs is not a rational Socrates, but one who represents professed ignorance as the most powerful critical tool.

the same loves the same', an error that is unavoidable in so far as, in order to expose it in other readings, we have to commit it again and again.[49]

The apostrophe to a sculpture, of wanting to make alive and give voice to what is not there, is in Hamann's text keyed to his own insistence, like that imputed to Plato, to meet the figure of Socrates with enthusiasm and thus to create a new, vivid type of history and knowledge. The one name that seems missing in this picture is that of Alcibiades. The Alcibiades we encounter especially in Plato's *Symposium* slots effortlessly into the paradox experienced by Hamann's Tsar, namely 'this embrace of a lifeless teacher, who realized miracles without looking to his own interest' (another stab at the utilitarian side of rationalism). The analogy brings out fully the ambivalence of Alcibiades, and thinking about the figure of Alcibiades adds the important element of pedagogy, knowledge, and subjective *Bildung* to the Pygmalion figure. The one-time relationship between the older Socrates and the younger Alcibiades, whether pedagogic, erotic, or both, was a narrative reference point in a number of sources on either of the two figures, often invoked in the context of whether Socrates played a part in Alcibiades's corruption and political downfall.[50]

In the *Symposium*, Alcibiades turns the tables on this topos of pedagogic failure, when he tells in his drunken speech of his own lack of success in engaging Socrates in the erotic-pedagogical relationship he has come to expect. In his speech, which is also the culmination of the praise of Eros in the shape of Socrates himself, he remembers his attempted encounters with Socrates, whom he likens to a statue in more than one way. Socrates is the obstinately unresponsive older man who, in an inversion of roles, turns into a desired beloved as Alcibiades spends an entire night physically lying close to him; but he is also the Silenus figure, whose deceptively sculpted exterior does not betray the riches of the interior.[51] Alcibiades is the involuntary lover who seeks to benefit from Socrates's wisdom, yet by his own acknowledgement fails to grasp the workings of the Socratic *eros*.

It remains a crucial question in critical readings of the dialogue, where to peg Alcibiades in the schema and sequence of erotic wisdom and self-knowledge that the *Symposium* builds throughout the speeches. Is he the

[49] Miller, *Versions of Pygmalion*, p. 11.
[50] For a discussion of the trope, its attractiveness, and its sources, see H. Tarrant, 'Improvement by Love: From Aeschines to the Old Academy', in Johnson and Tarrant, *Alcibiades*, pp. 147–63; V. Wohl, *Love among the Ruins: The Erotics of Democracy in Classical Athens* (Princeton University Press, 2002), pp. 129–70, gives a full account of the traditions surrounding Alcibiades, with a specific discussion of Socrates on pp. 158–70.
[51] To read those two points offered by Alcibiades in conjunction, see D. Steiner, 'For Love of a Statue: a Reading of Plato's Symposium 215A-B', *Ramus* 25.2 (1996), 89–111.

failed example of what Socrates's philosophical and pedagogical *eros* could and should achieve? Or does his understanding of the situation in hindsight, artfully recounted in his drunken yet clear-sighted speech, token his advanced knowledge and yet his and its limitations? And is this something that identifies him as the more realistic version of Socrates's ideal philosopher and thus as the key to the real ethics about knowledge and self-knowledge implied in the text?[52]

When Hamann mentions Erasmus's Socrates as a comparandum for his tsar's enthusiasm for the statue, he is already indirectly hinting at a tradition that links erotic striving for knowledge with the challenges of hermeneutic, textual, essentially philological understanding. Hamann may here clearly reference Erasmus's *Praise of Folly*, which already chimes with the *Symposium*'s topos of Socrates' external madness, or his ugliness hiding inner riches. Erasmus, in his *Adagia*, or annotated sayings, also has a long, specific entry on 'the Sileni of Alcibiades' (III.iii.1), which explicates in detail that structure of diverging exterior and interior meaning, and likens philosophers as much as Christ himself to the *silenoi* whose unassuming outer appearances hide inner riches that want discovering.[53] The sileni thus become self-referentially paradigmatic for the format of the *adagia* themselves, which despite their unassuming exterior warrant deeper unpacking, while Alcibiades's plight makes him already a similarly paradigmatic, self-referential figure for the difficult task of reading and interpreting of biblical scripture and pagan texts alike.

Thus for Hamann, Alcibiades as the figure that exemplifies the challenges of learning and *eros*, of *Bildung*, feeling, and hermeneutic deficiency, links up all those enthusiasts of sculpture whom he lines up in his *Memorabilia*, including himself among them, in an even more challenging variation on the Pygmalion theme. It is a variation that is highly appropriate for the context of the pursuit of knowledge, the context of the Socratic circle, and the context of studying that circle and its

---

[52] For a general overview of this issue, see M. S. Lane, *Plato's Progeny. How Plato and Socrates Still Captivate the Modern Mind* (London: Duckworth, 2001), pp. 76–88; more specifically, M. Nussbaum, *The Fragility of Goodness* (Cambridge University Press, 1986), pp. 165–95, for a seminal sympathetic reading of Alcibiades and the conditions of possibility of philosophy; F. C. C. Sheffield, *Plato's Symposium: The Ethics of Desire* (Oxford University Press, 2006), develops Nussbaum's lead by finding Alcibiades' position positively integrated into the narrative and philosophical argument of the dialogue; also S. Berg, *Eros and the Intoxications of Enlightenment: on Plato's Symposium* (Albany, NY: SUNY Press, 2010), pp. 131–50, offering a Straussian reading about the self-contradictions of enlightenment, and E. Belfiore, *Plato's Daimonic Art*, about the advances and deficiencies of *eros* and self-knowledge addressed across several dialogues.
[53] Erasmus, 'The Sileni of Alcibiades', in W. Barker (ed.), *The Adages of Erasmus* (Toronto University Press, 2001), pp. 241–68.

epistemology from a modern, scholarly perspective. It seems to have been Goethe who heard the echo of Alcibiades in Hamann's work particularly loudly.[54] In a letter that is quoted by Hamann's editors but not further remarked on apropos the Alcibiades motive, the young Goethe wrote the following enthusiastic recommendation to Herder in a letter at the end of 1771, fresh from reading Hamann's *Memorabilia*:

> Now I study the life and death of another hero, and dialogize it in my head. It still is but a dim presentiment. Socrates, the philosophical heroic mind, the joy of attack against all lies and vices, and especially where they claim there aren't any!; or rather, the divine profession of being a teacher to mankind ... I will need time to develop that into a feeling. And then also I do not know whether on this point I relate to Aesop and La Fontaine, in the sense that Hamann has it, and empathize with Socrates's greatest genius; whether I can lift myself above the adoration of the idol which Plato had painted and gilded and to whom Xenophon had made burnt offerings, whether I can lift myself up to the true religion that sees not the saint but the great man, whom I press to my bosom with loving enthusiasm and call friend and my brother. And to be able to say that with confidence to a *great* man! – If only I were Alcibiades for a day and a night, then I would gladly die.[55]

The dilemma of approach and lack of responsiveness, of the promise contained in the sculpture that is loved, and of lover turning into beloved, dead into animated, and vice versa, runs through Hamann's piece in its many further mentions of sculpture, too. These rearticulate the link between creating a figure and the confusions of intimacy when it comes to articulating the relation to this figure. In addition, it is the sculptural imagery that provides the hinge between Hamann's overall stated aim of reconceptualizing the history of philosophy and of doing so by way of the

---

[54] While Hamann may not have had the entire range of representations of Alcibiades in mind or indeed at hand, it is clear from his letters that he was familiar with the *Second Alcibiades* (or *Alcibiades minor*), the second of the Alcibiades dialogues attributed to Plato; Blanke, 'Einleitung', p. 43.

[55] 'Jetzo studir ich Leben und Todt eines andern Helden, und dialogisir's in meinem Gehirn. Noch ist's nur dunckle Ahndung. Den Sokrates, den philosophischen Heldengeist, die Eroberungslust aller Lügen und Laster besonders derer die keine scheinen wollen!; oder vielmehr den göttlichen Beruf zum Lehrer der Menschen ... Ich brauche Zeit das zum Gefühl zu entwickeln. Und dann weiss ich noch nicht, ob ich von der Seite mit Aesopen und La Fontainen verwandt binn, wo sie nach Hamannen mit dem besten Genius des Sokrates sympathisiren; ob ich mich von dem Dienste des Götzenbildes das Plato bemahlt und verguldet, dem Xenophon räuchert, zu der wahren Religion hinaufschwingen kann, der statt des Heiligen ein grosser Mensch erscheint, den ich nur mit Lieb Enthusiasmus an meine Brust drücke, und rufe mein Freund und mein Bruder. Und das mit Zuversicht zu einem *grossen* Mann sagen zu dürfen! – Wär ich einen Tag und eine Nacht Alzibiades, und dann wollt ich sterben'; cited in Hamann, *Denkwürdigkeiten*, pp. 33–4; the letter is in the Weimar edition of Goethe's *Werke*, section IV, *Goethes Briefe*, vol. 2, pp. 11–12.

example of Socrates. Thus Hamann makes reference, for example, to earlier and in his view misguided histories of philosophy, namely those by Johann Jacob Brucker (1742) and Thomas Stanely (1701). By linking their histories of philosophy, selective yet misguided in their selection, with a lapidary equivalent, he compares them to the composite sculpture of Helen, which the Greek artist Zeuxis had created by working from a range of female models, taking the most beautiful feature of each. In Hamann's judgement, this leaves the viewer with little more than estrangement and the aspect of a chimera, a monstrous aggregate rather than the icon of beauty.[56]

Further on in his essay, having established that history has to be studied by means other than reason, Hamann casts himself as a Pygmalion-like artist again.[57] To reach a clearer, distanced view of a form or 'Gestalt' – whether of the history of philosophy or Socrates is ambiguous in the German where *Gestalt* can mean both abstract shape and specifically human shape – he intends to step back like a painter, quoting a line from Euripides: ὡς γραφεὺς ἀποσταθεῖσ', 'standing at a distance like a painter' (*Hecuba*, 870).[58] In the same passage he speaks of the 'lover' of philosophy and its history, making use of the ambivalence of *Liebhaber* as both lover and as amateur, to champion a non-standard way of knowing.[59]

Hamann plays on this theme in yet more ways. In Diogenes Laertius he found the biographical topos that Socrates was the son of a sculptor, and himself practiced that trade, before Kriton (unsuccessfully) suggests that he pay for him to be educated as a sophist instead.[60] Hamann draws concentric circles around that invasion of sculpture imagery into his own account, and he speculates how Socrates's eye for beauty, well practised because of his initial training, played an active part in his appreciation of male physical beauty. Incidentally, Hamann here also critically engages some of the scholarship on Greek pederasty available in his time, which

---

[56] Hamann, *Denkwürdigkeiten*, p. 84; the Zeuxis story, like the one about Dibutades, is referred to in Pliny, *Hist. Nat.* 35, but also in Cicero, *De Inv.* ii.1, both contemporary staples of knowledge about ancient art and artistry.

[57] Hamann, *Denkwürdigkeiten*, p. 90. Hamann's turn of phrase is 'not plowing with the calf of reason', an allusion to *Judges* 14:18, where 'plowing with someone else's heifer' refers to the ability to solve a riddle – in other words, achieving understanding through thinking in someone else's terms.

[58] Hamann, *Denkwürdigkeiten*, p. 90. [59] Ibid., p. 92.

[60] *Diog. Laert.* II.18–21; Socrates's parentage is highly meaningful already in the biographical tradition: with his mother allegedly a midwife, and his father a sculptor, the twin methods of dialectic as midwifery and of pedagogy as formation mark his genealogy. Incidentally, Winckelmann and his circle were aware of the same tradition: the first edition of the *Thoughts on the Imitation of Greek Works of Art* had a vignette by the engraver Friedrich Oeser, which shows Socrates as the sculptor of a group of three graces.

had argued for a chaste Socrates in a society that (unfortunately) knew of
the vice of same-sex love. In Hamann's reading, Socrates freely acknowledges the inevitable involvement of the senses in friendship, at a time when
spiritual and bodily beauty shared a space, even though Socrates, he
concedes, would have struggled with it.[61]

Sliding from Socrates's own artistic approach to his own, Hamann
claims he would like to be able to paint a portrait of Socrates that would
be as well-crafted and realistic as one by a Hogarth or a Parrhasius. His own
skill, though, is closer to that of Tsar Peter in his attempt to elicit a response
from a statue: 'Here I am, lacking the secrets of palingenesis, over which
our historians have power, namely to raise out of the ashes of any given
human being and common man a spiritual figure, which we call a character
or historical portrait.'[62] To approach the writers and figures of antiquity by
giving a (slim) biographical summary was a traditional model. But to
reformulate the reliance on biographical information as part of a new desire
for character and character portrayal betrays a new historicizing attitude
both in Hamann and in his contemporaries, an attitude that looks for the
exemplary not so much in terms of the exceptional individual, but in terms
of looking for larger abstractions of human nature.[63]

For Hamann it is imperative to match his new critical epistemology with
his understanding of Socrates as a character, whose own biography in turn
serves as a figuration of his philosophical method. The writing style, which
such overlapping layers of figuration require, he glosses accordingly: 'I have
written about Socrates in a Socratic manner. *Analogy* was the soul of his
arguments (*war die Seele seiner Schlüsse*), and he made *irony* their body (*und
er gab ihnen die Ironie zu ihrem Leibe*)', states Hamann in his preface.[64]
Both Socrates's method and Hamann's own adaptation of it are an enormous act of figuration, of speaking ironically and through a figure, a giving
of face, voice, and body. Its success, as a critical tool, depends entirely on
the tension at the centre of *prosopopoeia*: namely, that in order to derive
critical value from it we need to accept it as a fiction first. Hamann has to
take Socrates at face value and understand him literally in order to show up

---

[61] Hamann, *Denkwürdigkeiten*, pp. 114–15. Charpentier's *Vie de Socrate* (1699), for example, was highly
critical of the 'shameful lust' that reigned all over Greece, but claims Socrates remained free of it;
similarly Heumann's *Acta philosophorum* (1715).

[62] Hamann, *Denkwürdigkeiten*, p. 163.

[63] *Charakter* and *Charakteristik* are not only frequently used words of the eighteenth and nineteenth
centuries, but they are terms that always associate a gathering of detail into a larger unit; see, for
example, the dictionary of the German language by the Brothers Grimm, the standard nineteenth-
century work.

[64] Hamann, *Denkwürdigkeiten*, p. 74.

the faultlines between history and myth, between the impotent Tsar and the strangely solipsistic Pygmalion enjoying his own creation.

Sculpture, however, is no guarantee of a successful approach. Hamann pointedly mentions the anecdote that the citizens of Athens tried to relieve the guilt of their persecution of Socrates by commissioning (not unlike Louis XIV) the famous sculptor Lysippus to build a statue of him and to erect it in a public place.[65] The fact that Hamann seeks the key to his polemic in a self-consciously historicizing and scholarly attitude to an individual of the ancient world – his classical readings may be patchy, but there is a consistent reliance on ancient source materials and contemporary scholarship – gives a preview of just how important such figurations of antiquity would continue to become as a comment on the value and the functions of scholarship and *Wissenschaft* itself.

In Hamann's writings, a sense persists of the eighteenth-century tradition of Socrates as both exceptional and exemplary, yet not without ambivalence and paradox. Readings of Socrates spanned the range from the philosopher as rationalist and as a source for all areas of knowledge, and to prefigurations of Christian values and true Christianity. Also, Socrates served as a paradigm of autonomy as much as of excessive self-love, as teacher and pedagogue, and as a charismatic leader.[66] Hamann describes an outsider's appreciation for an outsider figure whose attitude to traditional learning and knowing was provocative. The fact that the philosopher and critic Moses Mendelssohn, in a contemporary review of Hamann's *Denkwürdigkeiten*, felt reminded of Winckelmann's style, with a 'subtle but noble irony (*feine und edle Spott*), and the same familiarity (*vertraute Bekanntschaft*) with the spirit of antiquity', may underline that outsider status, or rather the distance that Hamann shared with Winckelmann from a growing field of disciplinary knowledge.[67] That Mendelssohn finds Hamann to have portrayed Socrates 'beautifully' and that the 'description of his character seems to be very life-like' adds to the effort of imagining understanding as reflected in the fuzzy oscillation of the lifeless and the

---

[65] *Diog. Laert.* II.43.

[66] For the transformations of Socrates since antiquity, see Lane, *Plato's Progeny*; Wilson, *Death of Socrates*; M. Trapp (ed.), *Socrates from Antiquity to the Enlightenment* (Aldershot: Ashgate, 2007). Socrates as charismatic leader also appears, for example, in Thomas Abbt's *On Merit* (1765), who was mentioned in Chapter 1 apropos the practice of affect; see, on Abbt specifically, Böhm, *Sokrates im achtzehnten Jahrhundert*, pp. 234–8.

[67] M. Mendelssohn, 'Ueber die kleine Schrift "Sokratische Denkwürdigkeiten für die lange Weile des Publikums", für deren Verfasser jetzt Joh. Georg Hamann gilt', in G. B. Mendelssohn (ed.) *Gesammelte Schriften*, vol. iv. 2 (Leipzig: Brockhaus, 1844), pp. 99–105, here p. 99 (quoted in Leonard, *Socrates and the Jews*, p. 31).

living figure in the exchange between sculpture and its observer and creator.

But Hamann also reflects a new, parallel move towards use of Socrates as a model and a figure for the process of knowledge itself, for understanding and interpretation as such. To understand a representative figure of antiquity thus becomes in its own right a figure for understanding. This links classical scholarship, as knowledge of the ancient past, with understanding in general, and it makes the success of historical insight coextensive with the possibility of hermeneutics. What we can know about classical antiquity – and it is a knowledge formulated through understanding antiquity's individuals and individuality – thus becomes a direct judgment on understanding *tout court*. This is also why the stakes in admitting ignorance about classical antiquity, in turn, are so high, and why a language for the act of striving for it is constantly explored.

Another way in which Hamann is symptomatic for the articulation of knowledge about antiquity as an other human figure, and self-knowledge as the projected aim of such a close encounter, lies in his emphatic upgrading of a language of inwardness. Hamann is deeply steeped in the emotive language and vocabulary of Pietism, the varied forms of Protestant theology and forms of community that had emerged to modify and often react against late Lutheran orthodoxy in the late seventeenth and early eighteenth centuries. The combination of intense spirituality and expectations of transcendence and renewal linked to the reading of texts, and the emphasis on perception, aesthetics, and experience as guides to understanding and moral virtue gave the language of interiority and of feeling a significant place to express 'true' knowledge.[68]

Hamann's praise of Socrates's ignorance also ties in with Pietist traditions of suspiciousness towards learning as pure learnedness, or *Gelehrsamkeit*, instead of the insight derived from a more intimate and immediate practice of understanding. Hamann's text has most commonly

---

[68] A. Langen, *Wortschatz des Deutschen Pietismus*, 2nd ed. (Tübingen: Niemeyer, 1968) is a standard source regarding usage of individual terms, though one should be cautious about claiming causal relationship; see S. Grote, 'Vom geistlichen zum guten Geschmack? Reflexionen zur Suche nach den pietistischen Wurzeln der Ästhetik', in A. Allerkamp and D. Mirbach (eds.), *Schönes Denken – Baumgartens Epoche (1714/2014)* (Hamburg: Meiner, 2016), pp. 365–80; J. Schrader, 'Die Sprache Canaan: Pietistische Sonderterminologie und Spezialsemantik als Auftrag der Forschung', in H. Lehmann (ed.), *Geschichte des Pietismus* (Göttingen: Vandenhoeck und Ruprecht, 2004), vol. iv, pp. 404–27; S. Grote, 'Theological Origins of Aesthetics', in M. Kelly (ed.), *Encyclopedia of Aesthetics*, 2nd ed., vol. 5 (Oxford University Press, 2014), pp. 51–4. For the impact of Pietism on educational models, see N. Hammerstein and U. Herrmann (eds.), *Handbuch der deutschen Bildungsgeschichte, Band II: 18. Jahrhundert. Vom späten 17. Jahrhundert bis zur Neuordnung Deutschlands um 1800* (Munich: Beck, 2005).

been read as a reaction against rationalist learning in religious or theological terms, and even the figure of Socrates could quite easily be integrated within such a revisionist tendency.[69] But the sibling relationship (complementarity and commonality as much as antagonism) of the discourses of a critical, sentimental theology and a critical, sentimental Hellenism allowed also for a shift towards a vision of knowledge and pedagogy as individual processes, in which classical sources and classical figures achieved paradigmatic status as catalysts.

'A True Academy, in the Socratic Sense': Platonic Programmes for a New University

One thinker who was highly aware of that sibling relationship and its development was Friedrich Schleiermacher, whose work is discussed in detail in the following chapter. Schleiermacher was one of several high-ranking thinkers, scholars, and administrators who, in the early 1800s and with a view to the state-sponsored foundation of a new Prussian university, sketched out their institutional visions in programmatic writings. Schleiermacher, in his 'Occasional thoughts on universities in a German sense, including one to be established' (1808), considers an institutional world in which former hierarchies and authorities are in the process of changing, a new social world, too, in which students, who may have very different aptitudes for pure *Wissenschaft*, have a choice of study and, regardless of quality, will need to be accommodated and measured in less predictable ways. In short, this is the socially differentiated world in which Luhmann saw a code of love operate as a catalyst and buffer. Schleiermacher, likewise, describes this as an academic and social community in which individual comprehension cannot be achieved through compulsion (*Zwang*), nor through external authority. The affects that do bind such a learning community are love, faith, and honor (*Liebe, Glaube, Ehre*), and it is 'passion and love' (*Lust und Liebe*) that have to keep learning and scholarly work from becoming empty appearance.[70]

---

[69] Thus, Socrates was used as a parameter for religious-pedagogical reform thinking and ways of teaching a sentimental rationalism in the Pietist reformer Nikolaus von Zinzendorf's journal *Teutscher Sokrates*.

[70] F. Schleiermacher, 'Gelegentliche Gedanken über Universitäten im deutschen Sinn. Nebst einem Anhang über eine neu zu errichtende' (1808), in E. Aurich (ed.), *Die Idee der deutschen Universität: die fünf Grundschriften aus der Zeit ihrer Neugründung durch klassischen Idealismus und romantischen Realismus* (Darmstadt: Wissenschaftliche Buchgesellschaft, 1956), pp. 219–308, here pp. 267, 271.

One other such thinker to contribute to the debate was the philosopher J. G. Fichte, already mentioned in Chapter 1. In his 'Deduction of a plan for an institution of higher learning, to be established in Berlin and connected to an Academy of Sciences' (1807), Fichte was even clearer about the need for positive affect as social and intellectual glue, and even more forward in linking it explicitly to the language of Platonic sociability in particular. Teacher and pupil have to work together, with the pupil learning gradually and the teacher 'addressing a subject not entirely unknown to him, but one that is constantly revealing itself (or: himself) to the point of complete transparency', which means that teaching distinguishes itself from the linear reasoning found in books by its dialogic form, 'and a true academy is to be erected, in the sense of the Socratic school, in memory of which we are using this particular term'.[71] Whether the 'subject' that is being addressed is academic subject matter or the human subjects in front of a teacher is initially ambiguous in the German phrasing. Fichte seems to toggle between both senses, but in his continuation emphasizes the latter: 'The teacher has to keep a known and specific subject in front of his eyes, as we said. But if, as is to be expected, this subject is not just one individual but many, and the teacher focuses on One single and particular subject, thus the individuals need to melt into an intellectual unit, forming one particular, organic body of learners (*zu einem bestimmten organischen Lehrlingskörper zusammenschmelzen*). That is why they have to remain in constant exchange with each other and in a form of scholarly symbiosis (*in fortgesetzter Mitteilung und in einem wissenschaftlichen Wechselleben*), in which each shows the other an individual perspective on grasping *Wissenschaft*.' The suggested method for such learning and such an elaboration of 'scholarly art' relies on exams and so-called *Konversatoria*, structured forms of exchange that create 'an expressly Socratic dialogue within the invisible dialogue that makes academic life'.[72]

Fichte, like many of his later successors, is well aware that one of the challenges is the immensity of material to be learned. That he expresses this pronounced worry about immensity (and the gradual progression that is meant to cushion it) in the imagery of an anxiety about 'drowning in the immense ocean' of the *wissenschaftliche* material may not coincidentally echo Platonic diction, too: Diotima's speech, outlining the progression from specific desired bodies to an increasingly abstracted notion of beauty, speaks of the sudden view that opens up over 'the sea of beauty'.[73] Likewise,

[71] Fichte, 'Deduzierter Plan', §7, pp. 35–6.   [72] Fichte, 'Deduzierter Plan', §8–9, pp. 36–7.
[73] Fichte's ocean of material: 'Deduzierter Plan', §10, p. 40; Diotima's 'sea of beauty', *Symp.* 210d4.

to remain in the world of Platonic imagery, Fichte next emphasizes that it is 'love' that allows the ascent of the art of scholarship to its proper height and animates (*belebt*) it, but that remains unpredictable depending on where it turns the 'wing' of its genius, hearkening back to the power of *eros*, described in the *Phaedrus*, to grow the soul's wings.[74] It is this love that for Fichte regenerates itself and inspires 'the most loving and joyful life of the pupil through those exercises and their material', and thus unites the individuals in forming (*bilden*) a 'learning, organic whole'.[75]

---

[74] Fichte, 'Deduzierter Plan', §11, p. 44; *Phaedrus* 249–51.
[75] Fichte, 'Deduzierter Plan', §11, p. 44.

CHAPTER 3

'So That He Unknowingly and Delicately Mirrors Himself in Front of Us, As the Beautiful Often Do'
Schleiermacher's Plato

The career of Friedrich Schleiermacher (1768–1834) exemplifies in many ways the confluence of various strands of philological, philosophical, literary, and theological thinking, and the gradual solidification of disciplinary frames. Schleiermacher is now mostly known as a Protestant theologian and philosopher and as an important proponent of the development of hermeneutics, the theory of interpretation, within philosophy. To the general reader he might be familiar as the thinker who coined the binary terms of 'domesticating' and 'foreignizing' translation, or, as he puts it with more attention to the human figure, the choice of 'moving the reader towards the author' or 'bringing the author closer to the reader'.[1] To the classicist reader he is likely to be known especially as a translator of Plato, though the two actually go together, since Schleiermacher based his then-and-now programmatic essay on translation for the most part on examples from his experience of translating the Platonic dialogues.

A theologian, preacher, and from 1810 professor of theology at the newly founded Friedrich-Wilhelm University of Berlin, Schleiermacher had received solid philological training, especially at the University of Halle, where he later taught between 1804 and 1807, before the university was closed during the French occupation. Schleiermacher had encountered a range of philological learning communities by the time he took on his teaching appointments at Halle and then Berlin: as a student at the pedagogical seminary of the Pietist Moravian communities in Niesky and Barby; as a student of both biblical and classical philology in lectures and *collegia* at the University of Halle; and, for a while, as a secular trainee teacher at the pedagogical seminar of the Graues Kloster gymnasium school in Berlin. The last, directed by the classicist Friedrich Gedike

---

[1] Schleiermacher gave 'On different methods of translating' (*Ueber die verschiedenen Methoden des Uebersetzens*) as a lecture in front of the Berlin Academy of Sciences in 1813; it was published in 1816.

with state funding, required its members to produce regular research work on classical subjects.

Schleiermacher was also a frequent guest and participant in a range of learned societies and salons in Berlin, and in the late 1790s he collaborated closely with Friedrich and August Wilhelm Schlegel and other members of their circle in the ambitious literary, philosophical, philological, and poetic programs of early Romanticism, especially the journal *Athenaeum*. His translations of the collected dialogues of Plato, originally begun with Friedrich Schlegel, proved seminal for modern Plato scholarship and were quickly and appreciatively integrated into contemporary classical scholarship, as was some of his work as an editor and historian of philosophical texts. Still, for all his success as a thinker, influential administrator, academy member, and educational policy-maker, Schleiermacher himself remained still somewhat at the margins of classical philology as a circumscribed field.[2]

Schleiermacher's work highlights in many ways the closeness of classical scholarship to the wider hermeneutic commitments of the period; or rather, the proximity in which the knowledge of antiquity and speculation about the theories and methods of interpretation operated. Schleiermacher's own theory of interpretation was first and foremost based on assumptions about language. Many of those assumptions in turn were in dialogue with those of Herder, and they suggested that words, and with words language, circumscribe and reflect thought, another pointer to how philology, as the critical study and use of language, comes to acquire its particular centrality and authority. On that basis, texts can reveal the thoughts expressed in them. At the same time, individual difference – the differences between individual people on a basic physiological, mental, historical, and temporal plane – makes complete understanding always challenging, though not outright impossible.[3] Both Hamann and Herder chose to think through the issues of understanding in the figurative language of the physical proximity and the intellectual intimacy provoked by the sequence of responses to a statue or by the representation of a human figure, be it that of Peter the Great, the writer of the *Socratic Memorabilia*, and the admirers of Socrates more generally in

---

[2] Wilamowitz's vignette of Schleiermacher in his *History of Philology* recurs nicely to the topos of unveiling the human figure and of making the voice of the dead heard again: 'His German Plato chased away the cloud of a halo and with it the fog that had, since his death, surrounded his true image, and with the treatises on Diogenes of Apollonia and Heraclitus alone he resurrected (*hat erweckt*) the study of the Presocratics'; U. von Wilamowitz-Moellendorff, *Geschichte der Philologie* (1921), ed. A. Henrichs (Wiesbaden: Springer, 1998), p. 51.

[3] M. N. Forster, 'Schleiermacher's Hermeneutics: Some Problems and Solutions', *The Harvard Review of Philosophy* 13.1 (2005), 100–22.

the case of Hamann; or the literary portrait of Thomas Abbt and the presence of sculpture for Herder. Schleiermacher, like them, returns to the Socratic theme to explore the limits of interpretation. Likewise he, too, employs images of the body and of personification, not only to analyse human interaction, mutual understanding, and self-understanding, but to think through the very challenges of understanding something that is past or otherwise inaccessible.

Schleiermacher's writings indicate a similar intellectual fascination with Socrates as a figure on the margins of traditional knowledge, and as a figure simultaneously within and outside science or *Wissenschaft* – both in the Socratic critique of traditional forms of knowing and in making the profession of ignorance into a tool of knowledge. Significantly, this is complemented by a broader transition from the figure and the example of Socrates as an intellectual towards Plato as his observer, his translator (of sorts), and as the creator of *Wissenschaft* in a new vein himself. From the sociability of the Socratic circle, the perspective is readjusted to Plato as its critic and mediator, who also established a way of knowing and of learning as the founder of the Academy in Athens.

To summarize, the tendency to separate the historical figure of Socrates from the figure of Plato and to move from Socrates's ambivalent knowledge to an account of Plato's more systematic philosophy increased throughout the nineteenth century, and it rested on the assumption that a systematic, coherent philosophy would necessarily respond to a coherent author, a coherent character of the author, and a coherent life of Plato the philosopher himself.[4] This assumption in turn makes good sense of the increasing amount of philological energy that was spent on questions of the authenticity and the order and sequence of Plato's works, as well as of whether there was an esoteric Plato, a body of knowledge not transmitted in the writings but reserved to the oral teachings at the Academy, a body of knowledge that would complement what is left unsaid in the extant dialogues.

The Introductions to Plato's Dialogues: Understanding, Feeling, Becoming Oneself

In a later university lecture course on the history of philosophy, Schleiermacher considered Socrates as the beginning and origin of

---

[4] A good and detailed account of this trajectory is found in E. N. Tigerstedt, *Interpreting Plato* (Stockholm: Almqvist and Wiksell International, 1977), the complement to his earlier *The Decline and Fall of the Neoplatonic Interpretation of Plato: An Outline and Some Observations* (Helsinki: Societas Scientiarum Fennica, 1974).

systematic philosophy, casting him as the quasi-embodiment of a philosophical first principle (*archê*), much as he remains elusive: 'The spirit, the whole character of philosophy was in him; yet of its execution, its reality, only a fraction. His spirit was not merely a popular and unscientific one. But it is difficult to determine what he truly was.'[5] In a slightly earlier lecture 'On the Value of Socrates as a Philosopher', held before the Prussian Academy of Sciences in 1814, Schleiermacher had already cast Socrates as a turning point in the development towards the 'becoming-conscious of knowledge' (*Bewusstsein des Wissens*), itself philosophy's main enterprise – something that chimes well with the reflective turn of his hermeneutics, urging us to become conscious of interpretation.[6] Where pre-Socratic philosophy had to rely on individual talent and instinctual knowledge, with Socrates we enter the realm of systematic understanding of knowledge itself.[7] In short, we enter the academy – even though Socrates himself could eventually be left outside its gates. Or rather, Schleiermacher postulates a trajectory that leaves Socrates ambivalently but deliberately on the cusp of a new 'science' and a way of knowing that would have been impossible without him. It is only with Plato as a scientist *and* a philosophical artist that the Socratic precedent is fully worked out.

Schleiermacher's translations of Plato's dialogues were the result of a literary and critical, 'symphilological' project of the kind Friedrich Schlegel had envisaged, and both thinkers would find ways to see their own ways of philosophizing reflected in the Platonic dialogue.[8] Schleiermacher was closely involved with the circle of young Romantics in Berlin, especially with Friedrich Schlegel, with whom he shared lodgings in Berlin for several months in 1798. It was Schlegel who sought to enlist Schleiermacher in his initiative for a translation of Plato in the name of a new critical philology, and against the background of both a new

---

[5] The script 'History of Philosophy: Lectures on Socrates and Plato (between 1819 and 1823)' is reprinted in F. D. E. Schleiermacher, *Über die Philosophie Platons*, ed. P. Steiner (Hamburg: Meiner, 1996), pp. 3–20, here p. 4.

[6] I owe this point to Kristin Gjesdal, with thanks.

[7] 'Über den Werth des Sokrates als Philosophen' (1818), originally published in *Abhandlungen der Königlich Preussischen Akademie der Wissenschaften zu Berlin 1814/15, Philosophische Klasse* (Berlin 1818), pp. 50–68; reprinted in F. Schleiermacher, *Sämmtliche Werke, 3. Abt.: Zur Philosophie*, ii (Berlin, 1838), pp. 287–308. For an evaluation, see A. Arndt, '"Ueber den Werth des Sokrates als Philosophen". Schleiermacher und Sokrates', in H. Dierkes et al. (eds.), *Schleiermacher, Romanticism, and the Critical Arts: A Festschrift in Honor of Herrmann Patsch* (Lewiston, NY: Edwin Mellen Press, 2007), pp. 293–302.

[8] For Schlegel's investment in Plato, especially with a view to the *Symposium*, see Matuschek, 'Die Macht des Gastmahls', and Mergenthaler, *Zwischen Eros und Mitteilung*, discussed in the previous chapter.

interest in Plato across Europe and a belief in the value of translation as a form of new critical and artistic thinking. Ultimately, the drive to get the project moving rather hastily was as much fuelled by Schlegel's financial needs as by the ideology of Romantic friendship and co-operation, after Schlegel in 1799 had breezily announced the forthcoming publication with his publisher Frommann in Jena for the following year. While both men had already set to work on Plato, Schlegel's many moves and other intervening projects meant a much slower progression rate than Schlegel had promised to his editor. Schlegel eventually dropped out of the project in breach of contract, leaving some drafts on the order of the dialogues and a short introduction to the *Phaedo* and the *Parmenides* each, even though he remained deeply invested in the idea and image of the project. Schleiermacher managed to resell it to his own publisher, Reimer, in Berlin, who published the first volume with a general introduction in 1804. Subsequent volumes appeared in 1805, 1807, 1809, and, after a hiatus, 1828, leaving the project, envisaged as a complete translation, well advanced but essentially incomplete.[9]

When the first volume of translations was republished with a new preface in 1816, the new emphasis on the character and development of Plato as key to the study of his systematic philosophy was already becoming the *status quo*. In the preface, Schleiermacher makes reference to the academic prize question of the Bavarian Royal Academy of Sciences in Munich in 1813, which sought an account of the authenticity and order of Plato's dialogues according to external and internal criteria, since 'the writings and teachings of Plato have in recent times become a main object of philological and philosophical inquiry, and its success partly depends on what can be determined about their authenticity and

---

[9] For a detailed account and timeline see W. Dilthey, *Das Leben Schleiermachers* (Berlin: Reimer, 1870), as well as Schleiermacher's own version of the genesis and progress in a letter to Boeckh of 18 June 1808, reprinted in H. Meisner (ed.), *Briefwechsel Friedrich Schleiermachers mit August Boeckh und Immanuel Bekker, 1806–1820* (Berlin: Litteraturarchiv-Gesellschaft, 1916), pp. 25–35; also, A. Arndt, 'Schleiermacher und Platon', in Schleiermacher, *Über die Philosophie Platons*, pp. vii–xxii; J. Rohls, 'Schleiermachers Platon', in N. J. Cappelørn et al. (eds.), *Schleiermacher und Kierkegaard: Subjektivität und Wahrheit* (Berlin: de Gruyter, 2008), pp. 709–32; for the mutual impact of Schleiermacher and Schlegel in terms of their hermeneutics, see H. Birus, 'Hermeneutische Wende? Anmerkungen zur Schleiermacher-Interpretation', *Euphorion* 74.2 (1980), pp. 213–22; H. Patsch, 'Friedrich Asts "Euthyphron"-Übersetzung im Nachlass Friedrich Schlegels. Ein Beitrag zur Platon-Rezeption in der Frühromantik', *Jahrbuch des Freien Deutschen Hochstifts* (1988), 112–27; J. Lamm, 'Schleiermacher as Plato Scholar', *Journal of Religion* 80.2 (2000), pp. 206–39; J. Lamm, 'The Art of Interpreting Plato', in J. Marina (ed.), *The Cambridge Companion to Schleiermacher* (Cambridge University Press, 2005), pp. 91–108; A. Laks, 'Schleiermacher on Plato: From Form (*Introduction to Plato's Works*) to Content (*Outlines of a Critique of Previous Ethical Theory*)', in A. Kim (ed.), *Brill's Companion to German Platonism* (Brill: Leiden, 2019), pp. 146–64.

sequence'.[10] Schleiermacher is at best lukewarm about the yield of that competition, but to have mentioned it at all indicates that the search for Plato's coherent body of works was becoming a priority with backing from authorized institutions and guardians of scholarship.

Schleiermacher makes it clear what in his opinion are the sources best used to give a coherent account of Plato, both as a character and as a writer, and he makes it equally clear that this is a departure from earlier studies. Right away he refers readers interested in Plato's life to W. G. Tennemann's *System der Platonischen Philosophie* (1792). Tennemann had prefaced his version of a systematic Plato with a detailed resumé of ancient biographical information, and he was, in Schleiermacher's view, trying to make the best of the 'crude and sorry effort' (*rohes Machwerk*) that is Diogenes Laertius's standardly used sketch.[11] Tennemann may be serviceable, and Schleiermacher's reference highlights the expectation that biographical information is relevant to the study of a philosopher, but he does not explicitly endorse a method that seeks to gather together disparate evidence when this technique does not add up to a careful integration of the biographical impetus with a fully grounded interpretation of the body of work at hand. A collection of disjointed details, in Schleiermacher's view, will throw no light on Plato's work as a whole, and from the perspective of the historicizing scholar it seems clear to him that what detail we could glean for a better understanding of his works is so far removed in time, and the evidence so shaky, that the yield would inevitably be too small.[12] If anything, Schleiermacher would prefer to see any such material integrated into contextual, historical information about the state of philosophical enquiry before and during the time of Plato – thus gesturing towards a type of nested biography of the 'life' of philosophical enquiry surrounding the life of the philosopher, a notion of identifying an individual as representative of an age that will shape biographical approaches increasingly towards the end of the nineteenth century.

August Boeckh, then a young professor of classical philology in Heidelberg and soon to be the inaugural and influential holder of the chair of classical philology at the newly founded Friedrich-Wilhelm University in Berlin, was Schleiermacher's former student at Halle and

---

[10] The exact text of the *Preisaufgabe* is reprinted in the editor's notes to Schleiermacher, *Über die Philosophie Platons*, p. 24.

[11] How self-evidently the biographical sketch was part of a scholarly presentation of Plato is reflected in the standard edition on which Schleiermacher bases his translations, the *Bipontina* or *Zweibrücker Ausgabe* of 1781–7 (discussed in the previous chapter), which included in its first volume Diogenes Laertius's 'Life of Socrates'.

[12] Schleiermacher, 'Die Einleitungen zu Übersetzungen des Platon (1804–1828)', in *Über die Philosophie Platons*, pp. 21–387, here p. 26.

an early reviewer of the first volume of his Plato translations. Boeckh rather regretted that Schleiermacher did not preface his work with a biography of Plato, since in his hands it would undoubtedly have turned out very well and much better than in his predecessors.[13] That this is indicative of a larger desire to put a biographical approach on new tracks, emphasizing the representativeness of the author's life as a figure for organic cohesion and developmental narrative, is nicely echoed in a letter Boeckh wrote to Schleiermacher in November 1807 from Heidelberg:

> I have about 18–20 auditors in my Plato colloquia. . . . I lecture on Plato four times a week; I have prefaced this with an introduction that deals exclusively with Plato's life; but I have continued this as a weekly session for one hour for the whole of the semester, so that we might understand the sum total together with understanding a single dialogue, namely the *Gorgias*; with both proceeding side by side, they shed light on each other in turn.[14]

For Schleiermacher, too, the language of individual coherence and a narrative line that models wholeness on the wholeness of the single human life and body remains his basic analytical frame – much as it remains shot through with the acknowledgement that understanding and interpretation necessarily must contain misunderstanding in order to proceed. When it comes to the understanding and interpretation of Plato (both man and text), Schleiermacher claims that the overall form of the works and their relation to each other are in fact constitutive of their content and meaning. In fact, he suggests a view of the whole that no longer distinguishes between form and content.[15] On this basis Schleiermacher criticizes earlier readings that either have claimed that the Platonic works are not coherent or have postulated an esoteric Plato with pieces of 'missing' doctrine to compensate for what was assumed lacking.[16] Schleiermacher contrasts his own approach with that of the anatomist who takes the body apart into vessels and bones for comparison with other bodies, or rather with that of the observer, who is left comparing the fragmented pieces without regaining a larger sense of the

---

[13] A. Boeckh, 'Kritik der Übersetzung des Platon von Schleiermacher' (1804/5), in F. Ascherson and P. Eichholtz (eds), *Gesammelte Kleine Schriften*, vii (Leipzig: Teubner, 1872), pp. 1–38, here p. 4.

[14] Letter of 12 November 1807 in Meisner, *Briefwechsel*, p. 9.

[15] 'It is in [Plato's philosophy], if anywhere, that form and content are inseparable, and each sentence can only be properly understood in its proper place, with its relations and distinctions, where Plato put it', Schleiermacher, 'Einleitungen', p. 38.

[16] T. A. Szlezak, 'Schleiermacher's "Einleitungen" zur Platon-Übersetzung von 1804. Ein Vergleich mit Tiedemann und Tennemann', *Antike und Abendland* 43 (1997), 46–62, is, unsurprisingly, largely unsympathetic to Schleiermacher's rejection of an esoteric Plato, but provides a useful overview of the debate on the topic both before and after Schleiermacher.

whole. Amassing individual pieces of Platonic doctrine is the opposite of Schleiermacher's offer of an entire corpus of translations to resist such dissection (*Zerlegung*).[17] Lutz Danneberg has examined the late-eighteenth- and early-nineteenth-century topos of 'dissection' and 'dis-memberment', a topos about being caught between trust in reasoned analysis and the revelation of inconsistencies, and about the resulting anxiety on display in those instances of reading where what is at stake is the critical and increasingly historical understanding of an authoritative text that resists expectations of structure, coherence, or beauty.[18] Biblical hermeneutics and text criticism, the understanding of an authoritative text that was increasingly seen as revealing historical strata, historical inconsistencies, and historical imperfections, was a template for this challenge, though other, secular kinds of reading responded to a similar need. Danneberg argues carefully that to outsource the com-plex aspect of a text with all its idiosyncrasies onto the individual character of an author behind the text was a strategy of dispelling the threat of the disintegration of text, while raising author personality and author intention to a central place in the hermeneutic demands of the late eighteenth century (and beyond).[19] In other words, a strong sense of an internally coherent author personality was an attractive antidote whenever textual inconsistencies became newly evident.

Schleiermacher's Platonic corpus is, similarly, an organic whole, a literal body of text: it is Plato the thinker himself who, as an indivi-dual, is inseparable from the coherence of the dialogues that form a continuous entity and reflect Plato's thought. Schleiermacher's emphasis is on organic unity grown in and over time, whose imprint manifests in the dialogic form itself, rather than on a Platonic system (in the sense of a rational-systematic philosophy) that exists outside time.

One tool for identifying the order, coherence, and unity of the works rested in critically evaluating the ancient sources on Plato and his corpus. Here Schleiermacher identifies as key what he calls a 'philological feeling',

---

[17] Schleiermacher alludes to the 'dissecting account' (*zerlegende Darstellung*) of Tennemann as an example of such literally analytic scholarship, 'Einleitungen', p. 38; Tennemann proceeds in his *System of Platonic Philosophy* mainly by relating the dialogues to external, historical evidence as a way to arrive at a chronology.

[18] L. Danneberg, 'Ganzheitsvorstellungen und Zerstückelungsphantasien. Zum Hintergrund und zur Entwicklung der Wahrnehmungen ästhetischer Eigenschaften in der zweiten Hälfte des 18. und zu Beginn des 19. Jahrhunderts', in J. Schönert and U. Zeuch (eds.), *Mimesis – Repräsentation – Imagination. Literaturtheoretische Positionen von Aristoteles bis zum Ende des 18. Jahrhunderts* (Berlin: de Gruyter, 2004), pp. 241–82.

[19] Danneberg, 'Ganzheitsvorstellungen', p. 264.

a *philologisches Gefühl.*[20] *Gefühl* represents what is mentally 'tentative', what one understands by feeling one's way along in an act of reasoning and arguing; but the underlying meaning of tentative as relying on touch (*fühlen*), already explored by Herder in his writings on sculpture, remains strong. At the same time, Schleiermacher confesses real philological scepticism when he discusses what we would now call the authentication of Platonic prose on stylistic grounds. Language alone cannot decide authenticity, as there is no *guaranteed* way for authorship to be reflected in the choice of language: 'so that [language] alone can decide hardly anything: a feeling can occur, which relies on no specific proof, but on a more general impression, which shows it to depend already more on composition than only on language'.[21] Form and composition together, in fact, must be the deciding parameter. Scholarly, philological 'feeling' therefore remains linked to technical and measurable grammatical knowledge as much as to a sense of intuition that feeds on and feeds back into an overall understanding.[22]

Schleiermacher suggested a rather extreme reordering of the dialogues (as did Schlegel, judging by the brief pieces we have of his contribution to the Plato project), firmly claiming the *Phaedrus* as the chronologically earliest and in some ways conceptually most fundamental of the works, containing all else as in a seed (a point to which I will return below).[23] This focus on the *Phaedrus* does in any case explain why Schleiermacher should mention it prominently in his general introduction to the dialogues, apropos Socrates's famous suspicion of writing and his praise of oral dialogue and the immediacy of human intercourse.[24] Schleiermacher puts at centre stage the Platonic feature of 'living teaching':

---

[20] Schleiermacher, 'Einleitungen', p. 53.   [21] Ibid., p. 56.

[22] Gjesdal outlines lucidly how the 'sympathetic-imaginative' aspect of understanding a 'You' or 'Thou' in Schleiermacher does not have to be thought philosophically inconsistent with his claims for grammatical understanding and a stricter sense of 'methodology', especially in view of Schleiermacher's knowledge of Herder; K. Gjesdal, 'Imagination, Divination, and Understanding: Schleiermacher and the Hermeneutics of the Second Person', in G. Gentry and K. Pollok (eds.), *The Imagination in German Idealism and Romanticism* (Cambridge University Press, 2019), pp. 190–207.

[23] For an overview of the suggested orderings of Plato's dialogues from antiquity to the late twentieth century, see H. Thesleff, *Studies in Platonic Chronology* (Helsinki: Societas Scientiarum Fennica, 1982); also L. Brandwood, *The Chronology of Plato's Dialogues* (Cambridge University Press, 1990); on Schleiermacher's ordering of the Platonic corpus, see J. Lamm, 'Reading Plato's Dialectics: Schleiermacher's Insistence on Dialectics as Dialogical', *Zeitschrift für Neuere Theologiegeschichte/Journal for the History of Modern Theology* 10.1 (2003), pp. 1–25; Lamm, 'The Art of Interpreting Plato'; J. Lamm, 'Schleiermacher's "Christmas Dialogue" as Platonic Dialogue', *Journal of Religion* 92.3 (2012), pp. 392–420, as well as Schleiermacher's account to Boeckh, where he elaborates specifically on this point and on his and Schlegel's diverging (though equally novel) views.

[24] *Phaedrus*, 275d-e.

so that here the one who teaches is in mutual, immediate, and vivid exchange with the one who learns, and could thus know at any given moment what he has understood, and thus support him where he has not yet comprehended; for this advantage to take effect, everyone would agree that spoken dialogue is the fundament that any living form of teaching (*ein lebendiger Unterricht*) needs must have.... Since Plato, disregarding those contentions, has written so great an amount, from his earliest manhood until his very last years, it is obvious that he must have sought to make written teaching as closely resemble the other, better one, and he must have succeeded in it.[25]

Rather than taking the passage as evidence for unwritten Platonic doctrine (as some later readers would like to do and would like him to do), Schleiermacher crafts an argument for the written dialogue as a translation and re-presentation of the oral mode of teaching, one that faithfully generates the same level of ambivalence and epistemological stumbling. The Platonic text, both in its time and by extension still for today's reader and scholar, *re-enacts* and reactivates the interpersonal situation that is the basis for understanding. The modern reader of works like Tennemann's, who comes to Plato by way of an edition that frontloads an account of the philosopher's life and follows it by a simple pronouncement of the sequence of works, cannot hope to experience freely and fully the very method that is exemplified in the dialogues: 'Even less will they grasp the man himself, and his own intention will least succeed with them, namely to present his own understanding vividly to others, but also to encourage them by this very act to stimulate and enhance their own (*nicht nur seinen eignen Sinn andern lebendig darzulegen, sondern eben dadurch auch den ihrigen lebendig aufzuregen und zu erheben*).'[26] The reader of Schleiermacher's translations, in contrast, is encouraged to be a living participant in the Platonic undertaking, which is essentially the same as that of modern critical reading – namely to forget all previous knowledge and accounts of his works, their content, and their order – and instead be exposed to the actual texts – to read, see, and discover their order by and for himself. In some sense there lingers a familiar language of emulation, self-formation, and exemplarity that looks back to ethical and readerly models from antiquity that maintained their traction certainly into the eighteenth century. When Plutarch emphasizes the importance of communing with exemplary figures from the past for moral and intellectual self-improvement, or of virtuous emulation and emulation of

[25] Schleiermacher, 'Einleitungen', p. 40.   [26] Ibid., p. 38.

virtue through reading and writing about the lives and works of great men, then attentive reading and acting are one possible form of such mimesis. For Schleiermacher and his contemporaries exemplarity alone was no longer enough: the power of self-formation becomes internalized, textualized, and historicized, modulated into modern individual *Bildung*, as Plato takes over from Plutarch, and dialectic re-enacted through hermeneutical understanding replaces narratives of self-fashioning.[27]

As for the open and ambiguous form of the dialogues, unsatisfactory to some at least, Schleiermacher suggests that this form corresponds deliberately to the tentative, Socratic dialectic of knowing and ignorance:

> this must have been of the greatest importance to [Plato], to calculate and to structure each conversation from the beginning in such a way that the reader is either forced to produce the intended idea in and of himself, or to experience the distinct feeling that he has found nothing and understood nothing. This makes it necessary that the outcome of the investigation not be explicitly articulated or spelled out word for word; this would be a stumbling block for the many who like to reassure themselves as long as they know the end; instead, the soul needs to be exposed to the need to seek, and to be set on the path of how to discover it.[28]

At this point, Schleiermacher goes one step further in his analysis: just like the choice of dialogue as an unsettling means to induce reflection, Plato uses the topics in which his characters engage, such as the definitions of various virtues, as mere fronts behind which lie the central questions of his philosophy, namely those of understanding and knowledge itself. This concealment, or the gentle introduction to the core issues of his philosophy by means of what look initially like more familiar issues, Schleiermacher describes effectively again as an act of personification, of a literal *prosopopoeia*: 'Or else, the true investigation is covered over by another one, not like a veil, but like a grown skin, which hides from the inattentive man, and only from him, what is truly to be observed and sought out; but for the attentive man, it additionally sharpens and clarifies his understanding of its inner cohesion.'[29] This is not quite Pygmalion bringing mute sculpted material to life; it is a more uncompromising view on the construction of dialogue, laying bare its mechanism. And yet it is the creation, as it were, of a body with its natural and organically grown and attached skin, which cannot be removed without damage, just as the dramatized epistemological fumblings of the dialogues' characters cannot be dissected and separated out without harming the overall integrity of the

---

[27] See also the discussion of Wilamowitz's Plutarch in Chapter 6.
[28] Schleiermacher, 'Einleitungen', p. 41.   [29] Ibid., pp. 41–2.

Platonic system. In fact, it is precisely the dramatic, figurative layout of Plato's works that gives them their particular, individual, and aesthetically impactful character (*besondere Eigentümlichkeit*): 'that is, its mimic and dramatic ingredient, which makes people and situations individual and which, all would agree, diffuses such beauty and grace within the dialogues of Plato'.[30]

That the Platonic dialogues, in form and content, are here singled out for their generally agreed-upon beauty and grace (grace, *Anmut*, signifying a quality specifically of human movement and expression) underlines even more strongly that Schleiermacher formulates Plato's hermeneutics as and with reference to the compelling, attractive human figure. Deliberately playing on Schleiermacher's imagery, August Boeckh, in the review mentioned above, speaks not only of the 'contours' (*Umrisse*) of the 'painting' (*Gemälde*) of Plato which Schleiermacher has presented. He also speaks of the tender skin with which Schleiermacher has covered the fragile naked body of the text's spirit in his translation, as if leaving it exposed still: 'The exterior of this inspired account (*die Hülle der genialen Darstellung*) is exceedingly tender, where its spirit appears as if undressed (*wie entblösset*), to speak with Schiller, and the sign merges into the signified (*das Zeichen ganz in dem Bezeichneten verschwindet*), and where language leaves the thought it seeks to express as if it were still naked.'[31] Boeckh may reference Schiller at this point, but he is also evoking once more the familiar Winckelmannian aesthetic structure of the beautiful body of antiquity and of those giving an account of it.

In Schleiermacher's reading, the strategy of the Platonic works is to encourage the reader to continue, mirroring the characters in the text, and in the act to confront the same reader with an equally continuing lack of knowledge.[32] These are therefore texts, as we would say, which deliberately refuse closure, an assumption generally in line with Schleiermacher's understanding of interpretation as an ongoing and approximative undertaking, conscious of the radical distance between self and other.[33]

---

[30] Ibid., p. 59. [31] Boeckh, 'Kritik', p. 17. [32] Schleiermacher, 'Einleitungen', p. 40.

[33] Forster, 'Schleiermacher's Hermeutics', p. 106, argues for this with reference to Schleiermacher's manuscript sources for his *Hermeneutik* lectures; by comparison, Matuschek's description of Schlegel's conception of Plato should offer a good reminder that the relative 'openness' of Schleiermacher's Plato is of a less radical kind than that of Schlegel; 'Die Macht des Gastmahls', pp. 82ff; for Schleiermacher's assumption of a fundamental distance between self and other, nonetheless, see G. Scholtz, 'Schleiermacher im Kontext der neuzeitlichen Hermeneutik-Entwicklung', in A. Arndt and J. Dierken (eds.), *Schleiermachers Hermeneutik: Interpretationen und Perspektiven* (Berlin: de Gruyter, 2016), pp. 1–26.

Schleiermacher's *Phaedrus* and *Symposium*

Philosophy, like interpretation, always happens in embodied form, and understanding is formulated with regard to the fact that individuals relate to each other. Or, as Schleiermacher rephrases it in his introduction to the translation of the *Symposium*, wisdom and philosophy are always embodied, and the aim of Plato's writings is to show the philosopher as an embodied human being, with wisdom manifest in the mortal life of the individual as it appears before us (*erscheinendes Leben*).[34] It is the terminology of love that captures the striving of the mortal for what is immortal. In fact, to look on this striving as love and to grant it generative power for the 'living formation' (*lebendiges Bilden*) of the correct notions of the good and just, and of understanding (*Erkenntnis*) tout court, should make it clear that this language of love is not a poetic image but a necessary reflection of the identity of spiritual and physical generation, simply on different, though related, planes.[35]

In fact, Schleiermacher discusses love not only with regard to specific Platonic operations, but rather he appears to integrate his interpretation of Plato with his own systematic outlook. In the series of linked prose reflections published under the title *Soliloquies* (*Monologen*), mentioned in Chapter 1, he closely links love and understanding of the other as key to a more broadly conceived *Bildung* and self-knowledge. The work was published anonymously by Spener in 1800, republished under Schleiermacher's own name by his usual publisher Reimer in 1810, then reprinted twice more, with some, though overall not a significant amount of additions in 1822 and 1829.[36] And while it has been called 'likely the least studied text among today's Schleiermacher scholars', it is also one that was reprinted multiple times during his lifetime and never renounced.[37] The text thus had a long gestation, but one that Schleiermacher himself thought signalled consistency underlying change. In his letters, he refers to the *Soliloquies* as a reliable and representative account of his personal opinions,

---

[34] Schleiermacher, 'Das Gastmahl', in *Über die Philosophie Platons*, pp. 273–86, here p. 276.

[35] Ibid., p. 276.

[36] The small changes mainly seem to help create a less uncompromising tone, according to G. Meckenstock, 'Die Wandlung der Monologen Schleiermachers', in G. Meckenstock and J. Ringleben (eds.), *Schleiermacher und die wissenschaftliche Kultur des Christentums* (Berlin: de Gruyter, 1991), pp. 403–18.

[37] R. Crouter, *Friedrich Schleiermacher: Between Enlightenment and Romanticism* (Cambridge University Press, 2005), p. 31. Though see now, for the importance of the text for Schleiermacher's ethics, literary form, and theology, R. Jackson-Ravenscroft, *The Veiled God: Friedrich Schleiermacher's Theology of Finitude* (Leiden: Brill, 2019), esp. part 2: 'Human Formation and Literary Form in Schleiermacher's Soliloquies (1800)', pp. 95–168.

character, and interior life.[38] In the growing number of prefaces to the later editions, it is both the continuous growth of his self as well as the underlying continuity that Schleiermacher stresses, not unlike his vision of Platonic revisions and developments he sees reflected in the order of the dialogues. In addition, the intellectual and personal development that accrues around the texts is couched in the language of mutual friendship and learning, adding yet another layer of individuals and texts interacting with each other, both in human intercourse and within texts, to the extent that the boundaries of figurative language become fluid. For Schleiermacher, texts really have agency. In the preface to the second edition of 1810, Schleiermacher claimed that the publication of the work made him friends he had not known before nor would have known otherwise. The new self, even if not the same, is still entirely consistent with the one described ten years earlier, 'so that all sentiments expressed therein are still so completely my own, just like any picture of an earlier time can and ought to resemble that of the older man'.[39]

In the preface to the third edition, added to, yet not replacing the previous one, he again justifies his writing, and again he does so by suggesting that friendship resulting from textual communication has acted as a catalyst for the continued submission of his self-portrait to a readership: 'an intimate friend of old has since told me what is most appropriate to mention here, that the life of each human being as we see it oscillates between its *Urbild* and a distortion (*Zerrbild*) of it. It is only the introspection which aims towards the first that can result in something that it is possible to communicate openly.'[40] Schleiermacher's self-reflection raises what is particular, namely himself, to a level of abstraction of the individual, whose embodiment he is, anticipating the method he will detect in the order and method of the Platonic corpus. There, the increasing evolution of a systematic philosophy in the name of exceeding what is phenomenal feeds back into an engagement with that phenomenal reality (Schleiermacher's *erscheinendes Leben*) – both in the dialectic movement that includes the oscillation between ideal and real, and actualized in the textual dialogue between more than one speaker, including the potential reader.

---

[38] Thus Schleiermacher in a letter to his sister, Charlotte von Kathen, in August 1809 – a passing reference to the effect that Charlotte surely knows about his character and his attitudes on friendship from her familiarity with the *Monologen*; G. Meckenstock, 'Historische Einführung' to Schleiermacher, 'Monologen', pp. VII–LXIX, here p. LXVII.
[39] Schleiermacher, 'Monologen', p. 325.   [40] Ibid., p. 326.

The whole of the *Soliloquies* is imagined as a gift made of the self. The opening section titled 'Offering' (*Darbietung*), is addressed to an abstracted You:

> Man cannot offer man a more intimate gift than that which he has spoken to himself in his innermost mind: for this gift offers what is the greatest secret, the open uninterrupted view onto another free individual. And there is no gift more assured: for life with you is filled with joy, provoked simply by looking upon what has become friendly and familiar; and inner truth holds your love close, so that you may want to return to observation often (*innere Wahrheit hält Deine Liebe fest, dass Du gern öfters zur Betrachtung zurükkehrst*).[41]

This recalls Schleiermacher's reading of the Platonic and Socratic attitude in both the *Phaedrus* and the *Symposium*: the attraction of the innermost man should encourage yet further engagement and a feedback loop to reflection. Maybe there is also once more the echo of Alcibiades and of the Silenus figure, in the intimate gift of looking into the most interior, secret, and hidden part of a man. What this most inward core reveals is not a thing, but dialectic itself: the words one has spoken in intimate dialogue with one's self. Interpersonal communication and affection are thus right at the heart of any figuration of Plato's philosophy, as understood by the modern reader. The *Soliloquies* were begun, written, and then certainly revisited and republished more or less exactly for the same period of time – a good twenty-five years – during which the Plato project was ongoing, and the structures of self-knowledge identified in the *Soliloquies* resonate especially with the Platonic works that treat on the structures of *eros*.

The dialogue which, following Schlegel's lead, Schleiermacher singled out from early on as seminal for Plato's work and its interpretation is the *Phaedrus*, to which he also devotes the longest introduction of any of the works.[42] Like the *Symposium*, *Phaedrus* is a dialogue framed by a discussion of *eros*, or rather by a discussion of speechmaking about *eros*. In Schleiermacher's reading, it becomes a dialogue about the dialectic principle itself. The often playful dialogue, within its frame of recounting inspiring speeches about love, returns repeatedly to the themes of rhetoric, poetry, and inspiration or madness, and it ostensibly falls into two sections, one dealing with *eros*, the other with rhetoric. Socrates's interlocutor Phaedrus recounts verbatim a speech he heard the orator Lysias make about the advantage of bestowing one's erotic favour on a dispassionate suitor rather than on one full of love. This in turn provokes three long

[41] Ibid., p. 328.   [42] Schleiermacher, 'Phaidros', in *Über die Philosophie Platons*, pp. 69–92.

speeches by Socrates: one, dismantling and improving on Lysias's speech on the effects of love on the lover; the second on inspiration in relation to *eros* and on the effects of inspiration on the soul; and the last on rhetoric and writing in their relation to passionate inspiration.

If the *Phaedrus* were simply a dialogue about love *or* rhetoric, Schleiermacher argues, the awkward position in which this would leave either part standing disjointed from the other would already sufficiently speak against that interpretation, '[b]ecause either suggestion would make the work, which is clearly beautifully and carefully crafted, appear unacceptably disfigured, quite contrary to the injunction that it be formed like a living being (*dass es wie ein lebendiges Wesen gebildet sein müsse*), with its body and its parts correlating to its spirit'.[43] The dialogue, Schleiermacher suggests, is best thought of as a beautiful organic body, and the image of the proportional parts of the body, through which he voices his objection, is itself taken from the *Phaedrus* (264c). Bodily integrity, as we saw, is an analogy that resonates more widely in Schleiermacher's frame of interpretation. Schleiermacher suggests a division into a first part, with the speeches on love as examples of rhetoric, followed in the second part by a theory of rhetoric, making the work altogether a dialogue about the *Wissenschaft* (his translation of *episteme*) of the art of rhetoric.[44] That the speeches in turn recommend first distanced and then enthusiastic attitudes of lover and beloved is seen as an instance of the flexible, interchangeable attitudes needed in rhetoric, the knowledge of rhetoric, and, eventually, pure knowledge. Seeing his own interpretation as mirroring Plato's systematic philosophy, Schleiermacher seeks to proceed by following a Russian doll principle, moving from the outside in. Thus he arrives at what he considers the real core of the dialogue, which is not about the art of rhetoric but the art of free thinking, that is, about the act of dialectic itself, of the 'formative act of communication' (*bildendes Mitteilen*) – this being the overall theme that in turn can include rhetoric, love, and all its other particular instances.[45]

This might stretch the interpretation that Schleiermacher is feeding back into his readings a notion and an imagination of interpersonal, embodied love, were it not for a strangely overdetermined comment he adds at this point. The object of dialectic is ideas, he claims, and this feature is represented by Plato through love: 'The original subject of dialectic is the ideas, which, therefore, he represents here with the warmth of first love';[46] the German of that last phrase, *welche er daher auch hier mit aller Wärme*

---

[43] Ibid., p. 71.   [44] Ibid., pp. 74–5.   [45] Ibid., p. 78.   [46] Ibid., p. 79.

der ersten Liebe darstellt, allows for a translation as either 'are represented through the warmth of first love' or 'are represented, with the warmth of first love'. The ambiguity must, if not calculated, at least have been welcome, as it captures precisely the double sense Schleiermacher attributes to Plato. Love articulates the striving that is part and parcel of philosophy – it *is* that striving, and it also represents it; but the sentence can also refer to the young Plato, in a dialogue that is meant to be foundational and in that sense 'early', who expresses in it the basic parts of his system. With that slide the Platonic notion of understanding is reattached to an image of Plato as an individual, whose emotional coherence is coextensive with the texts produced in his name.

In this notion of a personal and a philosophical *Bildung* working in creative tandem, Schleiermacher has found his principle of how to order the dialogues. The early dialogues are to him essentially about dialectic as such, often to the point of being a reflection of method devoid of specific content, which, however, increases over the course of Plato's text production. The textual corpus in turn is allowed, is even meant to bear the traces of that development, which explains for Schleiermacher its open yet consistent form. In fact, this principle of leaving earlier traces visible may even account for Schleiermacher's understanding of Socrates's place in the work of Plato and in the history of philosophy: as not fully part of 'academic' philosophy, yet as making it possible and therefore necessarily remaining present in it. In that sense, Schleiermacher's imagination of the textual configuration of Plato's thought is strangely resonant of the accruing prefaces to Schleiermacher's *Soliloquies*, where the author looked back over earlier editions, deliberately leaving earlier versions mostly the same and only subtly amended as testimony to his thought and his own process of individualization.

As Julia Lamm has carefully and persuasively argued, Schleiermacher himself conceived of Plato's works as a whole with a tripartite structure, each third composed of a trilogy, of which each was again dominated by one seminal work.[47] While the *Phaedrus* is the core dialogue of the first trilogy, and the *Republic* that of the third, the *Symposium* is not only the main player of the second part, but in fact the centre's centre, embedded in its own trilogy made up of *Sophist*, *Statesman*, and *Symposium*. Like the *Phaedrus*, the *Symposium* is treated in terms of its hermeneutically productive relation of form and content, on a smaller as much as on a grander

[47] Lamm, 'Reading Plato's Dialectics'; Lamm, 'Art of Interpreting Plato'; especially Lamm, 'Schleiermacher's "Christmas Dialogue"', pp. 398–400.

scale. That 'form' can also include the human form or figure gives the reading extra scope in its use of figuration and of individual development as a topos. The *Sophist* and *Statesman* are about the role of the sophist and the politician respectively; the *Symposium* is about the true philosopher, and its attempt to show the philosophical life in practice has to be seen together with the *Phaidon*, which, in counterpoint, is about the philosopher's death. The true philosopher here is personified by Socrates, who 'in our *Symposium* is praised just as he really was in Alcibiades's speech, which so obviously is the summit and crown of the entire dialogue; and which presents us a Socrates engaged in his untiring pursuit of reflection and in his joyous expression of it, in disdain of danger and in control over external phenomena . . . in short, in perfect valour of body and soul, and hence of all life'.[48] A subtle, but important readjustment occurs here. The drunken praise of Socrates's integrity, in body and soul, becomes for Schleiermacher the crowning centrepiece of the dialogue – not a self-evident interpretation, considering that Diotima's speech about the ladder of love might have been prized equally highly (and was so by Schlegel, among others). It is Alcibiades's insight that makes that crowning achievement possible – and it is, in view of Alcibiades's image of Socrates as a Silenus figurine, quite literally an 'insight'. With remarkable sleight of hand Schleiermacher next matches Alcibiades's unifying vision of the corporeal figure of Socrates, the true philosopher, with that of the modern interpreter of Plato, scholar or general reader, once more rendering Alcibiades as a counterpart for the modern interpreter of Plato:

> What is more, the affinity between [the *Symposium*] and the *Phaedo*, and the position we ascribe it, relies on the love speeches no less than on Alcibiades's contribution; it is only from that perspective that we see the whole as a whole, and it leads us to claim that whosoever views the *Symposium*, as is often done, outside its context and intention and just on its own, he will have seen of its composition only the outer form and, though beautiful and crafted with precision, the wanton figure of the Silenus, but not the infinitely more delightful divine image that is locked within.[49]

Wisdom and philosophy are both embodied, and they find a textual body to match. Procreation and love, therefore, are not just metaphors, but essentially link a lower and a higher level: 'this is not a poetic comparison; instead, it was altogether necessary for Plato to see both as one and the same, only viewing spiritual procreation as a higher step of the selfsame action; for natural birth also was to him nothing but a reproduction of the

---

[48] Schleiermacher, 'Das Gastmahl', p. 274.   [49] Ibid., p. 275.

same eternal form and idea, that is, its immortality within what is mortal'.[50]

Schleiermacher's subtle identification of the Plato reader and scholar with the Alcibiades figure as his closest equivalent still manages to integrate the rather more one-sided precepts of Diotima by extrapolating from her ladder to the great arch of the Platonic system overall:

> We find, in a remarkable way, yet another confirmation of our pattern writ large in what Diotima has to say about the gradual process of the mysteries of love. For this ascent chimes in the most precise manner with the developing presentation of philosophy in Plato's works, so that here he unknowingly and delicately mirrors himself in front of us, as the beautiful often do (*so dass er hier sich selbst, unwissend vielleicht wie die Schönen oft tun, auf das zierlichste vor uns bespiegelt*).[51]

In this final turn of the screw, it is the unselfconscious mirror image of a beautiful, attractive, youthful Plato that is revealed by the eye and to the eye of the observer, who, like Alcibiades, is firmly grounded in physical reality and who, also like Alcibiades, is confronted with the impossibility of knowing Socrates. If Socrates stands for the transition towards the academy, the modern descendants of those academicians retain an aspect, maybe already a nostalgic aspect, of the gate-crasher Alcibiades, youthful, beautiful, and possibly mistaken, vis-à-vis a Socratic Plato whose unselfconscious beauty contrasts with his critic's modern, conscious reflectiveness.

An echo of this knowing embrace can still be heard in August Boeckh's review of the first volume of the translations. Complimenting Schleiermacher on his portrayal of Plato like 'a painting, perfected before his soul', drawing its 'masterful contours', he singles out the 'introduction to Phaedrus, written with particular love', and he affirms that 'no one has understood Plato and taught others to understand him so completely as this man, who in a rare moment of grasping the highest does not forget to pay attention to the very smallest with the same care' – *Umfassung*, 'grasp', is a word meaning embrace even before, figuratively, it means intellectual comprehension.[52]

If Schleiermacher considered the *Phaedrus* foundational for a Platonic notion of dialectic, expressed in a language that works with the structures of *eros* and the image of the human figure, this is not without backing in the dialogues themselves, with their close inter-textual web between the

---

[50] Ibid., p. 276.   [51] Ibid., p. 285.   [52] Boeckh, 'Kritik', pp. 3, 12–14.

Phaedrus and the *Symposium*, the *Lysis* (which has Socrates quiz a beautiful boy on the nature of friendship and *eros*), and, arguably, the two *Alcibiades* dialogues. Schleiermacher was certainly aware that *Alcibiades I*, well into the later reaches of the Neoplatonic tradition in the early modern period, was considered an introductory dialogue to Platonic thought and pedagogy. Even so he himself, ironically, considered the dialogue in his introductions to be of lesser quality and likely spurious, thus contributing considerably to the scholarly marginalization of the dialogue in the nineteenth and twentieth centuries.[53] *Alcibiades I* is a dialogue about self-knowledge and self-care, making Alcibiades, the young, beautiful statesman-to-be, the central figure of pedagogical attention as he is being interrogated by Socrates.[54] One of its central images is that of the eye mirroring itself in the eye of another, just as the soul mirrors itself in another soul, as a route to an understanding of the self (133b). It is a topos that corresponds closely, despite Schleiermacher's criticism of the dialogue's coherence as a whole, to the self knowing itself only by way of reflection through an other, a notion which Schleiermacher himself explored in the *Soliloquies*.[55] The image of *eros* and beauty streaming in through the eyes, as a pre-rational but highly generative affect, is taken up again in the *Phaedrus* (255d), and it is possible to identify further points of overlap between the *Phaedrus* and the *Symposium* with specific regard to the figure of Alcibiades and to Alcibiades's speech in the *Symposium*. One such connecting point is the use of the sculptural image, of Socrates as an *agalma* as if of a god, which appears in the *Phaedrus* (251a1-7). Here, Socrates likens the enthusiasm of a lover for a boy to the admiration of an *agalma* – which resonates not only with Alcibiades's comparison to Socrates' inner beauty, but also, more importantly, with his analogy between philosophical arguments and the *silenoi* figures or *agalmata* contained in the outer, ugly shell (*Symp* 221e1-222a6).[56] In other words, the *Symposium* and its related dialogues provide an intricate model for

---

[53] Schleiermacher, 'Einführungen', pp. 319–26.

[54] For a detailed treatment of *Alcibiades I* as a dialogue about self-care, and an account of its later resurgence in, among others, Foucault's writing, see C. Moser, *Buchgestützte Subjektivität: Literarische Formen der Selbstsorge und der Selbsthermeneutik von Platon bis Montaigne* (Tübingen: Narr, 2006), pp. 79–124.

[55] That the cognitive challenge of the self mirroring itself in another's eye is a topos exercising not only Schleiermacher but a range of thinkers around 1800, I have tried to show with regard to Heinrich von Kleist in C. Güthenke, 'Postclassicism, Disturbed Philology, and Kleist's Fencing Bear', *Oxford German Studies* 47.2 (2018), 184–200.

[56] A careful comparison of the dialogues with specific reference to Alcibiades in C. D. C. Reeve, 'A Study in Violets. Alcibiades in the *Symposium*', in Lesher et al. (eds.), *Plato's Symposium*, pp. 124–46.

expressing abstract, conceptual terms or entities (such as philosophical thought, a body of work, or antiquity as whole) in terms of the sculptural figure whose appeal is as pronounced as its reciprocity or availability may be elusive.[57]

Schleiermacher treated Plato's *Phaedrus* as the 'seed' of all other Platonic dialogues, containing the seeds for all other dialectical thought.[58] This deliberately takes up the language of the dialogue itself, on the planting of actual and philosophical seeds (276b-277a). C. D. C. Reeve, incidentally, argued that in the *Phaedrus* the comparison of living *logoi* to living seeds (*spermata*) subtly and inter-textually also evokes the figure of Alcibiades. In the dialogue, the living *logoi* seeds contrast with the seeds planted annually in gardens during the festival of Adonis where they wither quickly instead of bearing fruit slowly. In Alcibiades, philosophical seeds withered quickly too; his figure can be historically linked with the Adonia festival, and his engagement with Socrates explicitly evokes the contrast between serious and playful efforts that marks the passage in the *Phaedrus*.[59] This, once more, makes Alcibiades a figure around whom the challenges of knowledge, formation of the self vis-à-vis beauty, and the epistemological implications of *eros* coalesce. At the same time, the language of 'seeds' as used by Schleiermacher, relying on Plato, links a biological organicism with scientific methods of knowing open to the philosopher and philologist in an even more integrated way. If the *Phaedrus* falls into two parts, one treating *eros* and the other rhetoric, Schleiermacher offered a unifying solution to the problem of the apparent bisection of the dialogue. His claim is that *impulse* and *method* stand, in this foundational, key dialogue, for the necessarily connected parts of Platonic dialectic as it appears throughout the dialogues: *eros* is the impulse presented early on that in turn leads to the actual enactment of dialectic in the second half.[60] The word Schleiermacher uses for impulse, *Trieb*, however, does not only suggest a psychological or physiological urge; it is also the term for 'shoot', as in the

---

[57] Reeve, 'A Study in Violets', p. 125 points out that the shadows of puppets projected against the wall of the cave in Plato's *Republic* VII (517d7) are also called *agalmata*, which adds both to the human affective closeness and to the illusionary quality of their appearance.

[58] Schleiermacher, 'Phaidros', p. 87; see also Lamm, 'Schleiermacher's "Christmas Dialogue"', pp. 402–3.

[59] Reeve, 'A Study in Violets', p. 131.

[60] I continue to follow here Lamm, 'Reading Plato's Dialectics', pp. 13–14 and Lamm, 'Schleiermacher's "Christmas Dialogue"', who makes her argument with reference to the introductions to *Phaedrus* and *Parmenides*. The latest commentary on *Phaedrus* by H. Yunis (Cambridge University Press, 2011) seems to suggest a not dissimilar strategy of how to understand the dialogue's structure, namely as the attempt on Socrates's part to move Phaedrus towards dialectic as method.

shoot of a plant or tree. He thus aligns a methodological and pedagogical claim about knowledge with organic developmental imagery throughout, and gives an affective stage an indispensable place within the practice of scientific understanding as exemplified first in Plato's text and ultimately mirrored in Schleiermacher's analysis.

Across his works, Schleiermacher applies several notions of organicism to describe how the process of thought, comprehension, and formation is structured. Aside from the trajectory of development and organic unity that, to him, forms the Platonic system, he operates elsewhere, especially in his *Hermeneutik und Kritik*, with a matching notion of a *Keimentschluss*, a 'seminal decision made by an author from which his text unfolds in a necessary fashion (at least in its main lines), and which it is the interpreter's job in psychological (or technical) interpretation to identify and trace in its necessary development'.[61] Michael Forster has pointed out that argument from organicism and its figurative language are central to Schleiermacher, but that the cracks in this argument, the fudging of several kinds of organicism, manifest particularly strongly in his introductions to the Platonic dialogues. The *Hermeneutik* conflates different notions of biological generation current at the time – one about preformation, where all parts of an organism are part of the seed and its subsequent development; and another, more primitivist one that assumes new, original generation with subsequent development rather than a gradual unfolding of a pre-existing seed.[62] This underlines that the topoi of originality and development are precisely interwoven in this strategy of imagining the text and its author as embodied individuals. This also chimes with Melissa Lane's suggestion that it is partly the preoccupation with originality that lies behind the Plato vogue of the early nineteenth century, understanding 'originality' in terms of both a developmental, seedlike starting point and individual genius. The search for Plato's authentic, original words thus presents itself as 'a function of Lutheran literalism about the Bible which was transferred to Plato', supplemented with an interest in Plato as the creative genius and mind.[63] Both notions of originality and of organicism are designed to evoke closeness imagined through distance and to project

---

[61] Forster, 'Schleiermacher's Hermeneutics', p. 112; on the 'Keimentschluss' as a metaphor used also by other hermeneutic and philological thinkers at the same time, see also L. Danneberg, 'Schleiermacher und die Hermeneutik', in A. M. Baertschi and C. G. King (eds.), *Die modernen Väter der Antike: die Entwicklung der Altertumswissenschaften an Akademie und Universität im Berlin des 19. Jahrhunderts* (Berlin: de Gruyter, 2009), pp. 211–76, here pp. 225–30.
[62] Forster, 'Schleiermacher's Hermeneutics', p. 112–13.   [63] Lane, *Plato's Progeny*, p. 8.

a sense of immediacy, of coming close to a source, an effect that in turn is easily reinforced by the focus on author personality.

An important point about Forster's careful philosophical rather than primarily historical analysis of Schleiermacher's organicism is his comment that neither of the two concepts, the harmonious unfolding or the original strike, is actually likely to do justice to what empirically goes on in intellectual and textual generation: namely, a process that is likely to be inflected by serendipity, unevenness, expectations of bias, and limitations of context.[64] This is a useful caveat when trying to evaluate the workings of the dominant organic and anthropomorphic model of treating textual formation and textual interpretation as if they manifested themselves as another human being, as was done rather matter-of-factly by many of the actors of scholarly knowledge in the long nineteenth century. Schleiermacher's insistent allusion to the hermeneutic longing and disappointment exemplified in Alcibiades suggests that confidence in the appropriateness of an organic analogy always remains tempered by an awareness of the limits of understanding, and it stresses the interpreter's potential for error as much as his express, exclusive devotion.

Schleiermacher arrived at an interpretation of Plato's unified corpus that stresses the role of interpersonal contact, and he read the Platonic project as a reflection on understanding formulated through interpersonal relationships. Luhmann defined the Romantic code of love as the means of communication that allows one to navigate the cognitive strain that is fundamental to a Romantic sense of self and other. Just so, love as an operative theme in Plato and in reading Plato becomes the medium of scholarly practice that lays bare and at the same time cushions incomprehension. At the same time, one of the most instructive impulses to come from Schleiermacher's configuration of the Platonic scene is the reminder that the active and reflective process of understanding represented in the dialogues triangulates with the situation of the reader of the dialogue as in effect another 'other'. It is precisely the reflective, distancing side of the Platonic dialogue that makes Plato attractive as a figure for modelling the modern critic. The Platonic dialogues, for all their direct speech, work hard to make their readers aware of difference and of indirectness, too: many of them, not least the *Symposium*, have complex, nested frames in which earlier conversations are recalled and retold, re-enacted from a distance, and thus draw attention to the very process of learning and the inevitably mediated nature of most knowledge in the human sphere. As Tigerstedt

---

[64] Forster, 'Schleiermacher's Hermeneutics', p. 112.

put it with regard to the crux of identifying the locus of any kind of authorial voice in the dialogues, Plato never speaks in his own voice, but 'the reader becomes as it were a silent listener to debates in which he does not join'.[65] In effect, this is the situation and function of scholarship, too. If the Socratic dialogues are scenes, or externalizations, of understanding, which model simultaneous observation and the turn of inquiry onto the self, then they come to mesh extremely richly with an understanding of scholarship as the creation of second-order knowledge with ambitions for primary *Bildung*.

---

[65] Tigerstedt, *Interpreting Plato*, p. 14.

CHAPTER 4

'Enthusiasm Dwells Only in One-Sidedness'
Knowledge of Antiquity and Professional Philology

Friedrich Creuzer (1771–1858) is known mostly for his role in the academic and Romantic study of mythology and his comprehensive, comparative, and contentious arguments about the cross-influences of symbolic and mythological themes and expressions in ancient cultures.[1] Especially in the English-speaking world, he may also be known as one of the figures hovering in the shadow of George Eliot's *Middlemarch* and its character Mr Casaubon, in search of a key to all mythologies. As professor of classical philology at the newly instituted philological seminar in Heidelberg, though, Creuzer was also a commentator on the task of philology as a field of study. And like Mr Casaubon, he offers an entry point to the question that drives this chapter: how did an increasingly institutionalized, established classical philology confront and put into words the (im)balance of feeling and reason, of empathy and technical skill, of one-sidedness and the dream of understanding?

Creuzer's academic programme 'On the Study of Antiquity' (1807) opens with an epigraph from (ps.-)Longinus's *On the Sublime*: χρὴ τὰς ψυχὰς ἀνατρέφειν πρὸς τὰ μεγέθη καὶ ὥσπερ ἐγκύμονας ἀεὶ ποιεῖν γενναίου παραστήματος – 'we have to turn the souls towards grand things and, as it were, make them over and over again pregnant with noble thoughts' (sect. 9).[2] Creuzer co-opts for the aims of professional scholarship the calculated borrowing from the *Symposium*'s language of spiritual

---

[1] F. Creuzer, *Symbolik und Mythologie der alten Völker, besonders der Griechen* (Leipzig and Darmstadt: Leske, 1810–12); for a discussion of his relevance for the study of ancient religion and mythology, see M. Konaris, *The Greek Gods in Modern Scholarship: Interpretation and Belief in Nineteenth and Early Twentieth Century Germany and Britain* (Oxford University Press, 2015), pp. 38–46; on the 'Creuzer debate', see J. Blok, 'Quests for a Scientific Mythology: F. Creuzer and K. O. Müller on History and Myth', *History and Theory* 33.4 (1994), pp. 26–52; S. Marchand, *German Orientalism in the Age of Empire* (Cambridge University Press, 2009), pp. 66–71.

[2] F. Creuzer, *Das Akademische Studium des Alterthums* (Heidelberg: Winter, 1807), p. 1; (ps-)Longinus, *De subl.* 9.

pregnancy (206 c-e, 209, 212a), which the author of *On the Sublime* had already transferred back from the realm of philosophy to that of poetry.

As the origins of Schleiermacher's Plato translations in the symphilosophical collaboration with Friedrich Schlegel showed, the Platonic texts were considered potential material to reimagine radically the role of the writer and critic, and of the philosopher as much as the philologist. This raises the question of how representative Schleiermacher was for the philology of his time, or rather of how much his investment in a Platonic pedagogic and organic model to think about the concerns of an increasingly professionalized and institutionalized philology resonated in other contemporary writings. This chapter will detail some examples of scholarly responses specifically to the Platonic erotic-pedagogical scene and the *Symposium* as a dialogue about knowledge, *Bildung*, and the epistemology of feeling. From there, I will examine a range of broader programmatic writings on the task and situation of philology as key to the study of antiquity (*Altertumswissenschaft*), writings that seek to define the autonomy of philology and its relationship with a necessary element of feeling that exceeds and complements a purely rational or technical set of skills. By making use of the idiom of individuality, including the individuality and autonomy of the philologist, this imagination of personal feeling as directed towards an other being helped to address the challenges of 'one-sidedness' as a characteristic of new disciplinary ways of knowing.

'Those Beautiful Days of the First Period of *Bildung*': Pedagogy and Genealogy

It is easy enough to see how the *Symposium*'s pedagogical *eros* might emerge as a suitable vehicle for articulating or framing the relevance of close relationships in the developing social sphere of education. We saw earlier that Wolf's references to the *Symposium* were paradigmatic of the task of aspirational learning and the organized sociability of the pedagogical encounter between increasingly institutionalized, professionalized, and disciplined participants. Another good example is Friedrich Thiersch (1784–1860), trained in theology and classical philology at the University of Leipzig, where he studied with Gottfried Hermann. After further training and a teaching stint in Göttingen he was called to a chair in Munich in 1809, where in 1812 he would become the influential founder of the philological seminar during a period of educational and political reform in Bavaria in which he took an active role. There he also rose to considerable prominence as an active advocate of political philhellenism

during the Greek War of Independence, as a seasoned traveler to Greece in
the 1830s, and as an advisor in the wings to the young Bavarian prince Otto,
who became the first king of the new Greek nation state in 1832.[3] Thiersch
had a lifelong interest in Plato's *Symposium*: his qualifying (habilitation)
thesis that granted him leave to teach at universities, *Specimen editionis
Symposii Platonis* (Sample of an Edition of Plato's *Symposium*), was a partial
commentary on the dialogue, with nested examinations of archaic poetry
as reflected down to Hellenistic writings apropos the use of certain lyrical
tropes in the dialogue itself. In addition, he lectured on or read the text in
colloquia regularly over the course of his career.[4] The fact that in the first
semester after being granted leave to teach in Göttingen he lectured on
both the *Symposium* and on an introduction to philology may be indicative
of the foundational status of the Platonic dialogue. The language of the
Symposium and the *Phaedrus*, which makes the *agalma*, the sculptural
object of loving admiration, instrumental on the path to knowledge, is
present in Thiersch's writing. The dedicatory verse preface to his dissertation that is addressed directly to his influential Göttingen teacher Heyne
indicates as much: in Greek trimeters (appreciatively noted by the
reviewers), Thiersch makes mention of *agalmata* not once, but twice, as
'shining agalmata of old wisdom' (ΣΟΦΙΑΣ.ΠΑΛΑΙΑΣ.ΑΓΛΑΟΙΣ.
ΑΓΑΛΜΑΣΙΝ) and as 'sweet agalmata by (or, through) the wise'
(ΓΛΥΚΕΙΑ.ΔΙΑ.ΣΟΦΩΝ.ΑΓΑΛΜΑΤΑ), the latter with specific reference
to Heyne. Heyne's archaeological interests, which themselves marked
a new, comprehensive notion of *Altertumswissenschaft*, make this an appropriate conceit in any case. In the context of a sample edition of the
Symposium, the allusiveness reaches beyond Heyne's research preferences
and suggests an analogy between the pedagogical energy of the work in
question and the actual situation of producing it as a qualification work in
a relatively new disciplinary field with new professional profiles.

Thiersch's *Specimen*, like the reviews of it that appeared soon after,
honed in on the question of Plato's reuse of other author's works and
styles, which suits the preoccupation with the practice of the philologist,
and the question of Plato's liminal status as both original poetic-

---

[3] An overview of Thiersch's significance as a cultural politician is in H.-M. Kirchner, *Friedrich
Thiersch: ein liberaler Kulturpolitiker und Philhellene in Bayern* (Munich: Hieronymus, 1996); a full
account typical of nineteenth-century biography, often by family members, was compiled by his son
H. W. J. Thiersch, *Friedrich Thiersch's Leben*, 2 vols. (Heidelberg: Winter, 1866).

[4] *Specimen editionis Symposii Platonis. Inest et quaestio qua Alcaeo carmen vindicatur quod vulgo
Theocriti putaverunt* (Göttingen: Dieterich, 1808); it is clear that Thiersch taught this text regularly,
from lecture catalogues as well as from multiple marked-up text copies and notebooks among his
papers kept at the Bayerische Staatsbibliothek Munich (BSB Thierschiana I, 27b, 27d).

philosophical thinker and second-order interpreter and collator of earlier thought.[5] Wolf in 1782 had reflected on Sydenham's overly keen identification of actual texts on which some of the Platonic speeches in the dialogue could have been modelled. Just so, Thiersch was invested in the extent to which Plato reworked other kinds of texts and genres (for example, medical treatises or lyric poetry). It is easy enough to log this as a general interest in source criticism, but it seems telling that an understanding of the dialogue as a model for learning should be balanced with a detailed investigation into Plato's practice as a kind of philologist himself, and that contemporary critics appreciated an account of a Plato who reconstructs and re-enacts Socrates's thought and speech after the fact, just as he offers a compendium of contemporary discourses for preservation, to be integrated into his philosophical, organic compound. It is no coincidence that Plato comes to offer a frame for considering the role of the third-person observer, witness, and interpreter, as much as the privileged, close intimate of Socrates whose task it is to develop and enact methods of knowledge and learning.

At the same time as considering Plato as a figure of the interpreter between faithful recollection and creative formation, Thiersch makes mention of the *Symposium* in another less obvious but all the more exposed context. In 1812, he publishes a *Greek Grammar, Especially of the Homeric Dialect*, which, as a successful school textbook, saw reprints in 1818 and 1826.[6] The first edition in 1812 contains a remarkable dedicatory preface, reprinted in all subsequent editions. This short prefatory text combines emotional closeness and loss, its catalytic epistemological function, and the business of perceiving, studying, and knowing antiquity in a way that suggests Winckelmann's love letters more than it does a qualifying exercise in grammatical criticism.[7] The preface is addressed to 'Andreas Freyherrn von Baranoff, auf Loal bey Reval', a young East Prussian nobleman to whom and to whose brother Thiersch had served as tutor in Leipzig and Göttingen, and it begins by an act of substitution:

---

[5] Anonymous reviews appeared, for example, in the *Göttingische Gelehrte Anzeigen* nr. 143, September 1808, pp. 1425–9, and the *Jenaische Allgemeine Literaturzeitung* nr. 23, January 1809, pp. 181–4.

[6] A review of the third, enlarged edition of 1826 suggests that 'all teachers of Greek among our readers can not unreasonably be assumed to be familiar with the 2nd edition of this work'; F. Schultze, 'Griechische Grammatik', *Jahrbücher für Philologie und Pädagogik* 1.1 (Leipzig: Teubner, 1826), 381–94, here p. 382.

[7] Katherine Harloe is currently preparing an edition and commentary on a selection of Winckelmann's love letters; see also K. Harloe and L. Russell, 'Life and (Love) Letters: Looking in on Winckelmann's Correspondence', *Proceedings of the English Goethe Society* 88.1 (2019), 1–20.

Instead of Plato's Symposium, my dearest friend, you receive here a Greek grammar of the common and Homeric dialect. ... As you know, my professional obligations have diverted me from engagement with Plato towards the examination of grammatical objects already during my employment at the gymnasium and then at the university in Göttingen, and the same held after our separation when you went on your travels to France and Italy and I took up a new position in Munich. In Paris, you collected for me material on Plato's Symposium from old manuscripts and rare books with a dedication and maturity that few of your age and a commitment of time that no one of your standing would have afforded, and I will make proper use of it only once I have some calm and free days so that my diligence not be surpassed by your enthusiasm.[8]

The deferred, disturbed scene of philological collaboration is then supplemented with the memory of the pedagogical encounter in which feeling and *Bildung* merge in the joint study of Greek antiquity:

I cannot take leave of you, my dearest and beloved Baranoff, without gratefully renewing the memory of the shared happiness of our days at Leipzig and Göttingen, and of the many pleasures which your company, your mind, and your *Bildung* afforded me, as well as of the essential services you did me to shape my fate and provoke some of its turns. Already in the earliest days of our acquaintance, when we quickly grew closer through the delightful contact resulting from your studies of antiquity under my guidance, your restless striving for higher *Bildung* filled your keen interest in every object worth your while, relying on your many rich talents of mind and some already existing knowledge; and not infrequently your interest was sublimated into the most beautiful enthusiasm, just as the purity and grace of your mind and character filled me with a growing respect which you provoked in the memory of your many friends in Germany. This feeling has been transformed into the most lasting love through our continued contact and our shared studies and fate when I followed you, on your request, to Göttingen, and this love,

---

[8] F. Thiersch, *Griechische Grammatik, vorzüglich des homerischen Dialekts* (Leipzig: Fleischer, 1812), p. iv. 'Du empfängst hier, mein theurer Freund, statt des platonischen Gastmahls eine griechische Grammatik des gemeinen und homerischen Dialektes. ... Meine Berufsarbeiten haben mich, wie Du weisst, schon in meinen Dienstverhälnissen an dem Gymnasium und der Universität zu Göttingen von der Beschäftigung mit dem Plato zu Untersuchungen über grammatische Gegenstände abgezogen, und auch nach unserer Trennung, als Du Deine Reise durch Frankreich und Italien, und ich später die meinige zu einem neuen Berufe in München antrat, war die Richtung meiner Arbeiten dieselbe geblieben. Was Du daher in Paris aus alten Handschriften und seltenen Büchern mit einem Fleisse und einer Einsicht, wie wenige von Deiner Jugend, und mit Aufopferung kostbarer Stunden, wie wohl kaum einer Deines Standes gethan hätte, für mich zum Symposion des Plato gesammelt hast, will ich erst dann verarbeiten, wenn mir ruhige und freye Tage kommen, damit meine Sorgfalt nicht von Deinem Eifer übertroffen werde.'

which no time or distance can lessen, is now only heightened by the pain of parting.[9]

Professions of friendly affect and loving admiration are common in the epistolary and dedicatory literary culture of the eighteenth and nineteenth centuries. But Thiersch's prominent preface frames the production of a comprehensive, functional, teaching instrument through looking back at emotional closeness in a pedagogical context and looking ahead to a continuation of this energy translated into a more complete commented edition of the Platonic *Symposium*. Thus it highlights the very moment in which the actual scholarly text at hand, the Greek grammar, exists: a moment marked by deferral and by longing for an incomplete, elusive alternative. The preface addressed to Thiersch's former pupil and companion allows the philological task at hand to be imagined as the riches of the *Symposium* dressed in the modest, uninspiring shell of a grammatical compendium, riches visible only to those who have experienced the company of shared study and the *Bildung* of feeling before. Thiersch's own marked-up copies of the Platonic text are preserved in the Bayerische Staatsbibliothek in Munich. They include Wolf's 1782 text edition and German commentary of the *Symposium*, interleaved with Thiersch's own handwritten comment sheets, and they underline the link between memory, knowledge, and interpretation, especially as it crystallizes around the figure of Alcibiades, torn between empirical needs and idealist aspirations. On the inside of the flyleaf is a handwritten reference to Alcibiades and Erasmus, presumably marking a reference to Erasmus's adage on the 'Sileni of Alcibiades' as symptomatic of interpretation.[10] Likewise, the speech of Alcibiades in which he recounts his encounters with and failed seduction of

---

[9] Thiersch, *Griechische Grammatik*, p. iv–v. 'Von Dir aber, mein theurer und geliebter Baranoff, kann ich nicht scheiden ohne die Erinnerung an das uns gemeinsame Glück der schönen Tage von Leipzig und Göttingen, an die mannigfaltigen Genüsse, welche mir Dein Umgang, Dein Geist und Deine Bildung gewährte, und an die wesentlichen Dienste, durch welche Du auf die Wendungen meines Schicksals Einfluss gehabt und sie zum Theil herbeygeführt hast, dankbar zu erneuern. Gleich in den ersten Zeiten unseres Umgangs, wo wir uns durch so erfreuliche Berührungen, wie Dein Studium des griechischen Alterthums unter meiner Leitung sie veranlasste, sehr bald nahe kamen, erfüllte Dein rastloses Bestreben um höhere Bildung, bey mannigfaltigem Reichthum des Geistes und schon erworbener Kenntnisse, Deine rege Theilnahme an jedem ihrer würdigen Gegenstande, die nicht selten zum schönsten Enthusiasmus sich verklärte, so wie die Reinheit und Anmuth Deines Sinnes und Charakters mich mit jener steigenden Achtung, welche Du in dem Andenken Deiner zahlreichen Freunde in Deutschland zurückgelassen hast. Die Fortsetzung unseres Umganges, als ich, durch Deine Wünsche veranlasst, Dir nach Göttingen nachfolgte, gemeinsame Studien und Schicksale, haben jenes Gefühl in die dauerndste Liebe zu Dir verwandelt, welche durch die Trauer des Abschieds nur erhöht und durch keine Zeit und keine Entfernung geschwächt worden ist.'

[10] See also the discussion of Erasmus's Alcibiades in Chapter 2.

Socrates has, among Thiersch's careful annotations, a reference to Alciphron's letters: here, a poor suitor evokes, after her death, the memory of a night spent freely under the same blanket with a courtesan, relived as a nostalgic memory in praise of her beauty.[11] Professional philology seems to have a need to articulate an imagined moment, lost and intimate, of the past as a reference point for a present, disciplined, and irreversibly changed situation of knowing.

Another good example to help determine some of the relations between Schleiermacher's imagery of the figure of antiquity and the disciplinary field of classical philology is the work of the philologist Friedrich Ast, also a one-time associate of Schlegel and a scholar of Plato in his own right. Ast, who since 1805 had been professor of classical philology at the University of Landshut (which transferred its location in 1826 to become newly incorporated as the University of Munich), published *Platos Leben und Schriften* in 1816, around the same time that the Bavarian Academy of Science published its prize question on the order of the dialogues. Schleiermacher mentions Ast's recently published work in the preface to his second edition of the dialogues in 1816 with friendly collegiality but also a distinct lack of enthusiasm. In the scholarly literature, Ast normally gets fairly short shrift both as a second-rank Platonist and a second-rank programmatic thinker about the hermeneutics of philology;[12] but his study represents nicely the contemporary academic standard in which is reflected the trickled-down centrality of the individual as both object and subject of classical scholarship.

The title alone, *Plato's Life and Works*, mirrors the changing tide away from the lives of Socrates as exception and exemplar and towards an integrated account of Plato the man and the individual author. Ast opens his work with the following programmatic statement: 'The works of a poetic genius are a faithful imprint of his spirit and of the particularity of his character (*Wesen*), which we call by the significant name of individuality.'[13] Unlike the static realism of his Eleatic predecessors, and unlike forms of a constantly shifting dualism, for Ast the essence of Platonism rests in postulating an 'essential character of being always

---

[11] Alciphron I.38.

[12] Patsch, 'Asts "Euthyphron"-Übersetzung'; Tigerstedt, *Interpreting Plato*, p. 19 is rather scathing on Ast's ruthless excising of dialogues as spurious. Boeckh categorizes him among those representing the fashion for florid, yet shallow criticism, 'Kritik von Schriften über Platon und Ausgaben Platonischer Dialoge', *Gesammelte Kleine Schriften* vii (1872), pp. 80–98, here p. 61; Schleiermacher, 'Einleitungen', pp. 24–5 is also rather lukewarm.

[13] Ast, *Platos Leben*, p. 3.

formative and always in the act of formation' (*ein ewig bildsames und sich bildendes Wesen*).[14] Plato stands out (*tritt uns entgegen*) among the 'spirits of genius' (*genialische Geister*) of antiquity for being on the cusp of myth and history, of art and science in perfect harmony; Plato as a figure of identification for the scholar thus embodies the very beginning of *Wissenschaft*.[15]

Ast argues that any criticism of Plato's work ought to rely on its relationship with Platonism and is therefore a question of authenticity and the sequence of thought across time, to which, in turn, biography as the 'history of life' is key: 'Chronology, in turn, is most intimately connected to the life story (*steht in engester Verbindung mit der Lebensgeschichte*).'[16] A first, extensive section on the 'Life of Plato' thus critically examines but also still refers in detail to the traditional biographical information found in Diogenes Laertius, Olympiodorus, and others – precisely the kind of collection that Schleiermacher had suggested his own readers go seek elsewhere and not in his own innovative work. Ast denies the interconnectedness of the dialogues in terms of a strictly sequential, external logical order. In fact, he argues for a rather indistinct 'inner coherence', which affects all areas of human, ethical, and physical 'life' and is the main objective of Platonism to articulate as an idea that 'lives' in and animates all the dialogues, as a kind of 'inner attitude' (*innere Gesinnung*).[17] We are probably inclined to read this as fairly run-of-the-mill idealist ventriloquizing more than anything else, but the insistently organic, personifying language that drives this inner coherence is notable exactly because it becomes so run-of-the-mill, as is his firm focus on Plato as individual genius, who shapes his texts in his own image.

For Ast, the *Symposium* belongs to the category of 'purely scientific' or epistemological (*wissenschaftliche*) 'Socratic-Platonic' dialogues, offering a harmonious mix of poetic (that is Socratic and individualistic) and dialectic (that is speculative, less concrete, and less clear) elements and arguments.[18] The dialogue, in Ast's reading, is a creative rewriting of much of the material of Xenophon's *Symposium*, and it shows up Plato's superior skill and 'spirit' in combining the dramatically exuberant with the philosophically speculative, linking the ideal and the real. This may seem much less intricate than Schleiermacher's boxed set of approximations where the Platonic imagery, his characters, his own individuality and that of his interpreter all throw light upon one another. But it also shows how pervasive the sense is of attaching interpretation to the integrity of a human individual that stands in for the object of study, and of thinking

---

[14] Ibid., p. 6.   [15] Ibid., p. 3.   [16] Ibid., p. 13.   [17] Ibid., p. 40.   [18] Ibid., p. 53, 299–318.

of the object of philological attention, in turn, in terms of a human individual. What Ast's more standard and much less sparkly account suggests is that Plato's works cannot be studied *other than* by way of giving an account of his individual character as a writer and thinker, with a biographical, narrative component, and of his works as behaving along the developmental lines of an individual. In addition, a comment in Ast's encyclopedic university textbook of Greek and Roman antiquity, his 'Outline of Philology' (*Grundriss der Philologie*) of 1808, makes plain how Plato is an attractive and authoritative role model of the interpreter and a figure of our own interpretation. Commenting on how Aristotle could well be considered the first philologist in the sense of cultivating a scientifically organized learnedness for its own sake, Ast then introduces Plato as the true representative of a philology in which individual *Bildung* in a universal human framework is the goal: 'If we understand philology in a higher sense, then Plato is the hero of all philologists.'[19]

Karl Friedrich Hermann's *Geschichte und System der Platonischen Philosophie* of 1839 – influential in its time even though K. F. Hermann is now largely a forgotten name – probably takes to an extreme this notion of Plato as hero in literary and physical terms:

> Just as the body of a Milo may never have developed the athletic beauty of his form and the full strength of his muscles to the same degree as when he tried to hold up the ceiling that buried him, just so Plato never developed the richness of genius as brilliantly as he did in those passages of his didactic structure that display the greatest inconsistencies in its fundamental assumptions; and if we are permitted to compare the philosophy of Aristotle with the measured progress of epic, that of Plato is like a tragedy where the greatness of its hero is bought at the price of his destruction; and for that reason, our true interest should in each case be on the development of all internal and external motives, personal and historical, which inexorably led to such necessity.[20]

As an account of Platonic thought this is considerably different from Schleiermacher, though its preoccupation with the consistency and coherence of Plato's philosophy is not. To imagine any philosophical shortcomings through the heroic body of the sixth-century athlete Milo of Croton, whom ancient sources linked with Pythagoras as his teacher, may seem, in its attention to the details of physical strength and beauty,

---

[19] Ast, *Grundriss*, p. 534; the topos of Plato as an artistic and not only a scientific writer, especially in comparison to Aristotle, is itself an old one reaching back to antiquity; for its long arm, see L. Danneberg, 'Schleiermacher und die Hermeneutik', p. 223.

[20] K. F. Hermann, *Geschichte und System der Platonischen Philosophie* (Heidelberg: Winter, 1839), p. 8.

indulgent or downright odd. Still, it is in line with several expectations: that a philosopher best be elucidated through a developmental life narrative; that heroic figures, whether sculptural or literary, best be understood through notions of individual character; and that ancient figures best be imagined through reference to the distance and closeness evoked by the sculptured body. Hermann's general model of a genetic and biographical interpretation remained popular for Platonic interpretation into the twentieth century. At the same time, the Platonic works were again and again highlighted as paradigmatic for the development of the classical scholar. That Milo's heroic act of holding up a roof allowed a group of Pythagoreans to escape unharmed reflects not only on Hermann's reading of Plato as catalyst for later philosophical developments, it also reappears in his own self-fashioning as a scholar. In his long preface Hermann situates his own controversial views within a scholarly community and concludes that, by relying on philological-historical tools, he will gladly admit defeat by the weapons he has forged if his views be disproven by those same rules.[21]

The preface to his substantial biographical project is dedicated to his own teacher Friedrich Creuzer, with whom this chapter started, and it contains a long description detailing the role of reading Plato in Hermann's own genesis as a *Wissenschaftler*. Creuzer is the teacher to whose dedication and love – 'such love, with which you met the pupil maturing into a youth' – he owes his first motivation for study and the first overview of antiquity, that is, a combination of personal affect and historical-scientific instruction. Just so, it was reading Plato, 'the writer whose wondrous attraction raised the gaze of the boy towards the eternal higher spheres of truth and beauty', that enabled him in the first place to follow Creuzer's lead in explicating Plato, and to follow 'the wings of your lectures and to grasp from your enthusiastic lips the meaning gleaned from the great objects of antiquity'.[22]

That Hermann is essentially angling for approval is clear from his insistence on the close relationship with Creuzer, despite their widely diverging views on Plato, and on the mutual appreciation of *Wissenschaft* and the 'individuality' which may be growing from its seeds. This itself is a return to the language of the *Phaedrus*, as was the mention of 'wings' just before, evoking the philosopher's soul pushing out feathers and taking flight when prompted by *eros* (*Phaed.* 249d-e, 251).

---

[21] Ibid., p. xi.   [22] Ibid., pp. v–vi.

Hermann further sets up his own Platonic research as a competitive and notably scientific undertaking when, right at the beginning of his preface, he contrasts his work with that of the Dutch scholar Philip Willem van Heusde. Van Heusde, a philologist and revivalist theologian and educator, had also dedicated his slightly earlier work on Plato, *Initia philosophiae Platonicae*, to Creuzer.[23] Hermann contrasts his own work 'as like the side of sober criticism and research, the obverse of this other work of artistic warmth and enthusiasm'.[24] Pitting the scientific, objective standards of his own work against the enthusiastic, intuitive character of van Heusde's, and at the same time invoking the inspiration he received from Creuzer during those 'beautiful days of the first period of *Bildung*',[25] Hermann's writing here again reflects the double function that the language of intimate Platonic learning could offer. Here is the creation of a nostalgic origin for an imagined epistemological community, and a template for its trajectory towards Plato as the emerging figure of the scientific interpreter standing at a distance. At the same time, the Platonic language of *eros* as a form of addressing the dynamic of lack, striving, idealism, and incompleteness helps to translate the unpredictability and elusiveness of knowledge and thus to shape a topos of endless approximation and imperfection that assumes an important, counterbalancing position within claims for scientific norms and methods.

Hermann contrasts the demands on his research time created by professional obligations and on his research orientation created by disciplinary standards with the inspirational, affective origins of his interest in Plato and, by extension, all of antiquity, and he is keen to highlight any shortcomings: this is only the first part of a larger projected work, it is marked by interruptions, it would be better if he had more time, and so forth. This is familiar territory and rhetoric to all scholars; but the concessive gesture of our modern academic acknowledgement pages that 'all remaining faults are my own' is genetically related to a topos of conscious incompleteness and imperfect and possibly even illusionary knowledge. What is more, it is deeply related to the structural paradoxes of philology as a modern field of *Wissenschaft*, matched in the Platonic language of idealist deficiency.

---

[23] P. W. van Heusde, *Initia philosophiae Platonicae*, vols. i–iii (Utrecht: Altheer, 1827–36).
[24] 'gleichsam die Kehrseite, die Seite der nüchternen Kritik und Forschung zu jenem Werke künstlerischer Wärme und Begeisterung', Hermann, *Geschichte und System*, p. v.
[25] Hermann, *Geschichte und System*, p. vii.

Philology and Its Limitations

With the emergence of philology as a professional, institutional, and disciplinary phenomenon came challenges, I argue, that found expression in a language of feeling, of individuality, and of personification. These in turn shaped the imagination of antiquity and of its sources, as much as philology sought precedents for its own language in some of those sources. This language could help to explicate, if not entirely remove, the constitutive tensions that marked philology and the study and knowledge of antiquity as a modern *Wissenschaft*. It could connect it to a developing notion of science between the poles of specialization and comprehensiveness, and of the individual and the universal, as well as balance the complex relationship between reason and feeling, objectivity and care of the self, rationality and inspiration, and historical contextualization and aesthetic response. *Bildung* was imagined as a parallelism between the modern individual and the ancient object of interpretation, as the parameter of organic coherence, and as a developmental narrative of character. All three underpinned the discourse of the pedagogical neohumanism that helped to establish the institutional structures of knowing antiquity and that remained structurally operative even as specialization and an empirical, historicist focus became ostensibly dominant.

German philology of the long nineteenth century was not short on programmatic writings, and those reflect the tensions just laid out.[26] At the same time, the observations suggested here were not a question of specific schools either. Hermann's affiliation with Creuzer, for example, could certainly suggest a particular 'Romantic' bent to his Platonic strategies. But Thiersch, who invests equally in such a textual dynamic studied with the decidedly un-Romantic text critic Gottfried Hermann in Leipzig (no relation to K. F. Hermann, incidentally, and certainly with no sympathy for Creuzer), as well as with Heyne in Göttingen before. Wolf and his sometime student Boeckh (on whose use of Platonic tropes more below) had very different intellectual backgrounds and contexts, as did the neo-Kantian educational historian and philosopher Friedrich Paulsen and the philologists, text-critics, and religious historians Friedrich Ritschl and Hermann Usener, just to name some of the voices that will appear

---

[26] On especially the format of the encyclopedia that in the nineteenth century changes from a universalist compendium towards a reflective, programmatic outline of the discipline, see C. Hackel, 'Philologische Fachenzyklopädien. Zu Charakter und Funktion eines wenig beachteten Genres', in C. Hackel und S. Seifert (eds.), *August Boeckh. Philologie, Hermeneutik und Wissenschaftspolitik* (Berlin: BVW, 2013), pp. 243–72.

throughout this chapter. The attractiveness of a classical language of epistemic desire and of its disavowals is a shared rhetorical idiom that connects very diverse voices within the discipline and it buffers the tensions between a historical and a subjective understanding of antiquity within the science of *Altertumswissenschaft* and of philology. If philology became the site of seeking unity and, at the same time, negotiating one-sidedness, then the idiom of loving attachment was able to redefine one-sidedness as a form of commitment and exclusive devotion, in line with the code of Romantic love and its exclusive focus on the relationship between two partners.

Friedrich Ritschl, with F. G. Welcker and Otto Jahn one of the founders of a historical-critical school of philology at the fairly new University of Bonn (founded in 1818), proclaimed that 'enthusiasm lies only in one-sidedness; the encyclopedic cannot enthrall' (*Enthusiasmus liegt nur in der Einseitigkeit; das Enzyklopädische kann nicht begeistern*).[27] *Einseitigkeit* is a double-edged sword, the intent focus of specialization as much as the blinkered one-sidedness of not seeing the forest for the trees, or rather a single tree. In fact, *Einseitigkeit* even raised exemplary tragic overtones and a classical genealogy. In his *Lectures on the Philosophy of Religion*, which Hegel had given several times between 1821 and 1831 in the last decade of his life, he had apropos ancient Greece and its 'religion of beauty' discussed the basic conflict represented in Sophoclean tragedy as one in which '[e]ach side only realizes one moral power, makes only one of them its content. This is *Einseitigkeit*, and the meaning (*Sinn*) of eternal justice is that both suffer injustice because they are *einseitig*, but thus also justice.'[28]

In Ritschl's lecture, *Einseitigkeit* is provocatively twinned with 'enthusiasm' and 'enthrallment', which itself sits uneasily with the demands of scientific method.[29] In his provocative aphorism Ritschl is pitting a controlled, creative *Einseitigkeit* against superficial encyclopedism as its own end, which only leads to mistaken pedagogy, and he advocates the

---

[27] Ritschl, 'Zur Methode', p. 24. For Ritschl, see C. Benne, *Nietzsche und die historisch-kritische Philologie* (Berlin: de Gruyter, 2005), pp. 46–68. In praise of Ritschl's approach, formatively translating *Einseitigkeit* as 'specialization' for the professionalizing American academy, see B. Gildersleeve, 'The Spiritual Rights of Minute Research [1895]', in W. W. Briggs Jr. (ed.), *Selected Classical Papers of Basil Lanneau Gildersleeve* (Atlanta: Scholars Press, 1992), pp. 93–105, here p. 95, and Güthenke, 'Enthusiasm dwells only in specialization', p. 267.

[28] G. F. W. Hegel, *Vorlesungen über die Philosophie der Religion II*, Werke, ed. E. Moldenhauer and K. M. Michel, vol. 17 (Frankfurt am Main: Suhrkamp, 1969), p. 132. My thanks to Henner Petin for drawing my attention to this passage.

[29] Friedrich August Wolf himself had acknowledged a 'sullen one-sidedness' (*mürrische Einseitigkeit*) for which the philologist is often blamed, 'Darstellung', p. 882.

profile of an independent professionalized researcher over that of the mere teacher, who will not take the 'wise detour of scientific insight'.[30] At the same time, he worries about a specialization that leads to the drifting apart of areas of expertise and of the individuals who practice them. In a lecture, 'On the Most Recent Developments of Philology', given in front of the *Philomathische Gesellschaft* in Breslau in 1833, Ritschl calls for the 'linking up of *Einseitigkeiten*' as the central task of a modern philology, a need 'to bring together in objective unity what had been spread variously as individual manifestations; as well as the true revitalization and reanimation of the dead bulk of material through a pervasive idea, material which had previously been categorized only by way of analytical, rational criticism (*sondernde Verstandeskritik*)'.[31] In this passage, the nuance of 'what had been spread variously as individual manifestations' (*des bisher in individueller Gestaltung zerstreuten Manigfaltigen*) is ambiguous: is Ritschl talking about the individual manifestations, texts, works of art of and in an ancient past, or about the individual, specialized approaches and insights of modern scholars, both of which need the unifying perspective of a science of antiquity? The ambiguity points again to the stereoscopy of ancient and modern individuality that under the terminology of *Bildung* gave the study of antiquity much of its conceptual traction.

Ritschl considered Wolf one of the earliest visionaries of such a 'linking up' of individualities, even though his programmatic *Darstellung der Alterthums-Wissenschaft*, thus originally published in 1807 in the inaugural volume of the short-lived journal *Museum der Alterthums-Wissenschaft* (which Wolf edited with Philipp Buttman in Berlin), had still fallen short of creating the unity Ritschl had hoped for.[32] In it, we can already see reflected the topics and questions that will reappear in theoretical or programmatic writings on philology in the course of the nineteenth century. These are as follows: the task of a broadly conceived philology that lays claim to the status of a professional discipline with its own canon of materials, techniques, and qualifications; the need for limitations and the kinds required; the

---

[30] Ritschl, 'Zur Methode', p. 25.
[31] Ritschl, 'Über die neueste Entwicklung', p. 3. The fact that this lecture was reprinted in the Brockhaus *Conversations-Lexicon*, vol. III, 1833 as the entry for 'Philology' shows the cultural authority given to Ritschl's programmatic statements.
[32] Ritschl, 'Über die neueste Entwicklung', p. 3. For sketches of Wolf's programmatic piece before 1807, see R. Markner and G. Veltri (eds.), *Friedrich August Wolf. Studien, Dokumente, Bibliografie* (Stuttgart: Steiner 1999), pp. 48–75.

definition of the scholar, and the boundaries between academic and nonacademic knowledge; and the relation between rationality and a nonrational element in the practices of philology.

Straightaway, Wolf subtly but authoritatively slides from offering 'an introduction to a revision or an encyclopedia of the knowledge usually known as *philological*' to declaring this an ambitious attempt to combine the individual opinions expressed at German universities in the past, present, and future into an organic whole, so as 'to raise everything which belongs to the complete knowledge of learned antiquity to the status of a well-ordered *philosophical-historical science*'.[33] This is the *Altertumswissenschaft* of his title – a comprehensive science of antiquity that combines various branches of knowledge but still gives pride of place to textual sources and to a philological way of reading even nontextual sources. It is an approach that is analytic and critical as well as synthetic, seeking to identify a larger idea that counters dispersion. Wolf's organic project aims to remedy fragmentation and magnifies the scope and range of philology at the same time. He is equally aware, right off the bat, that philology will need strategies of limitation. He pre-empts the question of how broadly to conceive of antiquity by claiming that while Oriental civilizations may have existed earlier, true 'spiritual culture', as opposed to the formation of civilizations, only began with the Greeks.[34]

Limitation goes further, in line with the dominant Hellenism that imagined antiquity as paradigmatically a Greek individual. Towards the end of the essay he comments on the paradigmatic quality of Greek culture (in essence, Winckelmann's Periclean Athens) as the confluence of free and beneficial conditions in political, artistic, and natural terms. Compared to this high point of humanity, though, and even within the already limited frame of the Greco-Roman world that for Wolf is the standard of value, Roman culture already raises a problematic counterpoint: the Romans cannot provide a fully desirable subject matter, since from the beginning they displayed some of the one-sidedness (*einseitige Richtungen*) – here is the term again – that has also, as he puts it with a stab against neighbouring France and its Roman tradition, 'in the last

[33] Wolf, 'Darstellung', pp. 810–11 (his emphasis).
[34] On the narrowing down and the exclusion of Oriental (and Jewish) cultures, see A. Grafton, 'Juden und Griechen bei Friedrich August Wolf', in Markner and Veltri, *Friedrich August Wolf*, pp. 9–31; Harloe, *Winckelmann*, pp. 197–8, suggests that Wolf did not introduce this limitation in 1807 but had hinted at it already in earlier comments. On the status of Oriental studies in Germany generally and on their development, see Marchand, *German Orientalism*.

centuries bedevilled some of the most highly respected nations'.[35] Wolf is, at the same time, conscious of the fact that the amount of ancient material is a challenge, one that will inevitably only grow more pronounced, always threatening a clear, organic, unifying contour or outline of the object of study. He estimates that some 1,600 writings in Greek and Latin are available in his time. That he explicitly discounts for the moment all Christian writings highlights the need for modification and immediately introduces another category of limitation.[36]

For Wolf and his contemporaries, being able to pin down a fairly precise number may still suggest an optimistic belief that a synoptic view is possible. We get a glimpse of the confidence of knowing and mastering all of classical antiquity, a belief in control that would become increasingly difficult to maintain. In many ways, it remains the anxiety-inducing ideal of many a classicist now – and it is already fraying at the edges in Wolf's own *Darstellung*. Quite aside from ancillary knowledge of other ancient and modern languages, the proper territory of *Altertumswissenschaft*, as he has it, 'has already become impossible to traverse in every direction even for the most diligent and optimistic'.[37] Thus he concedes that the philological scholar will have to negotiate constantly between 'drawing modest boundaries' and being able to engage extraneous materials fully when they present themselves, even if he has reduced the scope considerably.[38] Anthony Grafton has talked about the shifting balance between the polyhistor of the early modern period and the *philologus* of the world of professionalizing scholarship as two ends of a spectrum. Wolf seems to suggest that the task of the modern scholar is to be the philologist who knows enough about polyhistory to control it with his newfound skills when called upon. Translated to a model of inter-personality, the philologist needs to be selective in whom he engages with as his object of study.

All of this is to say that this supports the configuration of a relationship where the scholarly subject stands vis-à-vis a single, unified other that he aims to understand and that reflects back on the scholar – a configuration that conforms with contemporary assumptions about interpersonal, social, affective relationships as they relate to *Bildung*, the development of the self, and knowledge; or, as Wolf puts it later on in his *Darstellung*:

> To read and observe [the ancients'] works will steadily rejuvenate our mind
> and mood, not by treating them like historically positioned characters, but
> instead as in the intimacy with valued and dear people. In this way they will
> communicate their attitudes and sentiments and thus improve the

[35] Wolf, 'Darstellung', p. 887.   [36] Ibid., pp. 823–4.   [37] Ibid., p. 835.   [38] Ibid., pp. 835–6.

shortcomings of education in our corrupted times, lifting man above the many limitations of our age.[39]

Wolf is aware that the professional scholar – to match the developing, clearly delimited discipline – is another site where different, 'pre-professional' features of understanding and interpretation are provoked and shaped into a new profile. In his survey of justifications put forward for the engagement with antiquity, Wolf concedes that there have been and still exist amateurs, like those who have good historical knowledge without being historians proper. These, through a natural affinity with antiquity, can hit the mark more effectively in their understanding and in their thinking and doing than those who have devoted a lifetime to specialization and offered their services as mere translators, or *Dollmetscher*, that is, technical interpreters rather than masters of an art and science of scholarly interpretation.[40] Wolf here ostensibly pays homage to 'one of our kings, the pride of all Prussians and Germans', but he is also more indirectly referring to Johann Wolfgang von Goethe, already by 1800 a figure of authority as a poet and thinker, to whom the *Darstellung* is dedicated in an encomiastic preface.[41] This looks ahead to the enormous admiration for Goethe as an unreachable and inimitable role model by many later philologists, conscious that he embodies the comprehensively talented artist and scholar in perfect union, whose range lies beyond the expectations and possibilities of the trained philologist and whose extraordinary character helps to define the boundaries of the ordinary practitioner.

The scholar is confronted with different expectations, among them that he ought to enable others to gain access to antiquity (that is, pedagogy) and to fulfil the aims of science, which, as Wolf lays out in a long but significant footnote, can and should also stretch to moral improvement. Wolf here quotes a letter from Gronov to Heinsius stating that the purpose of reading the classics lies in emending one's character rather than the text's punctuation.[42] *Emendatio*, in other words, should not be considered synonymous with the work of 'dry critics' but should by extension be demanded of all branches of science. As for scientific standards, the scholar of *Altertumswissenschaft* is obliged to examine everything for himself and to

[39] Ibid., pp. 877–8.   [40] Ibid., p. 836.
[41] See also his aside in a section that deals with the value of material sources such as coins for illuminating periods with few direct textual sources, where Wolf refers to the clever insightfulness (*Scharfsinn*) and leadership of Goethe and his artistic friends; Wolf, 'Darstellung', p. 854.
[42] *Ego a prima aetate in lectione veterum id potissimum habui, ut mei mores emendarentur, non ut apices et puncta librorum*; Wolf, 'Darstellung', p. 837.

be ready to be reexamined in turn with a view to 'the knowledge of sources and their correct use'.[43]

Wolf's essay, a systematic survey of the branches of *Altertumswissenschaft* in their hierarchical and pedagogical relation and a historical and programmatic account of the value of studying antiquity, works itself up to formulate the highest aim of such study, the quasi-mystical *epopteia* – Wolf's term – of the sacred, comparable to that experienced by the initiates at Eleusis: 'This goal is *nothing other than the knowledge of the humankind of antiquity itself, a knowledge that is based on the study of its remains and emerges from observation of an organically grown meaningful national Bildung.'[44]* This national *Bildung* is exemplified, as in Humboldt's – and earlier in Winckelmann's – writings, by the Greek world (up to the period of Philip and Alexander) of 'peoples and states which had by nature most of those features on which a character's perfection of true humanity is based.'[45] Leaving aside the ostensibly objectivist tone in which highly subjectivist knowledge is turned into authoritative knowledge of human subjectivity, the Humboldtian tone of an anthropological – and anthropomorphic – mission of classical study is not accidental, and recent study has shown how deeply implicated with Humboldt's own writings Wolf is in this text.[46]

'As Philologists, We Are Not to Philosophize Like Plato': Boeckh's Comprehensive Philology

August Boeckh was one of the longest-serving professors, university administrators, and seminar directors at one of the flagship institutions of philology and of the German research university altogether, shaping the discipline at the Friedrich-Wilhelm University of Berlin for over fifty years, from 1810 to the early 1860s. He also integrated Platonic language carefully and deliberately as part of a highly conscious reflection on philological

---

[43] Ibid., p. 837.

[44] 'Es ist aber dieses Ziel kein anderes als *die Kenntniss der alterthümlichen Menschheit selbst, welche Kenntniss aus der durch das Studium der alten Ueberreste bedingten Beobachtung einer organisch entwickelten bedeutungsvollen National-Bildung hervorgeht*' (emphasis Wolf); 'Darstellung', p. 883.

[45] Ibid., p. 887.

[46] In an extensive footnote of the 'Darstellung', Wolf excerpts at length from Humboldt's essay 'On the Study of Antiquity', not naming Humboldt but instead portraying his rather systematic essay as the 'fragments' of a like-minded noble man (evoking classical standards: συμφιλολογοῦντός τινός ποθ' ἡμῖν καλοῦ κἀγαθοῦ), thus nostalgically praising shared sentiment and at the same time editing out the contribution of the 'amateur' scholar in favour of the programmatic account of a new discipline; see J. Trabant, 'Humboldt, eine Fussnote? Wilhelm von Humboldt als Gründergestalt der modernen Altertumswissenschaft', in Baertschi and King (eds.), *Die modernen Väter*, pp. 25–43.

theory and on the inherent lack of completeness that marks the knowledge of antiquity.

Boeckh articulated a program for a comprehensive *Altertumswissenschaft* that relied on philology as the royal road to any form of interpretation in the study of culture; in this, he deliberately went beyond his former teacher Wolf both in his suggestion of a more capacious notion of culture and in his insistence on the inner coherence of philology as a fundamental form of knowing rather than a collection or juxtaposition of subfields of inquiry. From its first mention in the opening section of Boeckh's lecture series *Encyklopädie und Methodologie der Philologischen Wissenschaften*, 'aggregate' (*Aggregat*) is a term that recurs frequently, and it marks a signature worry of textual interpretation that links Boeckh's text to the philological as much as the biblical criticism of the turn of the century.[47] This is a worry about the consequences of analytical criticism, especially historical criticism, making visible inconsistencies, faults, and blemishes in canonical texts and leading to a loss of coherence and wholeness. It makes it clear why images of text as a human being chime well with this concern over the 'appearance' of works and with the tendency to locate explanations for textual changes and developments in their authors rather than in their own ambiguous or inconsistent structures.[48]

Boeckh had studied not only with Wolf but also with Schleiermacher shortly after the latter arrived at the University of Halle, and he had heard his lectures on Plato and on ethics. During a fairly brief stint as a non-ordinary professor at Heidelberg, where Friedrich Creuzer had just established the philological *Seminar* as an institution, Boeckh also moved in broader literary and Romantic circles, including those of Achim von Arnim and Clemens Brentano. Boeckh was quickly appointed as one of the first professors at the newly founded University of Berlin in 1810, after Wilhelm von Humboldt had failed to move the increasingly intractable and peevish Friedrich August Wolf to accept the position. In Berlin he founded and directed his own *Seminar* and also continued to interact with Schleiermacher. He left his mark on a discipline which he taught there until his death in 1867 and which he represented as a high-ranking administrator at both the university and the Prussian Academy of Sciences, where he also instituted and oversaw big projects like the *Corpus Inscriptionum*

---

[47] A. Boeckh, *Encyklopädie und Methodologie der Philologischen Wissenschaften*, ed. E. Bratuschek (Leipzig: Teubner, 1877), p. 3, and passim.
[48] For a very detailed account of this worry, with its strong grounding in biblical hermeneutics, see, again, Danneberg, 'Ganzheitsvorstellungen'.

Graecarum.[49] His series of introductory lectures, which he delivered for twenty-six semesters spread over fifty years and which shaped genera-tions of students and professional scholars across the German-speaking world (the names of students listed as auditors over the years amounts to almost 1,700), was posthumously edited in 1877 as the *Encyklopädie und Methodologie der Philologischen Wissenschaften.*[50]

For Boeckh, philology is a general science of interpretation in which antiquity holds a privileged place, although it is not reducible to only its study. Science (*Wissenschaft*) as such is a whole, a philosophy or science of ideas, whose disciplinary differentiation is a reflection of the empha-sis we give to the material or ideal aspects of the world. Philology contains that entire spectrum yet does not belong to either category exclusively.[51] Philology offers a way into an understanding of all pre-vious thought covered by *Wissenschaft*, thus making it the meta-*Wissenschaft* par excellence, and of necessity historical in outlook too. This is what is expressed in the key term or phrase for which Boeckh is best known, namely that of philology as an *Erkenntnis des Erkannten*, an 'understanding' or 'cognition of what has once been understood before', or, as he glosses it a little further on, a 'reconstruction of the construc-tions of the human mind':

> Thus the proper task of philology is to recognize and understand the products of the human mind, and what it has understood (*das Erkennen des vom menschlichen Geist Producirten, d.h. des Erkannten*). Philology pre-supposes a given knowledge, which it sets out to recognize. The history of all sciences is thus philological.[52]

---

[49] On Boeckh, see most recently the contributions in Hackel and Seifert, *August Boeckh*; T. Poiss, 'Die unendliche Aufgabe. August Boeckh als Begründer des Philologischen Seminars', in Baertschi and King, *Die modernen Väter*, pp. 45–72; A. Horstmann, *Antike Theoria und moderne Wissenschaft. August Boeckhs Konzeption der Philologie* (Frankfurt am Main: Peter Lang, 1992); for the inscriptions, see S. Rebenich, 'Berlin und die antike Epigraphik', in W. Eck et al. (eds.), *XIV Congressus Internationalis Epigraphiae Graecae et Latinae* (Berlin: de Gruyter, 2014), pp. 7–75; for the correla-tion between very long tenures of individual chairs as directors of seminars and the importance of personality as a shaping factor of the institutional landscape, see Clark, *Academic Charisma*, pp. 164–6.

[50] On the complex textual status of Bratuschek's edition, as well as on the performative character of Boeckh's lecture, see C. Güthenke, 'Warum Boeckhs Encyklopädie lesen?', *Geschichte der Germanistik* 51/52 (2017), 83–97.

[51] '*Wissenschaft* altogether as a whole is philosophy, the *Wissenschaft* of ideas. According to the point of view whether to understand the universe from a material or ideal side, as nature or mind, as necessity or freedom, we arrive, aside from formal disciplines, at two different kinds of science, which we call physics and ethics. To which does philology belong? Philology includes both, so to speak, and yet it is neither', Boeckh, *Encyklopädie*, pp. 10–11.

[52] Boeckh, *Encyklopädie*, p. 10.

Philology thus covers material and ideal aspects of culture and is, fundamentally, a historical method; and since it examines the articulation and communication (*Mittheilung*) of knowledge and of anything intellectual or conceptual (*geistig*), it can cover as its subject matter also all historical events, which are nothing other than *Geistiges* changed into action.

Significantly, Boeckh's prime example through which he introduces this thought is the writings of Plato. Plato, to him, is a thinker whose range comprised all branches of knowledge, from the physical world to the ethical and spiritual, and whom we therefore should seek to understand rather than imitate, to reflect on rather than to produce original philosophy: 'As philologists, our task is not to philosophize like Plato, but to understand Plato's writings as works of art not only with respect to their form, but also in terms of their content. Explanation, which is fundamentally philological in nature, has predominantly to do with understanding content.'[53] Again, as with *Bildung*, in the figure of Plato the object of study dynamically mirrors the method of study.[54]

The advantage of making antiquity the body of material for such philological inquiry is its simultaneous completeness and distinct lack of completeness. In its linguistic, cultural, and historical distinctiveness antiquity is recognized as such from a later vantage point, which makes it different from more recent or even contemporary periods and cultures, marked by a still ongoing process of production. At the same time, the irreversible damage of historical distance and the loss incurred through it make antiquity paradoxically all the more exemplary and fruitful as the subject of philological reflection and reconstruction: 'antiquity is more remote, more alien, more incomprehensible and fragmentary and thus in need of reconstruction to a far higher degree'.[55] This is a thought that again is not so different from Winckelmann's insistence on the enhanced effect of antiquity's remoteness on our longing for and scholarly attentiveness to it. Even if Boeckh does not say this explicitly, antiquity's paradigmatic closeness through foreignness and its generative energy through lack of availability exemplify the paradox and tensions that are constitutive of philology, if and as soon as it is understood as practice or

---

[53] Ibid., p. 9.
[54] Just as the humanists, for example, relied on the ancient texts themselves to extract models of how to read and formulate approaches in line with tropes suggested in those texts, the nineteenth century in fact might not be so different; for the humanists' reapplication of reading techniques, see A. Grafton, 'Humanist Philologies: Texts, Antiquities, and their Scholarly Transformations in the Early Modern West', in Pollock et al. (eds.), *World Philology*, pp. 154–77.
[55] Boeckh, *Encyklopädie*, p. 12.

method of reflection, reconstruction, recovery, or representation. It contains within itself the tendency towards wholeness imagined through and because of fragmentation, with its brittle balance between synthesis and superficiality as much as its focused specialization and disaggregation.

For Boeckh, the philologist's approach to antiquity should be as that to a recognizable whole, and it would have to rely, aside from technical skills and knowledge, on a kind of scientific feeling, a principled philological intimacy that has the power to unite the fragments of the past and the fragmented knowledge of the past in the present. Like Wolf and Humboldt before him, Boeckh gestures towards the need for a unifying viewpoint to save philology from a fragmentation that goes beyond the present state of its materials. Just so, philology is always threatened by *Einseitigkeit* and is realized only in the sum total of its practitioners:

> in a thousand heads, partial, dismembered, broken, not to mention strange and in a broken tongue; but the great love alone, with which so many have embraced [philology] (*schon die grosse Liebe, mit der so viele sie umfasst haben*), guarantees the reality of the idea, which is nothing other than the reconstruction of the constructions of the human mind in their totality.[56]

This is not merely a reference to the fragmented sculptural body of antiquity reflected in collective study. Here, too, is an intimation of the lover of knowledge seeking to grasp the elusive human shape in front of him, and, just as Alcibiades and the romantic lover testify, consummation is never achieved:

> Philology, like every other science, is an infinite task of approximation (*eine unendliche Aufgabe der Approximation*). In philology, we will always be one-sided collectors (*wir werden in der Philologie immer einseitig sammeln*) and never bring to fruition a total union (*Vereinigung*) with speculation; for speculation, too, is always one-sided (*auch speculirn* [sic] *wird man einseitig*). And yet, incompleteness is no mistake; the only true deficiency is not to acknowledge it.[57]

The anxiety over one-sidedness as specialization is over one-sidedness as a failure of *Vereinigung*, of being unified, and merging disparate objects or elements into a larger whole as much as uniting, merging the self with an other – the same word applies in German. 'Becoming one' is also part of the vocabulary of feeling and desire, of sexual union, just as 'one-sidedness'

---

[56] Ibid., p. 16.   [57] Ibid.

signals not only a lack of broadness, but is also the term used of a love that is one-sided, unreciprocated, *einseitig*.

A vocabulary of love, familiar from the language of romantic attachment, emerges not only indirectly in this text, but also explicitly, and again with direct allusion to Plato. Boeckh glosses the terms *philologos* and *philologia* as 'the desire for and pleasure taken in scientific exchange' (*Lust zu und an wissenschaftlicher Mittheilung*) (22) – a meaning he takes, with exact reference, from *Phaedrus* 336e, whose every mention of *eros* he translates, like most of his contemporaries, as *Liebe*. The Platonic language keeps being redeployed consistently in order to capture the uncertainty of philological knowledge.

The language of *Gesamtheit*, of totality and wholeness, echoes in Boeckh's assessment of how any kind of insight can come about into what he significantly describes as an 'alien individuality' (*fremde Individualität*). Represented by any body of texts or any cultural materials, this 'individuality' makes clear how inseparable the language of philology is from imagining its subject matter as a reflection of coherent human agency. Boeckh's hermeneutic approach is one of approximation, and he reaffirms his earlier definition of philology: 'If, therefore, the foreign individuality can never be fully understood, then the objective of hermeneutics can only ever be met in an infinite approximation, that is to say through a gradual approach, advancing point by point, but never completed (*nie vollendete Annäherung*).'[58] In making such incomplete approximation the motor of all *Wissenschaft*, Boeckh also echoes Humboldt (whose thought had already underpinned Wolf's programmatic writing). Humboldt, in an essay of 1809–10 specifically dedicated to the establishment of new institutions of higher learning and science, glosses the task of *Wissenschaft* as follows:

> With this as a preface, one can see easily that the inner organization of institutions of higher learning relies on maintaining the principle that we view *Wissenschaft* as something that is not yet quite discovered and is never entirely to be discovered (*als etwas noch nicht ganz Gefundenes und nie ganz Aufzufindendes*), and to strive for *Wissenschaft* tirelessly as precisely that.[59]

[58] Ibid., p. 86.
[59] W. v. Humboldt, 'Über die innere und äussere Organisation der höheren wissenschaftlichen Anstalten in Berlin', in Königlich Preussische Akademie der Wissenschaften (ed.), *Wilhelm von Humboldts Gesammelte Schriften*, vol. 10 (Berlin: Behr, 1903), pp. 250–60, here p. 253; for the 'approximation' inherent in Humboldt's reform program, its normative rather than realized nature, and the narratives that accrued around the 'myth' of Humboldtian education up to now, see Wellmon, *Organizing Enlightenment*, pp. 211–13.

This incomplete approach (*Annäherung*), again a term that literally suggests physical closeness, is compensated for and articulated through the involvement of feeling, a feeling which can sometimes, though rarely, achieve a kind of unexpected, non-rational intimacy. 'In certain cases', Boeckh suggests,

> feeling can reach a complete form of understanding, and the hermeneutic artist (*hermeneutischer Künstler*) will be all the more perfectly accomplished the more he is in possession of such a feeling that can cut through a knot but cannot otherwise offer justification. It is this feeling, by means of which we can suddenly recognize (*mit einem Schlage wiedererkannt wird*) what someone else had once already understood, and without it there would indeed be no ability to communicate at all. Even though individuals are different from each other, they also harmonize in respect to many things; in that way, one can understand another individuality up to a point by way of calculation, but one can grasp completely certain of its expressions in a vivid intuition (*lebendige Anschauung*), which rests in feeling.[60]

This *lebendige Anschauung*, intuition understood in the Platonizing language of insight as a momentous, unpredictable recognition that lacks any justification beyond itself, sounds just like the description of the sudden intuition of the Beautiful itself – the idealizing yet unpredictable sublimation of erotic progress and erotic structure that Socrates ventriloquizes in the voice of Diotima in Plato's *Symposium*. Incidentally, Theodor Mommsen uses a quite similar image for the same sentiment in a public academic speech (*Rektoratsrede*) of 1874 on the possibilities of historical knowledge: 'The stroke that cuts through a thousand entanglements, the view into the individuality of humans and peoples, that is a stroke of genius that laughs at all teaching and learning. Maybe the historiographer belongs more among the artists than among the scholars.'[61]

Boeckh's mention of the 'hermeneutic artist', with its hint at the uncertainly defined interplay between the spheres of science and art, is a reminder that he had introduced the term 'vivid intuition' already earlier on. There, he had quoted Schelling's opinion that the philologist 'stands at the highest level together with the artist and the philosopher, or rather they merge in him. His task is the historical construction of works of art and

---

[60] Boeckh, *Encyklopädie*, p. 86.
[61] 'Rede bei Antritt des Rektorates 1874: Über das Geschichtsstudium', *Reden und Aufsätze von Theodor Mommsen* (Berlin: Weidmann, 1905), pp. 3–12, here p. 11.

science, the history of which he must grasp and represent in vivid intuition (*in lebendiger Anschauung*).'[62]

Boeckh's reference to Schelling comes at the point when he attempts to suggest his own definition of the characteristics required of the philologist, among which are:

> a pure heart and mind, open to everything that is good and beautiful, equally receptive to the most transcendental and to the smallest thing below, feeling and imagination combined with a sharp rational mind, a harmonious integration of feeling and thought, of life and knowledge, which, aside from unstinting industry, are the fundamentals of philology, as they are for any other science (*eine harmonische Ineinanderbildung des Gefühls und Denkens, des Lebens und Wissens, sind für jede Wissenschaft und nebst rastlosem Fleiss auch für die Philologie Grundbedingungen des wahren Studiums*).[63]

This is a familiar trope, glossed from Cicero's description of the ideal orator and by no means exclusive to Boeckh.[64] The scholar is thus part Ciceronian orator and part Platonic lover of knowledge, merging epistemological idealism with the appreciation of rhetorical professionalism, and a gesture towards the daring of Schlegel or Schelling with a view to the philologist as mediator between philosopher and artist.

Like many of his contemporaries, Boeckh integrates a historical genealogy of the scholar and philologist into the discussion of philology as scientific method or form of knowledge, and Plato, as he did for others, holds a generative position in this account, too.

Boeckh glosses philology first as an innate human drive, not unlike Aristotle's definition of *mimesis*, and again taking up the 'seminal' language of *Trieb* used by Schleiermacher:[65]

> The human spirit articulates itself in manifold signs and symbols, but the most adequate expression of understanding lies in language. To investigate

---

[62] Boeckh, *Encyklopädie*, pp. 25–6, with reference to Schelling's *Vorlesungen über die Methode des akademischen Studiums* (1803).

[63] Boeckh, *Encyklopädie*, p. 26.

[64] Harloe, *Winckelmann*, p. 172, with reference to C. G. Heyne and, before him, D. Ruhnken.

[65] How closely connected Boeckh thought his own thinking was to that of Schleiermacher is clear from his commentary in an essay on Pindar, in which he lays out the interdependent circle of judgment (*Urteil*) and critique (*Kritik*) as an ongoing challenge, and concludes: 'every philologist must acknowledge this if he is aware of what he is doing; even though this is not laid down in a theory, and I would not claim to have invented it either, since I learned it from Schleiermacher'; A. Boeckh, 'Über die kritische Behandlung der Pindarischen Gedichte' (1825), *Schriften*, v, pp. 248–396, here p. 249. My thanks to Thomas Poiss for showing me how explicit Boeckh is about his debt.

the spoken or written word is – as the name philology indicates – the most originally philological drive (*der ursprünglichste philologische Trieb*), and it is clear that it is universal and necessary from the fact that without communication not only science but life as a whole would be hard done by; this renders philology one of the primary conditions of life, an element which is inherent to human nature and fundamental in the chain of culture.

In the same breath, he suggests that the *Bildung* based on and in turn conditioning philology is already a token of civilization:

> It [philology] is a basic desire of civilized people (*ein Grundtrieb gebildeter Völker*); an untutored people (*ungebildete Volk*) can φιλοσοφεῖν, but not φιλολογεῖν. . . . In Greece, the first significant philology arose once production was relatively complete: this older era comes to a close with Aristotle, and it was Alexandrian philology which, with diligence and vigour, grasped reflection of this age which it had now brought to completion.[66]

This reinforces an imagination of Alexandrian scholarship as a predecessor of the philological work of modernity. This is a topos with its own genealogy: Wolf in his *Prolegomena to Homer* (1795) had not just put doubt on the recoverability of an 'original' text of Homer, but had instead singled out the Alexandrian scholars of Homer as our first available point of intersection between all earlier sources and the Homeric poems, and attributing to them interests similar to those of the scholars of Wolf's own time. Rudolf Pfeiffer's mid-twentieth-century historiography of classical scholarship, in which the Alexandrian scholars take up a pivotal position, invests the topos with a different postwar charge but essentially holds on to the identity-creating backward glance and pride for a bygone scholarly community.[67]

Boeckh makes philology explicitly an epiphenomenon, offering a self-historicizing gesture that makes 'coming after' programmatic for a disciplinary community that rediscovers its roots in the subject it studies. But it also leaves the time of Plato and his own organization of knowledge in a limbo where it is simultaneously *producirend* and *producirt*, active and reflected.[68]

---

[66] Boeckh, *Encyklopädie*, pp. 10–12.

[67] R. Pfeiffer, *History of Classical Scholarship: From the Beginnings to the End of the Hellenistic Age* (Oxford: Clarendon, 1968). For a more detailed discussion of Pfeiffer's and Wolf's respective genealogies, see C. Güthenke, '"The Alexandrian Scholar Poets Are Our Ancestors": Ancient Scholarship and Modern Self-Perception', in W. Beck, A. Kelly, T. Phillips (eds.), *The Ancient Scholia to Homer's Iliad: Exegesis and Interpretation*. Bulletin of the Institute of Classical Studies Supplements (London, forthcoming).

[68] Boeckh elaborates on Eratosthenes of Alexandria and, with reference to the Suda, his nickname as an 'eternal beta' – and a 'young Plato'; *Encyklopädie*, p. 13.

Hermann Usener, in his *Rektoratsrede* at Bonn in 1882 on 'Philology and History' (*Philologie und Geschichtswissenschaft*), echoes quite closely some of Boeckh's notion of *Erkenntnis des Erkannten* in his own anthropological definition of philology as something that is 'as eternal as the interest humans take in the human': 'φιλολογεῖν, the longing to re-experience and rethink (*das Streben nachzuempfinden und nachzudenken*) what significant men before us have experienced and thought, is an innate need of man, no less so than φιλοσοφεῖν, the search for truth'.[69] He also continues the thought of a philological *Urtrieb* by combining it with the notion of a philological feeling or 'tact' that not only signifies how knowledge is always deferred, but mirrors this approximation with postulating an element that eludes rational, technical, teachable skill, thus tying classical knowledge back to the all-important question of pedagogy. He explains:

> The specific grammatical tact of the philologist results from his *own* specific disposition, experience, and observation, conditioned and matured through longing (*Streben*) for a rational, historical understanding of linguistic expression. As much as knowledge and scientific knowing are essential to it, the ability itself cannot be transmitted. Only a drive, a desire, a longing can be awakened and trained up which, when strong enough, tends on its own towards acquiring such virtuosity (*Nur ein Trieb, ein Verlangen und Streben laesst sich erwecken und anerziehen, das, wenn es stark genug sich regt, von selbst zum Erwerb jener Virtuosität hindrängt*). 'Selbst ist der Mann' is true of the philologist even more so than of anyone else.[70]

The idiomatic motto *Selbst ist der Mann* is hard to translate – it is an exhortation to be a man of action, to rely on one's own talent and skill, to be self-made. Usener ironizes the genealogical, hierarchical thinking of organized science, but he does so in a way that flags strongly the place of individual affect in the system of classical knowing. It suits Usener well that one of the heroes to emerge in his genealogy of the modern knowledge of antiquity is Winckelmann, in whom archaeology, philology, and the science of history ostensibly come together in personal union: 'For the first time we see here the laws of organic life applied to an area of creative expression.'[71]

---

[69] H. Usener, 'Philologie und Geschichtswissenschaft' (1882), in *Vorträge und Aufsätze* (Leipzig: Teubner, 1907), pp. 1–36, here pp. 23–34. For the differences between Boeckh and Usener on philology as only a method or an independent science, see Gildenhard, 'Philologia Perennis?', pp. 163–6.

[70] Usener, 'Philologie und Geschichtswissenschaft', p. 22. On tact, see also T. Petraschka, 'Takt als heuristische Kategorie in Erkenntnis- und Interpretationsprozessen', in A. Arndt et al. (eds.), *Theorien, Methoden und Praktiken des Interpretierens* (Berlin: de Gruyter, 2015), pp. 591–608.

[71] Usener, 'Philologie und Geschichtswissenschaft', p. 6.

Usener was certainly attuned to self-reflexive disciplinary thinking: as the successor of Ritschl at the University of Bonn (founded in 1817, it, like Göttingen some time before, had the feel of a 'new' and more experimental university), he was invested in the comparative study of antiquity, especially the study of ancient religion.[72] In an 1884 lecture, 'On the Organization of Scientific Work', Usener, like Boeckh, takes up the trope of viewing the generation of Plato and Aristotle as hinges between productive and reflective cultural modes and of postulating scholarly knowledge as a direct result of this. He formulates even more pointedly a historical narrative of nostalgic genealogy, ideality, and analogy with modern scholarship when he reduces the ur-model of scholarly community and practice to the creative period that spans Plato's Academy and Aristotle's school: 'The creation of the science of Greek, in fact of all of classical antiquity, is the work of two or, to humour external appearances, of three generations: that of Plato, of Aristotle, and of the immediate students of the latter.'[73] The genitive 'of' in the phrase 'the science of Greek, in fact of all classical antiquity' is as ambiguous in English as it is in German: this is the scholarship produced *in* as much as *of* classical antiquity, leading him, in the *Rektoratsrede*, to call the Alexandrians confidently 'our colleagues in antiquity'.[74]

Usener in fact creates a complete template for an ancient equivalent to the modern university: this model responds to modern scholarship's structural needs with a bipartite or stereoscopic template that puts a Platonic, informal, egalitarian-elitist sociability next to an Aristotelian, taxonomic, project-driven community of scientific labour, thus safeguarding a place for nostalgic sublimation of individual striving at the same time as a modern skills-based division of labour, or for allowing to imagine humanistic *Bildung* alongside empirical grand-scale research.

To do so, he sketches a history of the Academy and the *Lykeion* that reaches into postclassical antiquity and the age of Justinian, and that looks ahead to all forms of *ritualized* scholarly communities that include the (pedagogical) relations between masters and disciples – something perfectly in line with his own interests in the history of religion:

---

[72] On Usener in his intellectual context, and on his importance within classical studies, see M. Espagne and P. Rabault-Feuerhahn (eds.), *Hermann Usener und die Metamorphosen der Philologie* (Wiesbaden: Harrassowitz, 2011); A. Wessels, *Ursprungszauber: zur Rezeption von Hermann Useners Lehre zur religiösen Begriffsbildung* (Berlin: de Gruyter, 2003).

[73] H. Usener, 'Organisation der wissenschaftlichen Arbeit. Bilder aus der Geschichte der Wissenschaft', in *Vorträge und Aufsätze* (Leipzig/Berlin: Teubner, 1907) pp. 67–102, here p. 73. The lecture was first published in *Preussische Jahrbücher* LIII (1884), 1–25.

[74] Usener, 'Philologie und Geschichtswissenschaft', p. 19.

Nothing could be further from the truth than to imagine the Academy and the Lykeion as mere groups of learners gathered around a teacher. Those schools were associations for shared research and work as much as they were for listening and learning. The number of their members included the entire gradation from the youth approaching science for the first time (*dem zum ersten mal an die Wissenschaft herantretenden Jüngling*) to the grown independent researcher (*bis zu dem selbständig forschenden Manne*). Those mature, actively co-researching members could equally form (*bilden*) their own students while subordinating themselves to the head of the school.[75]

And he continues, after distinguishing between the 'mass of mere pupils' and the 'smaller circle of research associates (*Forschungsgenossen*)', which together with the head constitute the school:

Here we have the solution of the riddle we faced regarding the Academy: the secret of the gigantic achievement of the 4th century BC to establish and develop almost all branches of science lies in the fact that the head/mind of the master had the different areas of science scrutinized, materials collected, and tasks executed according to commonly structured parameters and to one overriding and goal-oriented plan. In addition, he knew how to choose and appoint for each task a suitable person. Only such magnificent organization of shared work could have resulted in such magnificent results, and its foundation was laid in the institution of co-researching friends (*mitforschende Freunde*) who willingly defer to the unifying guidance by the master and at the same time already know how to bring up young helpers (*hilfreiche Jünger*) for their special tasks.[76]

This template responds well to the increasing challenges of *Einseitigkeit* as specialization and 'subcontracting' within an ambitious discipline striving for comprehensiveness, alternately highlighting technical cooperation and individual attention by way of this imagined genealogy. But it is especially notable that the imagination of a Platonic scholarly sociability of creation of knowledge affirms it as a central, common denominator. Throughout the Aristotelian schools, Alexandria, and other knowledge communities of late antiquity, the rule continues to apply:

For the humanely serene and spiritually uplifting character of such gatherings Plato created a classic model in his *Symposium*, maybe even deliberately: the tradition of imitation which it received among philosophers of the most

---

[75] Usener, 'Organisation der wissenschaftlichen Arbeit', p. 81.   [76] Ibid., p. 82.

different orientations, even among the grammarians, is itself a clue to the extent and durability of the custom.[77]

By the late nineteenth century, the link between symposium and seminar could be expressed in a narrative of historical development and affective relevance that integrated and arguably sublimated Platonic scenes of erotic knowledge into a story of the disciplinary, scholarly self.

This suggests that one of the standard narratives of nineteenth-century classical scholarship and its ideal humanism (or humanist idealism) might need modification. The standard narrative of the rise of philology in the nineteenth century posits an increasingly professionalized, institutionalized discipline within the secular university, where philology is outspokenly separated from theology. In addition, the traditional historiography of the discipline sees a shift from the 'ideal' neohumanist university, exemplified by Wilhelm von Humboldt's program for the newly founded Friedrich-Wilhelm University in Berlin and marked by a top-down administrative endorsement of *Bildung*, towards the highly successful yet tyrannically grinding academic machine of the latter part of the century. That machine is said to have favored increasing specialization and to have become increasingly bound by the stranglehold of a fraying empirical-positivist historicism; to have at once cultivated projects of the microscale (philological overspecialization) and the macroscale (big-science projects such as the ambitious collections of Latin and Greek inscriptions, made up of a multitude of microprojects); and to have paid only lip service to the notion of a comprehensive individual *Bildung*, with a brief flourishing of a new Third Humanism and re-examination of the classical in the 1920s, before the Second World War changed things for good.[78]

Such a narrative, however, underestimates the tensions *within* philology as a privileged scholarly method of approaching past or otherwise foreign cultures and the question of how to understand them as a key to understanding the self. Those were constitutive tensions, possibilities,

---

[77] Ibid., pp. 78–9.

[78] See, paradigmatically, Pfeiffer's *History of Classical Scholarship*; a similar canonical narrative is suggested in the supplementary volume on the history of the discipline of the revised *Neue Pauly*, the standard Classics encyclopedia (P. Kuhlmann and H. Schneider (eds.), *Geschichte der Altertumswissenschaften. Biographisches Lexikon. Der neue Pauly.* Supplemente 6 (Stuttgart: Metzler, 2013)); for a discussion of a 'myth' of Humboldt that has after-effects well into the present discussion over university reform, see Wellmon, *Organizing Enlightenment*, pp. 211–13. For the problematic continuities between the new Humanism of the 1920s and the post-war situation of Classics, including its very recent past, see J. Elsner, 'Paideia: Ancient Concept and Modern Perception', *International Journal of the Classical Tradition* 20.4 (2013), pp. 136–52.

and anxieties which were visible from the late eighteenth century onwards and they cannot simply be mapped onto a detached idealist superstructure increasingly lagging behind empirical philological practice. The two remained connected and should therefore not be reduced to the story of a failed idealism deteriorating into hyperspecialization.

Does the philology of the second half of the nineteenth century really simply jettison neohumanist intentions, replacing them with a narrow-minded historicism, the quasi-industrial production of historical fact and detail? The overspecialized, dust-blind 'micrologist' satirized by Nietzsche, and the antlike but somehow still spiritually beneficial condition of Ritschl's scholar who feels his own significance in 'participating in building the cathedral of science' (*sich zu wissen als Mitarbeiter am Dombau der Wissenschaft*) – both are figures of the scholar who continues to be defined through his own ability (or inability) to create a vision of a foreign or ancient individuality (a body of texts and cultural artefacts), which in turn stimulates reflection on the scholar's own individuality. The aim is still to see an overall, whole picture emerge, whether of a text, an author, a culture, or a nation. If the scope of individual works narrows down (as, for example, in the increasingly smaller and more-specific projects that make up such collaborative mammoths as the epigraphic collections), the belief persists that there is an overall understanding of a larger whole to emerge at a future point. The limited vision of the small-scale philological project depends structurally on the expectation that there is a larger whole that will manifest itself as a matter of fact, the vision of a meaningful individual writ large to match the individual engaged in observing and understanding it.

The concentration and focus of *Einseitigkeit* as specialization is one thing, and it tallies well with a rhetoric of focused exclusivity that also animates the Romantic discourse of mutual attention and increased self-knowledge. The worry over *Einseitigkeit* as lack of reciprocity is another, and it is made tangible and expressible in the persistent recourse to a Platonic and Platonizing language and to a model of erotic and epistemological approximation. The affinity of those discourses is well captured in one of the standard histories of German scholarship in the nineteenth century, Friedrich Paulsen's extensive *History of Learned Education in German Schools and Universities: from the End of the Middle Ages to the Present Day, with Special Regard to Classical Learning*. Published in 1885 and reprinted with revisions and additions in 1896 and 1921, it is still deservedly considered useful as a detailed source and compendium, though it is also valuable as a historiographical narrative in its own right and with its own agenda.[79]

Paulsen is sensitive to the lingering effect of Protestant-Pietist interiority and individualism in the late eighteenth century and to the literary-classicist assumptions that were made about a 'uniformity of inner experience' (*Gleichartigkeit inneren Erlebens*) between Greeks and modern Germans.[80] He is just as attuned to the imbrication of imagining antiquity and imagining pedagogy, captured by the structures of *Bildung*, and he has a good ear for the recurring language of desire: 'thus the neohumanist engagement with antiquity shared an inner affinity with education; enthusiastic devotion to an ideal always has something of the Socratic *eros* about it'.[81] Likewise, Paulsen relies on similar language when he describes the rise of both the historical sciences and modern philologies in the second half of the nineteenth century, a rebalancing that left Classics as both a more specialized and more isolated discipline: 'The period of inspired and inspiring first love was over, and with it the "rich business" of making plans, as Kant had called it; detailed work as evidence of technical skill was now the way to gain appreciation among a circle of peers.'[82]

In the context of discussing the philological school emerging at the University of Bonn, Paulsen casts Ritschl as an example of the change from neohumanist *Begeisterung* towards specialized realism. He does so in unexpectedly gendered terms: 'Philology has become very masculine, very scientific, very sober.'[83] At the same time, the success of Bonn in generating a school of thought is put down to the continuing work done by an inspired pedagogy: 'And yet, the efficiency of a teacher will depend on something other than technical training, namely first and foremost on love for the ancients and on a desire to sow new seeds of this love' (*nämlich jenes erste, dass er Liebe zu den Alten hat, und dass es ihn treibt, diese Liebe fortzupflanzen*).[84] It is not easy, with Paulsen, to pin down Ritschl only on the side of the scientific and austere. More in line with his phrase that 'enthusiasm dwells only in one-sidedness', quoted earlier in this chapter, Ritschl is explicit about the epistemological value of imagining and treating an ancient text as if it were another, affectively heightened individuality. As he puts it in a series of aphoristic notes:

---

[79] *Geschichte des Gelehrten Unterrichts auf den deutschen Schulen und Universitäten, vom Ausgang des Mittelalters bis zur Gegenwart. Mit besonderer Rücksicht auf den klassischen Unterricht* (Leipzig: Veit, 1885).

[80] He is no less sensitive to the simultaneous political aspects of such self-knowledge and of *Bildung* understood to have a national function; Paulsen, *Geschichte*, ii, pp. 5–7.

[81] Ibid., p. 393. [82] Ibid., p. 450. [83] Ibid., p. 451. [84] Ibid., p. 453.

Book knowledge. For a book just like with a human being: one must have seen it once, then go to the library every day and ask for one book after another to look at with infinite patience. *Anschauung* is worth a lot, even if only superficially, extent, aim, limits, structure are imprinted as something tangible, concrete, particular, as in fact like a living individual (*ein gleichsam lebendiges Individuum*). A mere title = dead abstraction, forgotten as quickly as it is perceived like a moving image with a fuzzy outline, or rather not as an image at all. Here in Bonn I am relieved of such dry efforts – rare happiness – indulging in its plenty![85]

Just as Usener is often quoted for his description of the specialized yet devoted scholar as a 'worker in the vineyard of philology', so Ritschl speaks of being a 'worker on the cathedral of science'. Aside from the religious undercurrents in both scholars, to balance professionalism with vocational, inner-driven energy, Ritschl's catchphrase is incomplete when it is not quoted in full. In the same group of aphorisms he states: 'The joy of life to "feel oneself" and the feeling of personal significance, to know one is a worker on the cathedral site of *Wissenschaft*' (*Lebensfreude 'sich zu fühlen' und Gefühl der persönlichen Bedeutsamkeit, sich zu wissen als Mitarbeiter am Dombau der Wissenschaft*).[86] At the same time that philology is firmly established in the university as a socially and scientifically qualifying and small-c conservative practice, it is 'life' that is emphasized as its necessary supplement.

---

[85] F. Ritschl, 'Zur Methode des philologischen Studiums (Bruchstücke und Aphorismen)', *Kleine philologische Schriften*, v, pp. 19–32, here p. 28.
[86] Ritschl, 'Zur Methode', p. 29.

CHAPTER 5

'The Most Instructive Form in Which We Encounter an Understanding of Life'
The Age of Biography

In his *Rektoratsrede* of 1882 on the relationship between history and philology, Hermann Usener had found strong words to describe the integral role of a philology that is inseparable from the study of history. This is a philology – and by extension also a history – which is to reach beyond the establishment of a text or of historical source material; instead, it ought to aim at an understanding, a making visible of relations and contexts, that is nourished by making the historical record come alive:

> Epigraphical materials remain mostly dead letters (*bleiben vielfach toter Buchstabe*) unless literary transmission allows them to be put back in their place, communicates a sense of their context (*den Zusammenhang vermittelt*), and endows the naked name with flesh and blood (*den nackten Namen mit Fleisch und Blut ausstattet*). One cannot write history from archival matters alone, even if they were Venetian diplomatic letters; it is literature which announces the forces that drive a period (*die Literatur ist es, welche die treibenden Kräfte der Zeit kündet*).[1]

The example Usener suggests here, 'even if they were Venetian diplomatic letters', is a not-so-hidden stab against Leopold von Ranke, the doyen of institutionalized German history and historiography, and his work on the Venetian *relazioni*, a rich archive of diplomatic correspondence which Ranke had, not without obstacles, studied in the late 1820s and early 1830s. In retrospect, Usener's criticism is on some level rather disingenuous, given that Ranke had repeatedly described the character of this research with the help of explicitly personifying, eroticized, life-oriented metaphors. In a letter he referred to the material, the 'object of his love', as a beautiful Italian woman with whom he hoped to procreate, and in a letter to Bettine von Arnim he famously speaks of the 'princesses' of the archives

---

[1] Usener, 'Philologie und Geschichtswissenschaft', p. 25.

that await rescuing by the male historian.[2] Ranke's emotionally charged rhetoric has increasingly become of interest to historians studying the gendering of the discipline of history as a 'masculine' effort that relies on the feminizing of the material record, among other things.[3] But the gendering as a form of 'enlivening' comes, importantly, with narrative strategies. When a living organism is made visible, it is through a story of development.

Leben and *Belebung*, feeling and making alive, as a balance to *Einseitigkeit* and the worry over the dead letter pored over in specialist, technical inquiry – this was the self-proclaimed dichotomy of historical inquiry, and its historiography, of the late nineteenth century. This dichotomy is between, on the one hand, historicism charged as guilty for embodying relativism and desiccated positivism, and, on the other hand, the advocacy for a new plea for historical study that stood in the service of modern, present life. In some sense, this amplified and summarized the tensions that had been part of historical scholarship and philology for a good while already and that were, in fact, constitutive of it.[4] *Leben* as an experiential category could capture and bring together subject and object. *Leben* as a narrative category gave the biographical a central role as a revitalizing act, one that was historicist, developmental, and experiential at the same time. It is hard to overestimate the rise and the importance of biography as a popular form of historical narrative. Both inside and outside the academy it was a successful phenomenon across Europe and across disciplines with a historical component. This

---

[2] Ranke to Heinrich Ritter, 28 October 1827, L. von Ranke, 'Zur eignenen Lebensgeschichte', A. Dove (ed.), in *Sämtliche Werke*, vol. 53/54 (Berlin: Duncker & Humblot, 1890), p. 175; Ranke to Bettine von Arnim, 6 February 1828, in L. von Ranke, *Das Briefwerk*, ed. W. P. Fuchs (Hamburg: Hoffman und Campe, 1949), p. 139. Both letters are quoted in P. Müller, 'Ranke in the Lobby of the Archive: Metaphors and Conditions of Historical Research', in S. Jobs and A. Lüdtke (eds.), *Unsettling History: Archiving and Narrating in Historiography* (Frankfurt am Main: Campus, 2010), pp. 109–25.

[3] See B. G. Smith, *The Gender of History: Men, Women, and Historical Practice* (Cambridge, MA: Harvard University Press, 1998); Müller, 'Ranke in the Lobby of the Archive'; F. Schnicke, *Die Männliche Disziplin: zur Vergeschlechtlichung der deutschen Geschichtswissenschaft 1780–1900* (Göttingen: Wallstein, 2015), pp. 408–10 with reference to earlier scholarly discussions of the passage.

[4] O. G. Oexle, '"Wissenschaft" und "Leben"', Geschichte in *Wissenschaft und Unterricht* 41 (1990), 145–61; also his 'Krise des Historismus – Krise der Wirklichkeit. Eine Problemgeschichte der Moderne', in O. G. Oexle (ed.), *Krise des Historismus – Krise der Wirklichkeit. Wissenschaft, Kunst und Literatur 1880–1932* (Göttingen: Vandenhoeck and Ruprecht, 2007), pp. 11–116; for the extension of this discussion into (modern) philologies and the professional study of literature, see H. Dainat, 'Überbietung der Philologie', in C. König and E. Lämmert (eds.), *Literaturwissenschaft und Geistesgeschichte 1910–1925* (Frankfurt am Main: Suhrkamp, 1993), pp. 232–9; and 'Ein Fach in der "Krise": Die "Methodendiskussion" in der Neueren deutschen Literaturwissenschaft', in Oexle (ed.), *Krise des Historismus*, pp. 247–72. For a recent and comprehensive discussion of the debates surrounding historicism and its representations, see F. Beiser, *The German Historicist Tradition* (Oxford University Press, 2011).

is reflected in the enormous popularity of, for example, Thomas Carlyle's writings inside and outside Victorian England; the reliance on author biography for academic and popular literary history in France, England, or Germany; or the phenomenon of the 'historian-novelist' and the writer of historical biography.[5] Within the context of classical philology, and with continuing recourse to the strand of Platonizing language and argument, biography here, too, could be shaped into a signature form of interpretation, including the interpretation of the classical scholar himself.

'Revitalization', like 'regeneration', was itself a term with complex social and political charges, especially around and from the mid-nineteenth century, when the dialectic between relative conservatism and revolutionary upheaval included in its force field the institutions of knowledge. Scholars of nineteenth-century cultural Romanticism have argued that the concern with historical presence or absence was one of the main parameters around which such dialectical debate crystallized. It was also one to which a range of affective stances, especially those marked by nostalgia and melancholy, aligned themselves, including a nostalgia for the earlier forms of 'regenerative' Romanticism around 1800, now reconceived later on in the century.[6] Classical philology, in its programmatic statements, fits remarkably well with what Virgil Nemoianu has described as a series of 'moderating discourses', including those of education and learning. Moderation involves, in his terms, 'the ability and willingness to use the beautiful as an epistemological vehicle and literary rhetoric as procedures for compressing and packaging knowledge; the stubborn remembrance of history and of the traditions it had engendered; the deft use of substitutive intertextuality

---

[5] For biography's status, narrative conventions, and functions as integrated into larger discourses about historiography and interpretation, see, for example, L. Marcus, *Auto/Biographical Discourse: Theory, Criticism, Practice* (Manchester University Press, 1994), M. Saunders, *Life-Writing, Autobiografiction, and the Forms of Modern Literature* (Oxford University Press, 2010); on the centrality of biography to Victorian Britain, see D. Amigoni, *Victorian Biography: Intellectuals and the Ordering of Discourse* (London: Routledge, 1993), T. L. Broughton, *Men of Letters, Writing Lives: Masculinity and Literary Auto/biography in the Late Victorian Period* (London: Routledge, 1999), S. Goldhill, *A Very Queer Family Indeed: Sex, Religion, and the Bensons in Victorian Britain* (Chicago University Press, 2016), with further bibliography; for France, see A. Jefferson, *Biography and the Question of Literature in France* (Oxford University Press, 2007); for the use of biography in German literary studies of the nineteenth century, see H.-M. Kruckis, 'Biographie als literaturwissenschaftliche Darstellungsform im 19. Jahrhundert', in J. Fohrmann and W. Vosskamp (eds.), *Wissenschaftsgeschichte der Germanistik im 19. Jahrhundert* (Stuttgart: Metzler), pp. 550–75; on the 'historian-novelist', see M.-G. Dehrmann, *Studierte Dichter: zum Spannungsverhältnis von Dichtung und philologisch-historischen Wissenschaften im 19. Jahrhundert* (Berlin: de Gruyter, 2015).
[6] T. Pfau, *Romantic Moods: Paranoia, Trauma, and Melancholy, 1790–1840* (Baltimore: Johns Hopkins University Press, 2005); V. Nemoianu, *The Triumph of Imperfection: The Silver Age of Sociocultural Moderation in Europe, 1815–1848* (Columbia: University of South Carolina Press, 2006).

and the techniques of analogy for the absorption of change; the vindica-
tion of interiority and subjectivity as enhancers of action and cognition;
[and] the utilitarian justification of emotional faculties'.[7] For sure, not
all philology was politically, socially, or culturally conservative. But its
acts of substitutive reading, the creation of organic narratives, and the
residual reliance on the beautiful fit the need for 'moderating' language
that helps to compute change. Biography itself is one such strategy of
substitution, and the biographical and autobiographical offer an
account that chimes with the promise, familiar since Humboldt, that
classical scholarship could communicate knowledge of the self, whether
that self is understood as an individual, a nation, or humankind *tout
court*. What gives the biographical momentum extra charge in the
context of philology is that it also offered a narrative of the professional
scholar. This chapter will examine this claim through a double reading
of Carl Justi's biography of Winckelmann, and Wilhelm Dilthey's
biography of Friedrich Schleiermacher.

Justi's Winckelmann

Carl Justi's Winckelmann biography, whose first volume was published in
1866, is a useful example of the status and function of biography as a self-
consciously modern tool of scholarly reflection and as a practice that integrates knowing antiquity.[8] Winckelmann's life had become the subject of
literary reflection almost from the moment of his premature death, entirely in
line with the premium put on *Bildung* and its narrative forms. Goethe's well-
known and oft-quoted comment that 'one does not learn anything from
Winckelmann, but we *become* something when we read him' suggests that an
encounter with Winckelmann offers quite literally an exercise in *Bildung*, an
act of reading and identification leading to self-fashioning. It also epitomized
the critical approach that was simultaneously taken to his historical arguments (increasingly found faulty), and the appreciation of his embodiment of
an aesthetic and ethical subjectivity developed in relation with antiquity.[9]
Both Herder and Heyne had submitted essays in response to a prize question

---

[7] Nemoianu, *The Triumph of Imperfection*, p. xi.

[8] C. Justi, *Winckelmann, sein Leben, seine Werke und seine Zeitgenossen: mit Skizzen zur Kunst- und
Gelehrtengeschichte des 18. Jahrhunderts* (Leipzig: Vogel) I: Winckelmann in Deutschland (1866); II:
Winckelmann in Italien (1872); from the second edition in 1898 onwards, the book was published in
three volumes under the reduced title *Winckelmann und seine Zeitgenossen*. Quotations in this
chapter, unless otherwise indicated, will be from Justi's first edition of 1866.

[9] 'Man lernt nichts wenn man ihn liest, aber man wird etwas'; the comment is reported in the
(carefully curated) conversations with Goethe which the writer Johann Peter Eckermann recorded

on Winckelmann's contribution, which included significant biographical and, in Herder's case, ekphrastic elements, presenting Winckelmann as a quasi-artwork in his own right. The best-known text within this comple-ment was probably Goethe's famous essay of 1805, *Winckelmann und sein Jahrhundert* ('Winckelmann and his Century'), which in turn became a reference point for the reception of Winckelmann within the institutiona-lized study of antiquity.[10] Wilamowitz, for example, picks up on it in the introductory parts to his commentary on Euripides' *Heracles*, a work that maintains its status as the paradigmatic work of the German commentary tradition. The commentary is prefaced with a life of Euripides (of which there is a fuller discussion in the next chapter), and it is here that Wilamowitz invokes Goethe's Winckelmann essay as a prime example of a 'discursive biography' (*erörternde Biografie*), one that is valid 'for his *Volk*, for us, for posterity and for eternity', and which he imagines could, ideally, be written about Euripides too.[11] He mentions in the same paragraph also the example of Justi's Winckelmann biography as a paradigmatic developmental narrative that, for lack of evidence, could unfortunately not be achieved for an ancient tragedian, a gesture which only confirms the central place of Winckelmann as a significant comparandum.

Carl Justi is mostly remembered as an art historian. He held the chair of Art History at the University of Bonn from 1872 (where he overlapped with Usener) and aside from the Winckelmann biography he also authored similar biography-oriented and widely read psychological studies of Velazquez and Michelangelo. It is worth remembering that his initial training was in theology and then philosophy. His first publication, based on his dissertation at Marburg, appeared in 1860 with the title *The aesthetic elements of Platonic philosophy, a historical-critical attempt*, and it presented an argument for a reading of Plato's works that emphasized the individuality of Plato as a literary artist.[12] The interest in artistic indivi-duality together with the transformative potential of Platonic philosophy is also reflected in his portrait of Winckelmann, reaffirming the overlapping narratives between the self-projections of the modern scholar of antiquity and the developmental arc of the philosophical subject. Once more,

---

in Goethe's last years; J. P. Eckermann, *Gespräche mit Goethe, in den letzten Jahren seines Lebens*, ed. G. Moldenhauer, i,1823–1827 (Leipzig: Reclam, 1884), p. 244.

[10] Harloe, *Winckelmann*, pp. 11–13; 133–6; Sünderhauf, *Griechensehnsucht*, passim.

[11] U. v. Wilamowitz-Moellendorff, *Euripides Herakles*, 2nd ed. (Berlin: Weidmann, 1889 [1868]), pp. 1–2.

[12] C. Justi, *Die aesthetischen Elemente in der platonischen Philosophie, ein historisch-philosophischer Versuch* (Marburg: Elwert, 1860).

Winckelmann in this context can become a touchstone for suggesting –
and at the same time keeping at arm's length – the competing demands of
scientific method and aspects of feeling.

Justi's account of Winckelmann's early years as a student, tutor and
scholar, up to the publication of his *Thoughts on the Imitation of Greek
Works of Art* essay in 1755, proposes a development towards the scholarly
commitment to Greek antiquity. Structurally, this is not only a development
and commitment equally marked by affect but also a narrative that has the
detailed description of Winckelmann's Greek studies follow directly on the
biographer's long disquisition on the role of friendship and desire. Feeling
and knowledge, in this account, are interdependent and they mark absence
and lack as much as renewed action as a result, quite like the dynamic
suggested in Winckelmann's image of the historian-lover gazing upon her
departing beloved. Justi's account, like the scholarly narratives of his contemporaries in the field of classical philology, is in equal parts individualizing
and historicizing, explicitly situating Winckelmann within his time, place,
and generation. In this way, he extends a continued invitation to his readers
to consider Winckelmann's significance against a general question of how to
calibrate an approach to the study of antiquity.

Winckelmann's instinctive turn to Greek texts after his arrival as a school
student in Berlin is described as a 'love ignited at first touch' (*dass sich die
Liebe schon bei der ersten Berührung entzündet hatte*), not against a backdrop
of personal loss but instead against a description of the general decline of
Greek studies in the German world. Here, access to Greek texts was provided
only in fragmented and indirect ways, through anthologies and chresto-
mathies as the standard instruments of instruction.[13] Winckelmann's newly
kindled love that leads him to independent study is thus in effect also a turn
to an alternative kind of pedagogy. This pedagogy will feed back into his
conflicted attitude first as a private tutor, especially to the Lamprecht family,
and then later as an official instructor and administrator at the gymnasium of
Seehausen, where his affective efforts, intellectually, socially, and emotionally, were thwarted.

Justi structures his narrative by outlining Winckelmann's stay at
Seehausen as a period marked by lack of freedom and the exercise of
a certain kind of asceticism, supplementing it by a chapter entitled
'Friendships' that leads on to a long chapter on Greek studies. The chapter
on friendship presents on the one hand the details of Winckelmann's
personal resignation and withdrawal from impossible or disappointingly

[13] Justi, *Winckelmann*, pp. 32–4.

one-sided emotional relationships (for example with his former pupil Lamprecht). On the other hand, Justi complements this deliberate turn away from particular attachments with reflection on and revaluation of friendship as a key to a sublimated form of scientifically and intellectually productive sociability – in short, invoking the model of the Platonic 'ladder of love' again. He describes Winckelmann's affective situation vis-à-vis his young friend Lamprecht thus:

> A letter sent from Hadmersleben of the 4th of June 1748, shortly before the end of this period of his life, is full of sad resignation. An ill star had alienated him from his friend, and so he revokes all his rights towards him. He recognizes that nature has made him ill-suited for stirring love; and thus he no longer wants to enter into close relation-ships with friends. He wants to rid himself of this passion (*Leidenschaft*) which destroys the calm of his soul and which is meant to live on only for an everlasting memory (*nun bloss noch einem ewigen Andenken fortleben soll*).[14]

In the same breath, Justi underlines the importance of friendship for Winckelmann's intellectual character and in Winckelmann's entire work. Justi is well aware of the personal attachments of Winckelmann and quotes liberally from his letters. In addition, he also uses those references to 'first and only love' as rhetorical instances, which he then transforms into an analytical vocabulary on the 'cult of friendship' and 'enthusiastic friendships'.[15] Those, in turn, he integrates into a historical excursus that sets out to make the appreciative case for a time-honoured intellectual and academic tradition. In other words, Winckelmann's own affective sublimation is suggested as part of a genealogy of such sublimations that reaches back to antiquity and, significantly, a Platonic form of both individual erotic progress and com-munal scholarly sociability:

> Often, friendship is the only available asylum of emotional life for the scholar (*das einzige Asyl des Gemütslebens*) – la passion du sage, as Voltaire called it – ; and as long as all human formation was educational and scholarly and therefore altogether male (*solange alle humane Bildung eine gelehrte und folglich eine ganz männliche war*), so long all intellectual and spiritual communities had to have the same character. It was only with the gradual rise of a modern kind of *Bildung* and literature, and with the spread of an esprit de société, that woman, in a kind of modern rehabilitation of chivalric devotion, became recognized as capable of a form of community that was not simply sensual.[16]

---

[14] Ibid., p. 130.   [15] Ibid., pp. 131–2.   [16] Ibid., p. 132.

Justi here expresses almost paradigmatically what Luhmann described as the anxieties and possibilities raised in a modern, differentiated society, which register in a code of romantic love: the break-up of older forms of sociability, a broadening of social participation, exhilarating and threatening in equal parts. It is all the more striking that Justi proposes his reflections on a modern code of love precisely in the context of the modern practices of knowledge and scholarship, and of the knowledge of antiquity. He does so in a remarkable, calculated conflation or recursive rearrangement of moments in the cultural history he has laid out so far:

> In the time of the Renaissance, the influence of ancient writers became prominent. Greek male love was the equivalent of Romanticism for republican antiquity (*die griechische Männerliebe war gleichsam die Romantik des republikanischen Altertums*), the ancient counterpart to medieval chivalry and its devotion to a woman; one could argue that both represent an attempt to neutralize an error, in one case an error of the senses, in the other one of morality: and not only to neutralize it, but to make it fertile for the highest ideal objectives (*für die höchsten idealen Zwecke fruchtbar zu machen*). The morally most sublime among the ancient philosophers never rose higher than in the love dialogues (*Liebesgespräche*) of Plato's *Symposium* and *Phaedrus*, and the greatest of Christian poets tried, in the most moving of episodes in his divine poem, to raise a memorial to a guilty couple.[17]

The reference to the 'Romantic' skilfully conflates the medieval and the modern (as nineteenth-century Romanticism did as well) and reflects the contemporary appreciation of Dante – his account of Francesca da Rimini and her lover Paolo Malatesta in Canto 5 of the *Inferno*, which Justi alludes to, is also a story of the erotic power of reading together and communicating love and desire through books. By making the articulation of friendship in erotic terminology an integral part of a positively valued genealogy of male academic sociability and *Bildung*, Justi's excursus also goes beyond familiar earlier strategies to make ancient pederasty palatable or at least explicable by treating it as a *de facto* analogue of more modern forms of socially acceptable, heterosexual displays of affect.

What is more, Justi styles this genealogy as a precondition for understanding and enacting a modern philology that is based on a similar kind of sublimation but holds on to its roots in feeling. Justi immediately follows his reflection on male academic friendship with a long exploration of Winckelmann's own readings of Platonic dialogues, a genre that he later

---

[17] Ibid., p. 132.

on specifically calls 'a drama of constant fleeing and befriending of the self' (*ein Schauspiel beständigen Sichfliehens und –befreundens*).[18] This is a judgement entirely in line with Justi's own previous work on Plato as essentially a dramatic artist. Justi's Winckelmann equates friendship and love and, more importantly, explicitly articulates an understanding of Plato that amounts to more than book knowledge. Platonic *eros* is reaffirmed as both the content of knowledge and its method, exemplified in the figure of Winckelmann and, in turn, recognized in the philologically rigorous close reading and meticulous listing of sources offered by Justi:

> It is in the spirit of Plato when he [Winckelmann] exclaims: "Friendship descended from heaven and it is not from human stirrings"; and when he believes that one has to ascend to the limits of the divine in order to imagine a true friend; and when he approaches such a friend with a certain awe; and when, at the first encounter, he feels an inexplicable pull which comes from the divinely ordained order of things that cannot be grasped (*unfasslich*).
>
> All this was not something that was felt or spoken after the model of books (*nichts aus Büchern Angefühltes und Nachgesprochenes*), but it was deeply rooted in his mental organization.[19]

The statement about approaching a true friend with awe carries a footnote in which Justi references Plato's *Phaedrus* 251a, the effect of looking on the face or body of a beautiful boy: εἶτα προσορῶν ὡς θεὸν σέβεται, καὶ εἰ μὴ ἐδεδίει τὴν τῆς σφόδρα μανίας δόξαν, θύοι ἂν ὡς ἀγάλματι καὶ θεῷ τοῖς παιδικοῖς ('either, looking at it, he reveres him like a god, and if he were not afraid to give the impression that he were almost insane, he would sacrifice to his beloved as if to the *agalma* of a god'). Justi deliberately, and with full philological panoply, returns to the image of the *agalma* precisely to underline the intellectual longing for something that 'cannot be grasped', while at the same time underplaying the sexually explicit term παίδικα, which denotes the beloved in a pederastic relationship.

The following chapter on Winckelmann's studies of Greek literature summarizes the simultaneous acts of renouncing the particular instances of human friendship and longing (note again the parallel to the 'ladder of love' in the *Symposium*) and the return to his independent study of Greek texts:

> As soon as Winckelmann had the security of a position and income, his old love for Greek literature reawakened, and he resolved once more to take up valiantly the battle against all sorts of obstacles. . . . And it was indeed his five

---

[18] Ibid., p. 159.   [19] Ibid., pp. 134–5.

years at Seehausen where his view of the Hellenic character and his personal relationship with Greek poets and writers were formed (*wo seine Anschauungen von hellenischem Wesen und sein persönliches Verhältnis zu hellenischen Dichtern und Schriftstellern sich gebildet haben*).[20]

Aside from the Platonic dialogues, Justi points out that Winckelmann's deliberate commitment to studying ancient forms and structures of *Bildung* meant particular attention to ancient biographical writers, detailing his enthusiasm for Diogenes Laertius (whose focus on Platonism as a fundamental and fundamentally Greek form of philosophy and pedagogy I have discussed in Chapter 2) and Plutarch, whom he keenly recommended to friends.

Winckelmann's readings proved a necessary step towards his identity as a historian of ancient art, and Justi gives deliberately ample space to following Winckelmann through them. Justi's method is that of a philological reading or rereading of Winckelmann's own readings reflected in his notes, an approach that allows him to chart the development of his studies and 'to enter into the workshop of the formation of his thoughts' (*in die Werkstätte seiner Gedankenbildung hineinzusehen*), a kind of reading by proxy to reflect and re-embody *Bildung*.[21]

Just as Plato's *Symposium* worked itself up to Alcibiades's praise speech with a turn to the sculptural qualities of Socrates as *agalma*, quasi-divine yet not by normal means responsive, so the rest of Justi's first volume details Winckelmann's path away from traditional philological practices of textual criticism towards the integration of archaeology and the material remains of art. This integration aims at 'increasing the understanding of the ancients' (*das Verständnis der Alten zu fördern*) but also underlines the contrast between Winckelmann's life-enhancing choices versus the necessities of text-critical and antiquarian labour:

> He can choose his favourite books (*Lieblingsbücher*) according to their significance and congeniality instead of the rather random requirements to have them cleaned up; instead of seeing texts as starting points for antiquarian and grammatical excursus he will connect them to his own views of the world, life, and everything that is dear and important to humankind (*was der Menschheit wert und wichtig ist*), and he will gain as

---

[20] Ibid., p. 136; the section is entitled 'Griechische Studien' in all editions; the later editions from 1898 onwards, though, deliberately add a new subtitle for the section describing in detail some of Winckelmann's favourite authors, as 'Griechische Lieblingsschriftsteller' (*Winckelmann und seine Zeitgenossen*, p. 162).

[21] Justi, *Winckelmann*, p. 4.

a human being what he loses as a learned scholar (*als Mensch gewinnen, was er als Gelehrter verliert*).[22]

Winckelmann's is an 'elective affinity with Greek essence ... which in this our case made up for a lack of instruments and methods through sympathy and divination' (*eine Wahlverwandtschaft mit griechischem Wesen ... die in diesem unseren Falle durch Sympathie und Divination den Mangel an Hülfsmitteln und Methode wettmachte*). It is a diagnosis and idealization of Winckelmann as simultaneously example and counterexample that chimes with the vocabulary of disciplinary self-scrutiny of contemporary philologists, even when instruments and methods seemed no longer to be lacking.[23]

This new conscious turn in Winckelmann's practice towards reading and viewing antiquity in a sublimated yet materially and sensuously perceptive way Justi expresses in diction that willingly returns to the Socratic and Platonic scenes of instruction, erotics, and imagined communality. Winckelmann engages with ancient authors 'as if with friends and companions' (*Umgang wie mit Freunden und Gefährten*),[24] and it is especially the figure of Xenophon – the young pupil who received his formation from Socrates and effectively became his biographer in turn – who attracts Winckelmann, and by extension Justi:

> The report about the 'tender and moral beauty' of the young Xenophon was significant to Winckelmann. He believed 'that we generally think the way we are made', and he was inclined to assume of beautiful people the best in taste and morals. The exquisite form (*herrliche Gestalt*), which had previously moved Socrates to want to make the mind of the youth equal to his body through *Bildung*, had assumed for Winckelmann the dimensions of an image that shone a positive light on the narrator (*hatte sich Winckelmann zu einem Bilde belebt, das einen Glanz auf den Erzähler warf*).[25]

By empathetically following Winckelmann through his readings, Justi charts Winckelmann's way towards becoming a published writer and scholar, 'who would have preferred to write for a select circle of sensitive souls, for a Platonic academy, and for posterity' (*der am liebsten für einen gewählten Kreis feinfühlender Seelen, für eine platonische Akademie und für den Nachruhm geschrieben hätte*).[26] The actual prompt for making the transition from independent, introverted scholar to published author is, in Justi's telling, twofold. For one, there is the exposure to ancient works of art in the cast gallery at Dresden:

[22] Ibid., pp. 140, 141–2.   [23] Ibid., p. 147.
[24] Ibid., p. 148. For the trope of books as friends see Eden, *Renaissance Rediscovery*, pp. 30–48.
[25] Justi, *Winckelmann*, pp. 157–8.   [26] Ibid., p. 164.

This was not merely a new spectacle for the senses and the mind, not simply a new content of knowledge. It was a new kind of knowledge, cognition coming from objects, not books, cognition coming from autopsy and intuition (*Anschauung und Empfindung*) instead of words and concepts. Winckelmann made himself consciously and passionately aware of this: and it would have a lasting impact on his life.[27]

On the other hand, there was the contact with the artist Adam Friedrich Oeser, whom Justi casts in a crucial, almost utopian pedagogical role: 'Oeser thought very highly of his pupil, and he could flatter himself that he midwifed his intellectual birth like a Socrates' (*er durfte sich schmeicheln, bei seiner geistigen Geburt sokratische Hebammendienste geleistet zu haben*).[28] Winckelmann's eventual publication of the seminal *Thoughts on the Imitation of Greek Works of Art* is thus imagined as the result of his Socratic birth as a public author and interpreter of antiquity.

Justi's biographical project, presented as a consciously appropriate form of scholarly inquiry and method, echoes tropes and discourses that characterize the assumptions and practices of the philological and historical disciplines of the nineteenth century, just like the figure of Winckelmann himself did. Among those tropes are the interlinking of *Bildung*, individuality, and personification as a strategy of interpretation; the expectation that individuality be expressed in and narrated as development; and the role of feeling as a complement and buffer for the challenge of scientifically accountable understanding. The reliance on an ideal of pedagogy and communication that is marked by Platonizing language and narrative tropes effectively reaffirms a nostalgic ur-scene that seeks to keep the antinomies of philology legible, and it reaffirms antiquity as a privileged object of philological inquiry. This is mirrored in Winckelmann as a nostalgic embodiment of the scholar as a model of 'becoming' and in Winckelmann himself as an 'asylum for the emotional life' of philology.

Justi's biography was widely read and a success, and the work saw several reprints over the next few decades. These show how the figure of Justi

---

[27] Ibid., p. 245.

[28] Ibid., p. 411. The reference to Socratic midwifery is obviously taken from the ancient biographical tradition; but it was also reinserted into the current of philosophical terminology by Kant, who speaks of the 'midwifery of thought' (*Hebammenkunst der Gedanken*) both in his *Metaphysics of Morals* (1797) and in his 1803 treatise *On Pedagogy*; for the traction of the Kantian use of this trope, together with Plato's, in German literature, see John H. Smith, 'Dialogic Midwifery in Kleist's *Marquise von O* and the Hermeneutics of Telling the Untold in Kant and Plato', *Proceedings of the Modern Language Association* 100.2 (1985), pp. 203–19.

became itself increasingly subsumed into the logic of biographical inquiry, affirming its potential as a resource for modelling both the scholar and scholarship itself. The biographical sketch of Justi by the art historian Wilhelm Waetzoldt, published in 1921 and later occasionally appended to Justi's Winckelmann book, is a case in point. 'Justi's great biographies are contributions to the phenomenology of genius', claims Waetzoldt, and their success is due to Justi's qualities and talents as scholar and interpreter, his 'ability for empathy' (*Einfühlungsmöglichkeit*). By extension, this includes the reader's ability: 'Möglichkeit' means 'possibility' and thus the phrase extends to call on every later reader's and scholar's empathetic response to reading Justi.[29] The Winckelmann biography, in fact, offers a biography of scholarship: '[it] narrates the coming into being of a science on the foundations of the spiritual movement of a century. It is a hymn to the power of the scholar (*das hohe Lied von der Macht des Gelehrten*) around whom a world revolves. This is the world of the mind. Ideas are the true heroes of this book.'[30] In other words, individual biography is representative of an age, something that echoes Wilhelm Dilthey's programmatic statement around the same time that Justi's *Winckelmann* is published:

> The centre point of biography, as much as of life, lies in the relationship of the individual to the totality in which he develops and on which he acts in turn; in addition, the biography of a thinker or artist has to address the big historical question of how it was that the scattered elements of a culture, which are given through the general environment, social and moral conditions, the influence of predecessors and contemporaries, are processed in the workshop of the individual mind and formed into an original unity (*zu einem originalen Ganzen gebildet werden*), which in turn intervenes creatively in the life of a community.[31]

In addition, the history of Winckelmann's *Bildung* is reprised in the description Waetzoldt gives of Justi's own turn from philosophy to art history, and from the interpreter of Plato's literary language towards a conscious producer of a narrative with artistic qualities. That this is also at least in part a Platonic *Bildung* is suggested by Waetzold's comment, apropos Justi's doctoral philosophical work, that 'Plato led him [Justi] to Winckelmann.'[32] That

---

[29] W. Waetzoldt, 'Carl Justi', in W. Waetzold (ed.), *Deutsche Kunsthistoriker. Zweiter Band: von Passavant bis Justi* (Seemann: Leipzig, 1921), pp. 239–78, here pp. 255–6.

[30] Waetzoldt, 'Justi', p. 271.

[31] Dilthey, *Leben Schleiermachers*, p. xxxiii. The *Leben* is quoted after the edition of Dilthey's *Gesammelte Schriften*, vol. 13 (with half-volumes 13.1 and 13.2), ed. M. Redeker (Göttingen: Vandenhock & Ruprecht, 3rd ed., 1991). Unless otherwise noted, references are to vol. 13.1.

[32] Waetzold, 'Justi', p. 245.

Winckelmann himself is singled out by both Justi and Waetzoldt for his use of
an artistic idiom, a *Kunstsprache*, to serve his acts of interpreting and understanding antiquity tightens the link of individual development, knowledge,
and the articulation of knowledge. It does so especially in the repeated
mention that Winckelmann himself had been making plans in the late
1760s for an autobiographical work.

Laura Marcus has talked of the promise of a 'self-transparency of
consciousness' reflected in the biographical and the autobiographical.[33]
This strategy by the end of the nineteenth century is probably most
strongly expressed in the theoretical language proposed by the philosopher
and critic Wilhelm Dilthey (1833–1911).[34] While Dilthey's main works on
hermeneutics appeared towards the turn of the century, one of his first
published works, an intellectual biography of Schleiermacher, was begun at
the same time as Justi's Winckelmann book.[35] It was this project on
Schleiermacher that Dilthey considered in retrospect representative of his
historical method,[36] and it is this book in which we also see biography as
a specifically philological act utilized to tell the story of the rise of the
modern scholar.

Dilthey's Schleiermacher

The rise of biography as an integral, heuristic part of historical understanding and criticism and its emphasis on the author as key to the work is not
restricted to the German-speaking academy and its cultural sphere nor to the
work of Dilthey.[37] What distinguishes the particular German constellation is

---

[33] Marcus, *Auto/biographical Discourses*, p. 147.

[34] For the importance of Dilthey's comments on autobiography, see also J. Popkin, *History, Historians and Autobiography* (Chicago University Press, 2005), pp. 17–19.

[35] Interestingly, the very first longer publication of Dilthey's was a review, in 1858, of the first three volumes of Hamann's collected and then newly edited works, prepared by C. H. Gildemeister. This review amounts to a discussion of Hamann's youthful development as a thinker, including a discussion of his *Denkwürdigkeiten* as a thinly veiled attempt to project his own, that is, Hamann's approach onto the figure of Socrates; an expanded version is printed as 'Johann Georg Hamann', in Dilthey, *Gesammelte Schriften*, vol. 11 (Leipzig: Teubner, 1936), pp. 1–39.

[36] 'Über das Studium der Geschichte der Wissenschaft vom Menschen, der Gesellschaft, und dem Staat' (1875), *Gesammelte Schriften*, vol. V 'Die Geistige Welt: Einleitung in die Philosophie des Lebens', ed. G. Misch (Göttingen: Vandenhoeck & Ruprecht, 1924), pp. 31–73, here p. 26.

[37] Across national philologies, with their notion of literature as a field of scientific inquiry, the 'author biography' had become a normative exercise already before Dilthey and across Europe. Saint-Beuve's 'l'homme et l'oeuvre', for example, is a popular formula that makes clear how intimately the terms of biography and literature were connected (as modern terms). Jefferson, *Biography* argues in detail that the terminology of biography and literature from the mid to late eighteenth century would develop as critical terms in corrective dialogue with each other. She treats both as quintessentially modern

the interaction of philology claiming a privileged institutional and educational place, the still available discourse of *Bildung*, and in addition the simultaneous emphasis on scientific method and organized scholarly practice. The latter also led to expectations to define the humanities as such vis-à-vis the (natural) sciences, which themselves were acquiring increasing dominance during that period. The particularly German nomenclature of the human sciences as *Geisteswissenschaften* belongs here, and Dilthey held an important position in shaping the terms of this debate.[38]

Dilthey's 'Human Sciences' inhabit their own domain compared to other sciences, and Dilthey found a place for autobiography and biography as an explicit tool of *Wissenschaft* and as the quintessential example for the relationship between historiography, lived experience, and interpretation. Dilthey's aim was nothing short of what he called, with a view to Kant, a 'critique of historical reason' – the plan for a comprehensive, systematic work of methodology, which he never finished. Scholarly opinion differs as to how systematic or scattered Dilthey's thought is. Arguably, his thinking is hard to pin down as offering one single and consistent approach. In any case it does seem clear that any appreciation of a more systematic nature of his writing happened mostly later in the twentieth century rather than in Dilthey's own lifetime.[39]

The task of the historian, for Dilthey, is to understand the meaning of human action and human interaction, which amounts to an understanding of individuals in relation to each other and to an understanding of life in the sense of lived experience. This hermeneutic approach that emphasizes *Erlebnis* (lived experience) stresses immediacy and the role of empathy as much as it ultimately stresses interpretation arising from distance. In fact, it operates with a very paradoxical and complex relationship between the two. What this means for historiography, most importantly, is that the individual of the past is the evident unit of historical study, and that lived experience is the element shared between past and present that allows scientific

notions, with ramifications for disciplinary development as much as for concepts of authorship across European literary culture; see also Kruckis, 'Biographie', pp. 550–75.

[38] J. Eckel, *Geist der Zeit: Deutsche Geisteswissenschaften seit 1870* (Göttingen: Vandenhoeck und Ruprecht, 2008); on the disciplinary structures and constellations emerging in the 'saddle period' of 1880–1920 as still valid and impactful for humanities into the late twentieth century, both in the German university landscape as well as a successful export model of the late nineteenth and twentieth centuries, see p. 12.

[39] For good general introductions to Dilthey's method and system, see R. A. Makkreel, *Dilthey: Philosopher of the Human Studies*, 3rd ed. (Princeton University Press, 1992 [1975]); M. Jung, *Dilthey zur Einführung*, Hamburg 1996; H.-U. Lessing, 'Dilthey als Historiker', in N. Hammerstein (ed.), *Deutsche Geschichtswissenschaft um 1900* (Wiesbaden: Harrassowitz, 1988), pp. 113–30.

interpretation specific to the humanities in the first place. For historiography and literary historiography this meant understanding historical and artistic events on a (modified Hegelian) model of *Geistesgeschichte*: the spirit of the age manifesting and crystallizing itself in strong personalities. The biographical descriptions of such characters and of their *Nachleben* are then the appropriate methodology for the interpretation of literary works, as they were part of that same manifestation – as articulated, for example, in Dilthey's widely received works *Introduction to the Sciences of the Spirit (Einleitung in die Geisteswissenschaften)* (1883) and the collection of literary-historical essays *Experience and Poetry (Das Erlebnis und die Dichtung)* (1905).[40]

As mentioned, it is arguable how consistent Dilthey's thought is, and there are clear differences between his earlier attempts at a psychological method of *Einfühlung* and a later, more differentiated, notion of a triad of experience (*Erlebnis*), expression (*Ausdruck*), and cognition (*Verstehen*). *Ausdruck* indicates the way lived experience is expressed, usually in textual and artistic ways, and *Verstehen* is the understanding of those expressions, the only object of understanding to which we do have access, rather than the lived experience itself. This is not to suggest that Dilthey's method is one of naïve empathizing with the past, of a complete 're-feeling' or *Nacherleben*. However systematic his thought is (or not), he is clearly aware of a complex dynamic between closeness and distance, and the necessity of distance for acts of understanding.[41] At the same time, the language of empathy, immediacy, and closeness features prominently to describe the methodological attitude which the scholarly individual should take, however approximative this may be.

While not a classicist in the strict sense, Dilthey had enjoyed a traditional classical upbringing with solid school training in Latin and Greek. In Berlin he had also been a student of August Boeckh, and his familiarity with

---

[40] Works such as the slightly later Goethe biography (1920) by Friedrich Gundolf, professor of German literature and member of the circle around the poet Stefan George, as well as Gundolf's works on Shakespeare and Caesar were representative of this notion of *Geistesgeschichte* as scientific method (and as work of art, in the case of the George-Kreis in particular), as well as of the success of historical biography as an extraordinarily popular genre of literature in the decade(s) around 1900. Significantly, it is mostly artists and thinkers that Dilthey focuses on, unlike the members of the George-Kreis a little later, who included statesmen such as Friedrich Barbarossa or Julius Caesar in their horizon. Gundolf, in turn, had considerable impact on the classicist Albrecht Dihle's work on biography in the 1950s, who reprised the theme of Socrates as a charismatic personality and model for the auto/biographical tradition; on contextualizing the latter, see A. Momigliano, *The Development of Greek Biography* (Cambridge, MA: Harvard University Press, 1993), pp. 16–21.

[41] See, for example, D. Morat, 'Verstehen als Gefühlsmethode. Zu Wilhelm Diltheys hermeneutischer Grundlegung der Geisteswissenschaften', in U. Jensen and D. Morat (eds.), *Rationalisierungen des Gefühls. Zum Verhältnis von Wissenschaft und Emotionen 1880–1930* (Munich: Fink, 2008), pp. 101–18.

developments in the world of classical scholarship was later maintained through family relations with Hermann Usener, who was married to Dilthey's sister Lily. His first large-scale publication in 1870, the extensive *Life of Schleiermacher*, was conceived as the intellectual biography of a thinker and his age and it was intended to appear in at least two volumes. As with others of Dilthey's works, only the first volume was published in complete form.[42] The first volume, though, was not only widely read but also well received by classical scholars.[43]

What sets the Schleiermacher biography apart is the particular spin Dilthey gives to his interpretation of Schleiermacher's importance. Dilthey had begun work on the life and thought of the theologian, philosopher, and translator first in his doctoral dissertation of 1864 on Schleiermacher's ethics, and then subsequently as an editor of some of his letters. By then Schleiermacher was mostly known, and highly respected, for his mature work and as a theological thinker. Dilthey shifted the focus decidedly back to Schleiermacher's early years, to his integration into the social and cultural environment of Berlin Romanticism around 1800, and to its personal networks. His Schleiermacher is a thinker who made the discussion and the understanding and interpretation of individuality his highest goal, the foundation of his own systematic thought, and its ethical centrepiece. In Dilthey's biographical account, Schleiermacher combines in exemplary fashion religion, aesthetics, the force of life, and the freedom of science or *Wissenschaft*, viewing individuality as itself a mirror and symbol of the divine and of the world suffused by the divine, a knowledge that can ultimately only be gathered through an element of inner apperception or intuition (*innere Anschauung*).

Just like Dilthey himself, his Schleiermacher appears as a figure who attempts a synthesis of intellectual and creative understanding that is qualitatively different from scientific, technical and rational knowledge *alone*. In short, Schleiermacher becomes a model for the modern *Wissenschaftler* as imagined by Dilthey, a scholar of life in whom all branches of knowledge combine into a whole:

---

[42] Late in life, Dilthey tried unsuccessfully to finish both the *Einleitung in die Geisteswissenschaften* and the second volume of the Schleiermacher biography as summaries respectively of his overall theoretical and historical thought. The drafts to the second volume (running to almost eight hundred print pages) are available as volume 14 of Dilthey's *Gesammelte Schriften. Leben Schleiermachers. Zweiter Band: Schleiermachers System als Philosophie und Theologie* (Göttingen: Vandenhoeck & Ruprecht, 1985).

[43] For Dilthey's readership and the reception of the Schleiermacher biography, see Lessing, 'Dilthey als Historiker'.

> Schleiermacher's drive (*Drang*) . . . had an effect on all areas of knowledge: it
> claimed for itself sociability, aesthetic pleasure and the expressions of artistic
> form, family life, pedagogy, and political action. Schleiermacher, deeply
> thoughtful and surrounded by the highest achievements of a scholarly spirit,
> elevated this universal experience and understanding to philosophical con-
> sciousness, and tried to grasp the central element of every aspect of life, and
> in this way reached a universal intuition of the world of culture . . . A mild
> and clear light seemed to shine forth from him, illuminating all the creative
> acts of life (*alles Gestalten des Lebens zu erhellen*).[44]

This Schleiermacher, as a strong individual and the representative of
a generation as much as of a nation (itself an individual writ large), is
a child of the post-Enlightenment world. For Dilthey, this is
a world – and he means a German world – in which the philosophers
of rationalism were followed by a talented generation just before
Schleiermacher's, who translated that philosophical and rational
impetus into the realm of poetry. To him, this is the world of
German classicism, of Lessing and especially Goethe – an exceptional
group of individuals in whom poetic drive and reflective thought
came together in harmony. The wording consciously recalls the
image of classical Athens as imagined in that generation, idealistically
situated at the point of perfect confluence of new political, intellectual, and aesthetic liberties. This is the life of a generation who, not
yet part of a politically 'strong nation' but still of a 'mighty spiritual
nation' (*kräftig geistvolle Nation*), have to turn inwards, where their
vital spirit (*Lebensdrang*) is expressed in poetry complemented by
thought.

Significantly, Dilthey does not couch this opposition in a terminology
of *Dichtung* and *Denken*, or reflexivity, but instead in a language of poetry
as opposed to or rather completed and in the first place provoked by
Wissenschaft. By 1870 *Wissenschaft* was no longer a term simply synonymous with knowledge but a term that had obvious associations with
science and with institutionalized forms of knowledge:[45]

> And thus our [classicizing] poets are not simply scientific thinkers alongside
> their poetic acts; instead, their development as poets is indeed shaped by the
> progress of their thinking. They create out of themselves a great, immediate

---

[44] Dilthey, *Leben Schleiermachers*, p. xxxvi.
[45] Throughout the nineteenth century, the semantic range of *Wissenschaft* as more generally knowledge, skill, and even art narrows down to a predominant meaning of discipline and structured
scholarly knowledge, or expertise, within a given discipline. See, for example, the German dictionary
of the Brothers Grimm.

scientific movement, new ways of investigation, in short, a new worldview. Which explains why the generation that followed them [i.e., Schleiermacher's] was less fortunate in its poetry, but all the more creative in its research (*schöpferisch in wissenschaftlicher Forschung*), its ethical views, and its formation of a worldview – creations which were the perfection of what the earlier generation had begun.[46]

Schleiermacher's own generation, then, is one that is 'less fortunate in poetry, but all the more creative in scholarly research' – a generation that, more one-sidedly, fulfils what the preceding one had begun. As he puts it: 'From poetry now arises *Wissenschaft*' (*Aus der Poesie erhebt sich jetzt die Wissenschaft*).[47] Schleiermacher's Romantic circle, as Dilthey will lay out in detail, was full of gifted young men who had less poetic success, a reading that may owe to the contemporary admiration of Goethe and Goethe's own misgivings about the young Romantics. Still, some of those artistic thinkers – especially Schleiermacher – embodied to Dilthey the true and new meaning of their generation as creatively gifted *Wissenschaftler* for whom and for whose *Wissenschaft* 'active life' (*handelndes Leben*) was an important feature.[48]

Schleiermacher himself, in this context, was to Dilthey's mind not a particularly gifted poet himself, despite his youthful attempts and aspirations, but someone with the right receptive sensitivity and admiration for music and poetry. He emerges as a perceptive, talented critic and reader, an interlocutor who turns his passive artistic understanding into active artistic *Wissenschaft*. In this way, Dilthey may be trying to articulate something akin to an apologia of philology as, again, something essentially belated and 'coming after', a gesture we already saw, among others, in Boeckh: poetry sublimated into scholarship.[49] Dilthey quotes Schleiermacher's own thoughts on his likely failure as an artist, were he ever to become one: 'It is too much of a dilemma, either to form mankind into a definite shape in one's self and then to express it in many actions, or to represent (*abzubilden*) it in external form by making works of art, so that everybody is compelled to recognize what one

---

[46] Dilthey, *Leben Schleiermachers*, pp. xxxix–xl.   [47] Ibid., p. 285.

[48] Dilthey gathers around the description of Schleiermacher a whole wreath of individual mini-biographies or portraits of his fellow Romantics, a narrative strategy that recalls Justi's full title *Winckelmann and His Contemporaries*. Compare also Makkreel's comment on Dilthey's output: 'Before the *Einleitung* [*in die Geisteswissenschaften*; 1883], Dilthey had already written more than seventy publications, but the great majority of them had appeared in lay journals and under various pseudonyms. These early writings were mainly reviews and scholarly articles dealing with the life and work of prominent figures in the history of philosophy and literature. Generally, they were more expository than critical', Makkreel, *Dilthey*, pp. 44–5.

[49] Thanks to Joshua Billings for helping me to tease out this point.

wanted to show.'[50] The middle ground between becoming a representative human individual and representing individuality in works of art seems to be occupied by the practice of *Wissenschaft*. The *Wissenschaftler* of Schleiermacher's calibre are in the business of representation just as much as artists are, but a representation of the other in an act of *inner* understanding in which the individual self forms the ground of knowledge.

Dilthey takes this last quotation from Schleiermacher's *Soliloquies*, the set of four linked personal reflections discussed above with regard to Schleiermacher's account of the process of becoming an individual as the highest good. Their strongly autobiographical tone predestined them to become a paradigmatic work in Dilthey's eyes, for whom they qualify as a 'serious study in the ethics of love, friendship, and sociability' (*ernstes Studium der Ethik von Liebe, Freundschaft und Geselligkeit*).[51] In fact, he describes their genesis from a plan by Schleiermacher to write a novel, not unlike Rousseau, Goethe, and Schleiermacher's friend Friedrich Schlegel had done, offering religious thoughts about love, marriage, and friendship, so that, to quote Schleiermacher again, 'inner *Bildung* may translate into external representation' (*die innere Bildung auch übergeh' in äussere Darstellung*).[52] Instead of a novel, Schleiermacher creates a different form of artistic prose, which Dilthey reads as the 'yield of his scientific worldview and view of life for the question of ethics' (*Ertrag seiner wissenschaftlichen Welt- und Lebensansicht für die sittliche Frage*).[53]

The aim of the *Soliloquies* is the self-consciousness of the individual, and

> [i]t follows from this scientific thought, that it needs the work of art in order to be fully represented (*sich ganz darzustellen*). For life is the expression of our true higher self, life in which man gives perfect reality to his self (*in dem ihm der Mensch vollendete Wirklichkeit geben soll*), together with the artwork, which anticipates this perfection and represents it in the illustrative shape of character (*in der anschaulichen Form des Charakters*), which can never quite become reality (*was so, ganz so niemals Wirklichkeit werden kann*). The novel is able to represent this 'inner human-ness' ('*innere Menschheit*') by way of development, of 'an external sequence of changing circumstances'. But if the character is to emerge as a complete ideal image, one needs to find an artistic

---

[50] Dilthey, *Leben Schleiermachers*, p. 307.   [51] Ibid., p. 312.

[52] Ibid., p. 460. Schleiermacher was certainly *au fait* with contemporary theories of the novel; he had also come to the defense of his friend Schlegel after his novel *Lucinde* had caused a scandal. Part of Schleiermacher's attempt was the belief in the novel as a quintessentially modern phenomenon, with Goethe's *Wilhelm Meister*, in Schlegel's famous formulation, as one of the three great tendencies of the age.

[53] Dilthey, *Leben Schleiermachers*, p. 463.

form that puts him right into reality, like the hero of a drama, or the way Plato put his Socrates. We have to view the *Monologen* as an artistic creation of that kind, however much they fell short of that ambition.[54]

Once more, we seem to be oscillating between Schleiermacher's goals and Dilthey's own reflections on the art and science of biography.[55] The representation of the individual in a post-poetic generation cannot be externalized in the novel (*pace* Schlegel, who tried to achieve just that in his *Lucinde*), but it wants to be captured in an artistic form particular to its needs. The best *comparanda* Dilthey can invoke here are, not accidentally, the Platonic dialogues, and Plato's representation of the figure of Socrates as an ideal, ungraspable character, a return to the trope of Plato as the philosopher who exemplifies a position of reflective, *wissenschaftlich* distance gained from experience formerly had. Dilthey is insistent about the artistic qualities of Schleiermacher's innovative work, calling to attention his lyrical prose (*dem Lyrischen sich nähernde Prosa*) and quoting additional evidence from Schleiermacher's letters that he was thinking carefully about metrics and prosody during the composition of the work.[56] At the same time, Dilthey insists that it is fundamental to emphasize the scientific attitude that is perfectly clothed in artistic form: 'The basis of the *Monologen* is formed by a scientific view of the world and of life, its form is artistic, its aim ethical' (*Die Grundlage der Monologen bildet eine wissenschaftliche Welt- und Lebensansicht, ihre Form ist künstlerisch, ihr Ziel ist ethisch*).[57]

This harmony of scientific and artistic insight, both experienced and exemplified in the process of being an individual and of describing it, carries over into what takes up a large amount of Dilthey's account, namely Schleiermacher's translation of Plato. Even though the bulk of this section in 1870 remained unpublished as part of the materials collected for a second volume of Dilthey's extensive study, Schleiermacher's project holds an important place.[58] Dilthey positions Schleiermacher's Plato, described as a proven milestone in Plato scholarship, at the moment of convergence of Romantic philosophy and textual criticism, that is to say at the point of the

---

[54] Ibid., pp. 463–4.
[55] This is in line with Crouter's suggestion that we might want to read Dilthey's biographical interest in Schleiermacher as a reflection of Schleiermacher's own emphasis on the interaction of life and thought; Crouter, *Friedrich Schleiermacher*, ch. 1, 'Revisiting Dilthey on Schleiermacher and biography', pp. 21–38.
[56] Ibid., p. 465.   [57] Ibid., p. 466.
[58] The materials, according to their editor reasonably complete and not too fragmentary, can be found in the second half-volume of the edition of *Das Leben Schleiermachers* in *Gesammelte Schriften*, vol. 13.2, as 'Schleiermachers Übersetzung des Platon', pp. 37–75.

new philology around 1800. For Dilthey, philological-historical criticism in general was one of the main forces of modern scientific consciousness, a consciousness *representative* of the modern individual in search of reconstructing a historical world from scientifically sound sources. Not only does he put Schleiermacher in line with Friedrich August Wolf and his textual approach to Homer, and the Brothers Grimm with their ambitious German philology, but more importantly he again commends Schleiermacher for beginning to realize a type of modern *Wissenschaft* that culminates in Dilthey's own methodology of *Geistesgeschichte*. He praises him for a 'combination of philological criticism, artistic spirit, and systematic philosophical thought' (*Verbindung von philologischer Kritik, künstlerischem Geist und systematischem, philologischen Denken*) that leads to a 'conscious-artistic treatment of interpretation as the hermeneutic task' (*bewusst-kunstmässige Behandlung der Interpretation als der hermeneutischen Aufgabe*).[59]

If Dilthey contextualizes Schleiermacher within a German idealism that unfolded in poetry, philosophy, and literature, then the Plato he imagines emerging in Schleiermacher's work belongs, in turn, to a generation with similar characteristics. Unlike Wolf's Homer, whose edition came at a time of great poetry (namely in the age of Goethe), Schleiermacher's Plato stands, for Dilthey, for a flourishing of philosophy and epistemology in the wake of great poetry. And just like Schleiermacher's generation, the generation of Plato, with Plato as its prime representative, is again one of the philosophical artist and of a reflexive and scientific attitude inspired by artistic form: 'Plato is not only a philosopher, but also the greatest prose artist of antiquity. The age of Schleiermacher was particularly conditioned to grasp that unity of philosopher and artist. The emergence (*Ausbildung*) of German artistic prose was followed by reflection on its artistic form; Friedrich Schlegel and Novalis had used *Wilhelm Meister* to formulate their initial insights.'[60] In other words, Schleiermacher himself, like Plato (and like Dilthey), is the necessary *wissenschaftliche* (and quite Hegelian-sounding) 'Vollendung' of a poetic age.

Dilthey emphasizes Schleiermacher's attention to the overall structures of Plato's thought, rather than the meaning of individual dialogues, in terms of their 'inner form' (*innere Form*). Both consider Plato a thinker whose thought develops organically and unfolds dialectically in the artistic form of the dialogue. But Dilthey also matches what he identifies as one of Schleiermacher's main contributions with his own working method. At the

[59] Dilthey, *Leben Schleiermachers*, 13.2, p. 38.   [60] Ibid., p. 42.

end of his drafts on Schleiermacher's Plato project he lays out his own attempt to find the 'inner form' of the Plato project as it developed between the two friends and was later continued by Schleiermacher alone. To this end, his main sources are mostly unpublished documents such as letters and diaries, which were given to him by Schleiermacher's family, with whom he had cooperated before on an edition of the theologian's letters.

Dilthey thus justifies his method as both intensely philological and intensely personal, just as Justi did in painstakingly reliving Winckelmann's reading experience and, incidentally, Bratuschek did in comprehensively drawing together all of Boeckh's scripts and performances into a publishable version of the *Encyklopädie* lectures:

> Hardly less important than the letters appear to be diaries and unpublished materials. It is regrettable that what we have preserved of Friedrich Schlegel and Novalis's work in this regard has been published without a fuller examination of its genesis. I hope that the unspeakably labour-intensive and exhausting work of going through Schleiermacher's papers several times has allowed me to discover their true timeline. In the *Denkmale* I have presented them in their chronological order and in their essential content.[61]

Dilthey underlines the extensiveness of the source material and the degree of personal knowledge and contact this has enabled: the material, which stretched 'as far as the most confidential letters' (*bis in die vertraulichsten Briefblätter*), is 'so comprehensive and well-ordered as hardly any other available for a life's history' (*so umfassend und wohlgeordnet, wie wohl kaum eines zu einer anderen Lebensgeschichte vorliegt*). He sums up: 'And thus I dare to hope that I have reached truly objective insight (*So darf ich hoffen, eine wahrhaft objective Einsicht gewonnen zu haben*).'[62] At the same time, Dilthey projects an image of himself as a counterpart, or rather as a student, a successor to the scientific yet personal engagement which Schleiermacher, like a new Plato, had encouraged in his own disciples and readership. This makes re-experience and recovery of the inner form, achieved through personal encounter as well as laborious, painstaking philological effort, the essence of the scholarly task.

Dilthey's objectivity is compatible, even interdependent with a personal, subjective aspect. In the preface to an unnamed systematic work that is included with the draft materials Dilthey recalls his own experience apropos his work on Schleiermacher:

[61] Ibid., p. xliv.   [62] Ibid., pp. xliii–xliv; see also Lessing, 'Dilthey als Historiker', p. 124.

An irresistible pull had driven this youth, as if towards Plato, towards this most ideal personality of contemporary philosophy (*Ein unwiderstehlicher Zug hatte schon den Jüngling wie zu Platon zu dieser idealsten Persönlichkeit der neueren Philosophie hingetrieben*). [...] I noticed that this rich, great personality related to abstract concepts and truths in a way completely different from other modern philosophers, comparable only to the behaviour of some poets, Wilhelm v. Humboldt, and the Historical School; he did not leave to us the totality of his character (*die Totalität seines Wesens*) as something incidental, but instead he recognized intelligence in its living relationship to that totality.[63]

Wissenschaft and feeling coexist in the Platonic scene. Putting forward, like Schleiermacher, a vision of Platonic dialogue as arising 'out of life and out of conversation' (*aus dem Leben und dem mündlichen Gespräch*),[64] and only truly understandable through re-experiencing the sequence of learning, Dilthey projects a Plato whose own hermeneutic demands – appealing to intellectual rigor, universal validity, and aesthetic experience – can be perfectly captured by the kind of *Geistesgeschichte* Dilthey himself promotes. Its aim is the formation of a modern individual ideally poised to understand the sequence of dialogues, complemented in a sequence of individual interpreters that reaches from Plato to the present.

Dilthey is very clear in his draft materials for the biography that this modern scientific and empathetic method is exemplified by Schleiermacher but holds at the same time as a general model for the persona of the *Wissenschaftler*. Again, in the generation of Herder, Lessing, and Goethe lie the seeds of such scientific productivity. In a draft to the introduction of the section on Schleiermacher's Plato translation, Dilthey argues:

Aesthetic sensibility became scientifically productive in them (*Das ästhetische Vermögen wurde in ihnen wissenschaftlich produktiv*). And how could this method of seeing not separate itself from artistic production and make figures appear in whom their poetic ability was surpassed by new tasks? This turn was most noticeable in the understanding of literature, its criticism, and the history of art, in Winckelmann, Friedrich August Wolf, and others. The most intimate fusion (*am innigsten durchdringen sich*) of artistic skill and scientific task happened in the translations that incorporated Homer, Shakespeare, and Cervantes into German literature, allowing us to gain an overview of world literature. A next step was to advance to a historical understanding of these phenomena by way of a congenial imagination. Here, the re-experiencing of forms led the way, an empathy

---

[63] Dilthey, *Gesammelte Schriften*, vol. 14: *Leben Schleiermachers. Zweiter Band: Schleiermachers System als Philosophie und Theologie*, p. 32.
[64] Dilthey, *Leben Schleiermachers*, p. 50.

based on putting one's inner self into another time, place, and mood (*das Nachfühlen der Formen, das getragen war von einem inneren Sichversetzen in Zeit, Ort, Seelenverfassung*).[65]

This is not so far from Schelling's definition of the philologist, which Dilthey quotes in another draft, and which his former teacher Boeckh had also referenced in his *Encyklopädie* lectures:

> To call the mere scholar of languages a philologist is a misnomer; the philologist stands at the highest level with the artist and the philosopher, or rather they both fuse in him (*vielmehr durchdringen sich beide in ihm*). His task is to reconstruct historically the works of art and of science, whose history he has to grasp and to represent in an act of vivid intuition (*lebendige Anschauung*).[66]

For Dilthey, Schleiermacher's contribution is not least to a genealogy of scholars and *Wissenschaftler*, of which he himself, with his historical method, is a current endpoint – maybe Dilthey's own indirect confirmation about the dream of autobiography as the most privileged form of access to the self. Dilthey's account, importantly, does not stop with Schleiermacher; the lineage he traces is one specifically involving classical philologists, whose discipline, by Dilthey's time, could claim the status of a *Geisteswissenschaft* par excellence. In Dilthey's terms:

> Just as Schleiermacher in his Heraclitus applied his own method to the arrangement of fragments, so did Boeckh, a pupil of both Wolf and Schleiermacher, apply the same method to Philolaos; and when Boeckh linked Schleiermacher's hermeneutic ideal with the general thoughts of Friedrich August Wolf's 'Darstellung der Altertumswissenschaft', he created his most influential lecture series at the University of Berlin, his *Enzyklopädie und Methodologie der philologischen Wissenschaften*. The impetus of those ideas then significantly shaped Dissen, the theoretician of the art of interpretation, Otfried Müller, and Welcker.[67]

The genealogy of *Geisteswissenschaft*, which Dilthey suggests in his biographical project, is one in which philology, and classical philology in particular turns out to play a prominent role. His own work in turn fed back

---

[65] Dilthey, *Gesammelte Schriften*, vol. 14, p. 62.
[66] Dilthey, *Gesammelte Schriften*, vol. 14, p. 45. The quotation is from Schelling's 'Vorlesungen über die Methode des akademischen Studiums' (1803), in M. Schröter (ed.), *Schellings Werke* (Munich: Beck, 1927), vol. iii, p. 246.
[67] Dilthey, *Gesammelte Schriften*, vol. 14, pp. 38–9.

into the discourse and hermeneutic expectations of classical philology, especially with regard to the biographical as a key to historical practice.

Georg Misch's *History of Autobiography* (1907)

In 1907, the philosopher and historian of philosophy Georg Misch, who was Dilthey's student and later editor and interpreter of some of his works, published the first volume of what would turn into a long-term project, *The History of Autobiography*. Misch, who had Jewish roots, spent the Second World War as a refugee scholar in the UK before he returned to Germany. His work was translated into English relatively quickly after the war, including some of his writings on the history of autobiography and on phenomenology and Heidegger in relation to Dilthey and the philosophy of life.[68]

The first volume of the *History*, a project which ultimately amounted to nearly four thousand pages and for which he is still known among historians of life writing, was devoted to antiquity. For Misch, we live and do research in an academic age of (auto)biography: 'The renewal of the *Geisteswissenschaften* in the nineteenth century', he says, 'also brought a specialization of the scientific interest in autobiography.'[69] For Misch, autobiography, *Selbstbiographie*, as much as biography is essentially a modern parameter and a modern method: it relies on a developed sense of self and on a quasi-Aristotelian tendency towards expressiveness or *Lebensäusserung*. It is a desire which describes a historical trajectory of the 'great spectacle of a continuous development of spirit or mind (*Geist*)', which Misch sees move from Egypt to the Ancient Near East, to Greece and Rome: and from there, in short, as the standard path of Western civilization.[70] For him, western history is about the development of individuality, and autobiographical writings are the sources used in tracing the 'sense of individuality (*Persönlichkeitsbewusstsein*) of western humankind'.[71] On this point

---

[68] The most contextual information regarding Misch, aside from an appreciation of his philosophical and historical work, is probably gathered in H. Weingarten (ed.), *Eine "andere" Hermeneutik. Georg Misch zum 70. Geburtstag. Festschrift aus dem Jahr 1948* (Bielefeld: transcript, 2005), a volume put together in 1948 yet not published for almost sixty years. One of Misch's students, who contributed to the volume, was the classicist Bruno Snell.

[69] G. Misch, *Geschichte der Autobiographie. Erster Band: Das Altertum* (Leipzig: Teubner, 1907), p. 4.

[70] Ibid., p. 66.

[71] Ibid., p. 5. On the topos that we can understand only what we produce ourselves, see Danneberg, 'Schleiermacher's Hermeneutik', p. 275, n. 75, with detailed reference to precedent in Schelling and Kant.

Misch explicitly quotes Dilthey: 'Autobiography is the highest and most instructive form in which we encounter an understanding of life.'[72]

In the heavily revised and expanded third edition of 1949 – Misch's monumental history of autobiography had at this point itself turned into a life's work – Misch extends his praise of autobiography as a tool of historical empathy and hence understanding to the usefulness of biography as its second-in-command. It is a mode that is properly situated in the realm of *Wissenschaft*:

> In remembering facts, the autobiographer experiences a spontaneous resur-gence of emotions and tendencies (*Gefühle und Strebungen*) that were part of the original experience (*die zu dem einstigen vollen Erlebnis gehörten*); the heterobiographer by contrast needs to bring a high degree of imagination and empathy (*Phantasie und Einfühlungsvermögen*) in order to offer a re-presentation of such feelings (*solche Regungen zu vergegenwärtigen*) stimu-lated by the telling of past events, in a way that is not artificial. After all, he who writes the history of his own life sees its totality before him and the meaning it contains.[73]

And yet, Misch's monumental study also reveals a tension: on the one hand, there is his insight that ancient biography is in many ways radically different from modern expectations of the biographical as a narrative unfolding of character development; on the other hand, there is his desire to see Greek writing as a highly developed stage of accounting for the individual self in the modern sense. The solution which he proposes to resolve this tension is to treat the genre of *bioi* as one whose roots lay in philosophy – and to stress Socrates and Plato as the figures who could guarantee that modern parameters of individuality and of the biographical remained applicable to ancient materials.[74] His tendentious argument runs

---

[72] 'Die Selbstbiographie ist die höchste und am meisten instruktive Form, in welcher uns das Verstehen des Lebens entgegentritt', Dilthey, *Der Aufbau der geschichtlichen Welt in den Geisteswissenschaften* (Berlin, 1910), p. 10. Misch had written his *Habilitation* under the supervision of Dilthey, who then also (not untypically for German academic filiation) later became his father-in-law. For a detailed yet succinct account of the impact of Dilthey on Misch, see M. Mezzanzanica, 'Die Lebenskategorien, das Problem der Individualität und die Logik des historischen Geschehens in der *Geschichte der Autobiographie* von Georg Misch, in *Dilthey-Jahrbuch für Philosophie und Geschichte der Geisteswissenschaften* 12 (1999–2000), 107–19; M. Jaeger, *Autobiographie und Geschichte: Wilhelm Dilthey, Georg Misch, Karl Löwith, Gottfried Benn, Alfred Döblin* (Stuttgart: Metzler, 1995), pp. 71–132.

[73] Misch, *Geschichte*, 3rd rev. ed. (Frankfurt am Main: Schulte-Bulmke, 1949), pp. 9–10.

[74] This is a strategy familiar since the late eighteenth century, and one which Misch would continue to share with some of his successors; see Momigliano, *Development of Greek Biography*, and T. Hägg, *The Art of Biography in Antiquity* (Cambridge University Press, 2012).

that while there is a wide range of ancient texts before the fourth century BC that contain narrative elements of the self and others, it is only with Socrates that the self becomes the centre of reflection and inquiry.

The Socratic example ostensibly puts a narrative of personal development and the reflective, examined life centre stage, linking the individual with the universal. The relation of the soul with a higher order of things is imagined as an ultimate moment of empathy and understanding writ large – in short, a historical hermeneutic based on lived experience is once again rediscovered and rewritten as a philosophical *eros*. Misch, too, homes in on a text such as Plato's *Symposium* as the basic expression of an individually representative, developmental 'history of the soul' (*Seelengeschichte*). More than that, he imagines such a lived experience, reflected in autobiographical-philosophical discourse, as an 'effect of love' (*Liebeseffekt*) in which rational thought is transcended in ongoing 'longing' (*Sehnsucht*) and the power of intuition.[75]

Another example shows even more strongly how Misch's insight into the difference of ancient biographical materials struggles with his overarching paradigm – even in the case of Plato and Socrates. This is the case of Plato's *Seventh Letter*, which is allotted a remarkable forty-four pages in the third, expanded edition of the *History*.[76] The authenticity of the letter, one of a good dozen transmitted in the Platonic corpus, has been and continues to be a bone of contention, though Misch is representative of his time when he treats its authenticity as a matter of (recent) contemporary academic consensus, even though not a unanimous one.[77] The letter is organized around Plato's ostensibly autobiographical account of his visits to the court of Dionysius II, tyrant of Syracuse, and his entanglement with political intrigue. Just as much, it is about his educational effort at making Dionysius a philosopher-king in behalf of his peer and rival Dion, who in turn becomes an important reference and friendship figure for Plato.[78] That we appear to be

---

[75] Misch, *Geschichte*, pp. 81–2.

[76] Misch, *Geschichte* (1949), pp. 114–58. That Misch should give so much room to Plato's letter indicates his continuing engagement with this particular author and the role of Plato as a central figure for intellectual history in classical scholarship.

[77] The consensus Misch speaks of is a question of majority opinion rather than absolute consensus, though; for an overview of the (mostly German) literature before the 1910s, see R. Hackforth, *The Authorship of the Platonic Epistles* (Manchester University Press, 1913), esp. pp. 84–131. Hackforth himself defends the authenticity of the Seventh Letter. The discussion is ongoing; see most recently, with a detailed survey of the debate, M. Burnyeat and M. Frede, *The Pseudo-Platonic Seventh Letter*, ed. D. Scott (Oxford University Press, 2015).

[78] The fact that Plutarch's *Dion* seemed to complement the letter by offering similar biographical materials only cemented the place of that epistle in the gallery of texts treated as essentially biographical in tone and content.

dealing here with a Plato drawn between the spheres of public, political life, and the intellectual world of the academy might well have given the text extra urgency for a scholarly readership preoccupied with the standing and role of the institutionalized academic, especially so in the immediate post-War period in Germany during which Misch added this long section. It brings into even greater focus how attractive and how enduring the figure of the (Platonic) philosopher seems to have been as a model of identification and projection for the modern scholar.

Misch himself is critically aware that the material cannot simply be used for a biography of the philosopher 'as some eminent classical scholars want it to be'.[79] He leaves open the question of authorship, and he is sceptical about what constitutes true 'biographical' or autobiographical elements:

> That Plato does not fashion himself as the philosopher the same way he fashions Dionysius as the tyrant and Dion as the ideal statesman may seem quite true to life (*lebenswahr*) to the modern reader, who considers himself closest to the reality of life when he sees a man in all his inconsistencies. But to approach this apologia with such a positivist understanding of realism means to misunderstand altogether its literary character and to sever its link with the realm of Platonic philosophy. Analysis shows that the material is deliberately shaped: just not out of the entirety of Plato's personality (*nicht aus dem Ganzen von Platos Persönlichkeit hinaus*), but instead in pieces, according to the stances he takes and the roles he plays. We are handed parts of an image of Plato, yet without the intellectual and spiritual bond that unites them. . . . All together this suggests to us that self-representation has a different function than the one we are familiar with: it does not include the autobiographical intention which to us gives a certain philosophical dignity to self-presentation, namely to understand life from life itself (*das Leben aus dem Leben selbst zu verstehen*).[80]

Misch wants the *Seventh Letter* to show a Plato whose complexity we can understand as a modern phenomenon, but he also readily acknowledges that the *Letter* does not fit his own, modern, categories as it ought to. He sees in the *Letter* material that seems disconnected and constructed with a clear agenda in mind yet no real 'spiritual link' or narrative-reflective cohesion. His diagnosis, though, is not that which might now be ours, namely that ancient biography has its own rationale that might explain and value what to us looks disjointed. Misch appears to come close enough to this position when he concludes that the gulf between ancient and modern biography is not one of degree, to be bridged by the Socratic or Platonic

---

[79] Misch, *Geschichte* (1949), p. 126.   [80] Ibid., pp. 157–8.

narrative of the self, but that instead it is one of quality and of a historically differentiated functionality. This conclusion would render the grand arc of the development of the biographical, self-reflective account of Misch and others an inappropriate parameter and so, instead, Misch's ultimate conclusion is that the claim of authenticity of the *Seventh Letter* must – unfortunately, that much he admits – be wrong.

The modern notion of (auto)biography as a hermeneutic method of the kind Misch imagines it to be thus turns out to be dominant enough to shape the data rather than let itself and its assumptions be worried by it. The modern expectations about individuality and its reflection in the biographical process override interpretation shaped solely by the textual record of antiquity. This is not so much because of an unreflected reliance on modern parameters or an unwillingness to acknowledge historical difference (quite the contrary in Misch's case), but rather because the imperative of biography as a developmentally coherent and self-reflective narrative had come to enjoy a particular central place within the method of philological interpretation as, itself, modern.

Misch was not the only one to struggle with the difficulty of giving an account of ancient lives that exposed the rifts between modern narrative expectations and ancient life-writing strategies and genres. His *History of Autobiography* belongs to a reorientation of works invested in the historical study of ancient biography that appeared close to the turn of the century, works that suggested a developmental story of biography as a genre, in which the Socratic-Platonic tradition held an important place but that also often ended up by sidelining a large amount of ancient biographical texts as comparatively deficient.

Ivo Bruns's *Das Literarische Porträt der Griechen im Fünften und Vierten Jahrhundert vor Christi Geburt* (1896) is a good example of both the centrality of representing individuals and of Platonic writing as significant in this respect. The preface makes clear that 'the plan for this book arose through examining particular instances of attaching importance to individuality in antiquity. Wherever such work put its starting point, it would be drawn back to the literary monuments of the Attic fifth and fourth century.'[81] While Thucydides' descriptions of historical characters is an important starting point for him, Bruns structures his volume around four categories of writers – historians, comedians, philosophers,

---

[81] Bruns, *Das Literarische Porträt*, p. v. The work is dedicated to Hermann Diels, the author of *Doxographi Graeci* (1879), itself a work that addressed the ancient biographical tradition in the historiography of philosophy.

and orators – across which the longest section by far is dedicated to Socrates and Plato (with significant spillage into the section on comedy, where he discusses Aristophanes' portrayal of Socrates in *Clouds*). Bruns's central argument in this long section is that Plato's artistic prose, with the literary strategies and complex narrative framing devices of the dialogues, is motivated by the insight (Plato's as much as Bruns's) that a purely historical account could not adequately and fully represent the personality of Socrates: 'At the root of this choice of [literary] form is the thought, a thought which Plato's later works will confirm, that a historical report is not at all able to represent the essence of a personality to perfection' (*das Wesen einer Persönlichkeit vollkommen wiederzugeben*).[82]

He returns to this argument with thorough cross-referencing a hundred pages later when he discusses in detail Plato's *Symposium* as the work in which Plato has achieved the perfect writerly distance from his subject. In this dialogue Socrates is presented as one, albeit important, participant integrated into a group, represented through the eyes of others who speak with emotional investment but, in terms of narrative frame and ventriloquizing, establish sufficient distance for Plato to make his portrayal efficient and truthful. Alcibiades's speech in particular is for Bruns paradigmatic of his argument that 'all those characterizations show time and again that they are based on one specific Platonic theory, which I have already formulated above. By this I mean the conviction that the language and forms of science (*Wissenschaft*) are not able to represent the essence of a human being exhaustively (*das Wesen eines Menschen erschöpfend wiederzugeben*).'[83]

Bruns here blurs the boundary between the theorizing attributed to Plato and his own reflections on the task, the potential, and the anxiously observed deficiency of *Wissenschaft* to account for the individual. He does so with particular vehemence when prompted by Alcibiades's autotelic, autoerotic, autobiographical speech that is a narrative of the self as much as of Socrates, and that feeds on the impossibility of achieving full knowledge.

If biographical writing expresses the challenge of understanding and representing fully the 'essence' of another individual (whatever such 'essence', which is not further qualified, consists in), then it is easy to see

---

[82] Bruns, *Das Literarische Porträt*, p. 212; the German term *vollkommen* indicates completeness as much as perfection.
[83] Ibid., p. 335.

how the discourse of biography as a historical and scientific tool can be
absorbed into the central assumptions of a philological hermeneutics.
But it also becomes evident that against the background of such methodological assumptions a good number of ancient biographical models
look at the least unfamiliar, if not outright problematic. This is particularly visible in the treatment of ancient 'academic' biographizing.
Here, we see a projection of post-Platonic proto-scholars at work, who
may fall short of his near-perfect reflective investment in individuality,
yet at the same time offer a space for considering the role of familiar,
necessary philological practices in a minor and more conflicted key.

One of Misch's 'eminent scholars who want [the *Seventh Letter*] to be
[authentic]' was Ulrich von Wilamowitz-Moellendorff, who offered his
own 500-page biography of Plato in 1919 (discussed in more detail in the
next chapter) and whom Misch might therefore have had very much in
mind when he devoted this long section to the *Letter* in the 1949 edition.
Wilamowitz reviewed Misch's *History* the same year it was published,
and he recognized and fully acknowledged Dilthey's influence on it.[84]
Following Misch, he, too, commented on the strand of scholarly-
scientific life writing of the Alexandrian kind – and he, even more
explicitly, finds it surprisingly wanting. His criticism, in fact, amounts
to the strongly worded and remarkably far-reaching claim that the
Greeks simply never understood real individualism:

> Learned or scholarly biography collects separate character traits, arranges
> them into categories, and makes no real effort to connect them into a whole
> (*Die gelehrte Biographie sammelt Einzelzüge, ordnet sie nach bestimmten
> Kategorien und versucht kaum ihre Zusammenfassung zur Einheit*). The
> school of Aristotle, which knows so well how to observe and classify plants
> and animals, attempts the same for human beings. It perceives the particu-
> lar, the character (it gave us the term itself), and traces them through an
> entire life as it is lived. But there is never enough attention to what is

[84] The review was published as 'Die Autobiographie im Altertum', in *Internationale Wochenschrift für Wissenschaft, Kunst und Technik* 1 (1907), reprinted in, and here quoted after, U. von Wilamowitz-Moellendorff, *Kleine Schriften*, vol. 6 (Berlin: Weidmann, 1972), pp. 120–7. In the scant literature on Wilamowitz and Dilthey, Wilamowitz is usually portrayed as entirely disconnected from the contemporary debate about the *Geisteswissenschaften* – unjustifiably so; see, for example, K. Oehler, 'Dilthey und die Klassische Philologie', in H. Flashar et al. (eds.), *Philologie und Hermeneutik im 19. Jahrhundert: Zur Geschichte und Methodologie der Geisteswissenschaften* (Göttingen: Vandenhoeck und Ruprecht, 1979), pp. 181–98 and, *contra*, M. Landfester, 'Ulrich von Wilamowitz-Moellendorff und die hermeneutische Tradition des 19. Jahrhunderts', in Flashar et al. (eds.), *Philologie*, pp. 156–80; similarly, W. Calder and S. Rugullis, 'Ulrich von Wilamowitz-Moellendorff on Wilhelm Dilthey: His letters to Georg Misch (1914–1928)', *Illinois Classical Studies*, 17/2 (1992), pp. 337–45.

individual. . . . Hellenistic scholarship knows how to see what is typical; but there is no progress in that. . . . We must not deny that Greeks have never truly understood how to understand and grasp a man, just as they have not been able to produce true historiography. The observer always remains aloof instead of putting himself into the place of another's soul (*wo er sich doch in die fremde Seele versetzen sollte*). Instead of understanding, he praises or criticizes. What is more, another man is always treated as something finished, or whole, never as something in the process of Becoming. Where is there ever an insight into the complexities and tensions that are part of a rich soul and that together make up its true individuality?[85]

For Wilamowitz, there are two exceptions to this rule: tragedy and Plato, for tragedy created 'entire human beings who let us experience how they became who they are' (*ganze Menschen, bei denen wir empfinden, wie sie so werden mussten*).[86] In his description of the Alexandrian scholars and their learned biographies, Wilamowitz reprises the anxiety over philological-historical one-sidedness, a specialization and particularism that leads to a lack of understanding an overall life. In the next chapter, I will detail how Wilamowitz's responses to the assumed challenges of 'capturing' individuality exemplify the dominance of the organic, individualizing, personifying rhetoric that arose out of a discourse of sentimental *Bildung* but maintained its hold on the professionalized, specialized, and disciplined world of scholarship.

---

[85] Wilamowitz, 'Autobiographie', pp. 123–4.   [86] Ibid., p. 124.

CHAPTER 6

The Life of the Centaur
Wilamowitz, Biography, Nietzsche

Scholarly Lives

Scholarly biography, scholarship on biography, and scholarship utilizing tropes of biographizing its object are ultimately all forms of commentary on the role and identity of the scholar. That this is a role potentially in contrast with that of the artist underlines the status of the biographer as both scholar and creative writer. As such, it contributes to exploring the same, often anxiously examined, relationship between scientific method and reason on the one side, and creativity, feeling, and intuition on the other. This chapter looks at both Ulrich von Wilamowitz-Moellendorff and Friedrich Nietzsche as proponents of making the biographical a key to modern scholarship, emphasizing the similarities of their concerns rather than their usually affirmed differences in the perception of philology's *status quo* and of their own scholarly selves.

In his 1976 Sather lectures on Greek biography, which remain in many ways a seminal guide to the genre of ancient biography, Arnaldo Momigliano pointed with characteristic attention to the historiography of his topic in a number of German works around 1900. This cluster, which signalled particular interest in the nature of *bioi* as a genre, he saw represented, for example, by the studies of Ivo Bruns, mentioned at the end of the previous chapter, Friedrich Leo's account of Greek and Roman biography *Die griechisch-römische Biographie nach ihrer literarischen Form* (1901), and also Georg Misch's *History*.[1] Momigliano does not indicate that, of the writers he groups together, both Bruns and Leo had a link to the University of Bonn as students of Bücheler and Usener. But he explicitly makes echoing room for the now familiar trope, dear to Usener among others, of seeking important precedent for modern scholarly and

[1] A. Momigliano, *The Development of Greek Biography*, chapter 1.

disciplinary practice in the work of the generation of Plato and Aristotle's students and the Alexandrian professional critics relating to them.

Momigliano engages closely with the question about the importance of an Aristotelian and Peripatetic model for the development of Hellenistic and ultimately Roman-era biographical writing, and while he seeks to modify and adjust it, he revisits what is essentially the argument of Friedrich Leo's work on the development of Greco-Roman biographical form. For Leo, the teleological thinking about character that distinguished the Peripatetic School was at the root of a subsequent forking into two 'traditions'. On the one hand, there was that of the Alexandrian grammarians and their part doxographical, part anecdotal compilations of lives and opinions of especially poets and philosophers, an attitude that later still gave Suetonius a grid of categories on which information could be variably distributed; on the other hand, there was what would become the narrative elaboration of a Plutarch who aimed at presenting the 'overall image of a personality'.[2]

Momigliano shrewdly discerns that Leo's Alexandrians, set on compilation, on classification, and on a 'scientific form that disregards beauty and rhetorical strategies of representation',[3] bear a touching or ironic resemblance to Leo's own present generation of scholars as workers in the vineyard of positivist history. Leo's Alexandrians could be students of a Mommsen-like Aristotle figure, who had left to them the details of data collecting that still needed completing, and Momigliano also invokes Usener's 1884 lecture on the organization of scientific work in the Academy and Peripatos (discussed earlier in Chapter 4), where Usener had made the parallels with current scholarly practice explicit.[4]

---

[2] F. Leo, *Die griechisch-römische Biographie nach ihrer literarischen Form* (Leipzig: Teubner, 1901) p. 187.

[3] Ibid., p. 178.

[4] 'There are enough indications that the early Peripatetics collected biographical material, wrote definite biographies, and generally stimulated what we call Alexandrian scholarship. But anyone who reads Leo's chapters on the Peripatos carefully will have to admit that Leo sees Aristotle as an ancient Mommsen urging his pupils to do what he had no time to do himself and creating the conditions for new branches of learning to develop', Momigliano, *The Development of Greek Biography*, p. 20. Aristotle himself became a focal point of classical and philosophical scholarship towards the end of the nineteenth century, including the complete edition project at Berlin under the direction of F. A. Trendelenburg, a Boeckh student and, incidentally, the initially planned dedicatee of the first volume of Dilthey's Schleiermacher biography; on Dilthey's dedication, see Lessing, 'Dilthey als Historiker', p. 128; on Aristotle, D. Thouard, 'Von Schleiermacher zu Trendelenburg. Die Voraussetzungen der Renaissance des Aristoteles im 19. Jahrhundert', in Baertschi and King (ed.), *Die modernen Väter*, pp. 303–28, together with the collected volumes D. Thouard (ed.), *Aristote au XIXe Siècle* (Villeneuve d'Ascq: Septentrion, 2004), and G. Hartung, C. G. King, and C. Rapp (eds.), *Aristotelian Studies in the 19th Century* (Berlin, New York: de Gruyter 2018). This is not the place to map out a more detailed

William Clark has suggested that the strong biographical focus was reflected in the practices of classical scholarship and translated into specific genres. He sees it exemplified in one of the standard models for a philological doctoral dissertation, a model that peaked in popularity in the mid-nineteenth century. This is the type of dissertation that takes a little-known writer and collates all the fragments, biographical sources, and testimonia of this author as fully as possible: a type that generated a veritable industry in prosopography as a qualifying disciplinary practice.[5] Clark links this suggestively, though all too briefly, with contemporary Romantic notions of authorship and individuality, but also with the cultivation of an institutionalized individualism that was tamed, cumulative, and collective. As such it was not unlike the ethos which Leo, too, suggests in his view of the scientific biographers of antiquity.[6]

One could, in addition, easily extend this mirroring of practices to the contemporary biographies of classical scholars that were framed in strikingly similar terms. Arnold Heeren's biography of C. G. Heyne (1813), Wilhelm Körte's account of F. A. Wolf (1833), and Hermann Köchly's biography of Gottfried Hermann (1874) are a representative cross-section. In each case they are explicitly based on a selection of personal documents as comprehensive as possible, either integrated into a narrative or added in long appendices. In each case, they are also described as having grown into their present shape through philological diligence. And in each case they are based on explicit and literal familiarity (all three are curated by sons-in-law, who were philologists in their own right).[7] Köchly's account of Hermann is a good case in point: grown out of a *Gedenkrede*, a memorial, extended to a one-hundred-page biographical narrative, there are an additional one hundred fifty pages of supporting documents, including letters, unpublished scholarly works, and notes, in fact not unlike the standard format of dissertation identified by Clark. The *Biographisches Jahrbuch für Alterthumskunde*, founded in 1879 by Conrad Bursian, began as an addition to the annual *Jahresbericht über die Fortschritte der klassischen Altertumswissenschaft* and it published obituaries.

If this is an example of the translation between scholarly labour, ancient models, and contemporary cultural expectations, Leo's typology of ancient

comparison between him and Plato as figures of and for the classical scholar, including their respective biographical traditions, but such comparison deserves fuller examination.
[5] Clark, *Academic Charisma*, p. 227.   [6] Clark, *Academic Charisma*, pp. 210–11.
[7] A good discussion of the genre and its heroic features is found in M. Espagne, 'De Heyne à Lachmann. Biographies héroïques de philologues allemands', in C. König and D. Thouard (eds.), *La philologie au present: pour Jean Bollack* (Villeneuve d'Ascq: Septentrion, 2010), pp. 127–39.

biographical writers plays equally on the trope of how to calibrate the relationship between scientific and artistic aspects of the scholarly task. He divides biographical traditions into the scientific, no-frills accounts of the grammarians versus the extended narrative of Plutarch's *Lives* where aesthetic effect is one of the chief structuring principles. This distinction pits *Wissenschaft* against art (*Kunst*), and the scholar (*Wissenschaftler*) against the writer (*Schriftsteller*), offering a frame to articulate some of the anxieties over scholarly biography as a genre between science and literature.

A look at the fate of Plutarch in the nineteenth century will show that both the compilatory works of the Alexandrians and Plutarch's narrative, in the end, were found equally lacking when they were measured against the parameter of understanding individuality. A case in point is the trajectory of scholarship on Plutarch during the nineteenth century, which is marked by the relative disappearance of Plutarch as a prominent reference point and his continued use as mostly a historical and linguistic source only.[8] Again, it is Plato who takes over the position of prime pedagogical model and of being the canonical writer who can most appropriately encourage reflection and suggest moral precepts for the developing self. A writer like Plutarch became simply too wide-ranging to match the kind of focused, narrative organicism that shaped the neo-humanist outlook and its translation into disciplinary priorities. For sure, Plutarch was the biographer *par excellence*, but his narratives were not those of a modern character with an emphasis on development and *Bildung*. They were not considered unified in the way of the Socratic 'examined life' or the path of dialectic that could be attributed to the Platonic dialogues. Nor did they sit easily with the aim to achieve 'knowledge of ancient mankind itself, a knowledge that arises from the study of the remains of antiquity and the observation of an organically developed, meaningful national Bildung', as F. A. Wolf formulated the highest objective for his *Altertumswissenschaft*.[9] That alone need not have excluded Plutarch: Amyot had stressed in his early modern translation of Plutarch, as did Aristotle in the *Nicomachean Ethics*, that for a life to have unity it needed to be whole in terms of the narrative.[10] What changed was the assumption

---

[8] For a more detailed account of the historiography of Plutarchan scholarship, including Wilamowitz's role in it, see C. Güthenke, 'After Exemplarity. A Map of Plutarchan Scholarship', in P. Mack and J. North (eds), in *The Afterlife of Plutarch*, *Bulletin of the Institute of Classical Studies Supplement* 137 (2018), pp. 191–203.

[9] F. A. Wolf, 'Darstellung der Alterthumswissenschaft', p. 893.

[10] For Amyot, see his preface 'Au lecteur' in his edition of Plutarch's *Vies parallèles* (Paris, 1559); for Aristotle's reference to a 'complete life' (*bios teleios*) as the basis of judging a life, *NE* 1.7.32.

that the work as a whole ought to mirror the same sense of unity (which, incidentally, is not meant here as an argument for or against the absolute structural unity of Plutarch's works).

Within a new, modern regimen, though, one that made any identitarian potential for reading Plutarch (or other texts) dependent on the balance between the organic and developmental coherence of the text and of its reader, such earlier models of reading must have provoked resistance, or at the very least created tensions. While the emphasis on the individual as a parameter of interpretation and on the biographical as a way of charting individuality *could* still have left room for Plutarch, the expectations about coherence and development shifted the focus and ultimately favoured investment in a writer like Plato and in a body of works such as his.

Wilamowitz's Plutarch

Wilamowitz's 'Plutarch as a Biographer', originally published in 1922, is an essay which seems to sum up the fate of Plutarch in the nineteenth century.[11] In its explicit statements and its unspoken assumptions it is extremely revealing, since it apparently rescues Plutarch from the charges levelled against him by the historians, insisting on his role as a biographer, but reconsidering it in a new light. *Pace* the 'historians' he collectively invokes here, Wilamowitz reminds the reader of the literary coherence and artistic structures of the *bios* as genre, which is emphatically far from being a historical chronology. Thus, Wilamowitz vindicates a Plutarch who is more systematic than he might at first appear. He also praises his essential 'Greekness' and broadly understood loyalty to the Romans as much as to an image of classicism and Hellenism that he, Plutarch, helped to create.[12]

At the same time, the short piece seems to be no less an exercise in damning with faint praise. Plutarch is 'Hellenic', that is to say he is 'more Hellenic than all the others [of his time]', such as Apollonius of Tyana, Nicomachus of Gerasa, Dio of Prusa, and Phrygian Epictetus, but he is not original.[13] He is better than Pausanias, but given Wilamowitz's dislike for Pausanias, this is not much of a compliment.[14] He is Platonic, but Platonic

---

[11] U. von Wilamowitz-Moellendorff, 'Plutarch als Biograph' (1922), in *Reden und Vorträge*, vol. ii (Berlin 1926), pp. 247–79; reprinted as 'Plutarch as Biographer', in B. Scardigli (ed.), *Essays on Plutarch's Lives* (Oxford University Press, 1995), pp. 47–74; page references are to the German version.

[12] Wilamowitz, 'Plutarch', p. 269.   [13] Ibid., p. 255.

[14] Most explicitly articulated in U. von Wilamowitz-Moellendorff, 'Die Thukydideslegende', *Hermes* 12 (1877), 326–67, esp. pp. 344–7; for a good account of Wilamowitz's influential hostility towards

in a practical, domesticated sense. He is *wissenschaftlich*, but he is also like a genial amateur, appreciated and upstanding, representing the values of diligence (*Tüchtigkeit*), education (*Bildung*), and enjoying a good reputation (*Ansehen*) and a certain material comfort (*Wohlstand*), the equivalent of someone who has gotten a good classical education and knows how to make the best of it. In sum, this is Plutarch as a bourgeois *Bildungsbürger*.

Wilamowitz makes the point that modern scholarship, namely the discipline arising out of the German neo-Humanist tradition that began with Winckelmann and Humboldt, shifted the focus decisively back from a Roman and Greco-Roman world to a Greek one.[15] This Greek world was classical or, at any rate, considered 'original', thus implying a return to the classical sources exemplified by Homer, tragedy, Plato, and Aristotle. In this context, a writer like Plutarch who is not only 'late' but also mixes Greek and Roman is easy to push aside for a new canon. Wilamowitz makes his judgments clear, stating expressly that others took over as models for the self-reflection of the discipline: 'The other half [of Plutarch's writing] inevitably had to fall into oblivion, not only because time produced new whole systems of philosophy, but also because we finally found our way back to Plato and Aristotle.'[16]

The essay falls into three sections: a biographical description of Plutarch himself and of his character as a writer; a genealogy of his genre of *bios* and comparison with other earlier, contemporary, and later kinds of ancient biographical writing; and a last, third part that is essentially about limitations. 'There is plenty to praise in him as a narrator and biographer', states Wilamowitz, 'even though it is precisely in his role as biographer that we feel most pressingly the narrow confines imposed in Hellenic biography.'[17] This last section states a grievance that Wilamowitz would express in other publications as well (for example, in the review of Misch's *History of Autobiography*, mentioned in the previous chapter), namely that Greek writing, with few exceptions, had not understood individuality properly speaking. The chief limitation of Greek biography, which it shares with much other Greek writing, was that it looked for the same 'human' across time and regardless of context and context-dependent values. This is not to say that Wilamowitz is presenting a relativist, post-humanistic approach

Pausanias, C. Habicht, *Pausanias' Guide to Ancient Greece* (Berkeley: University of California Press, 1985), pp. 165–75. R. Hirzel, *Plutarch* (Leipzig: Dieterich, 1912), p. 196, recognizes that Plutarch shares this delegation from once-popular writer to second-rank status with Pausanias and Xenophon, thanks to the dominance of an overcritical, somewhat limiting source criticism and historiography in the late nineteenth century.
[15] Wilamowitz, 'Plutarch', p. 248.   [16] Ibid., p. 248.   [17] Ibid., p. 273.

(and there is a certain amount of the pot calling the kettle black). Instead, what he chiefly misses is the familiar due emphasis given to character *development* – that is to say, a specific understanding of temporality and of narrative such as would distinguish a concept of individuality that is essentially modern, approved, and recognizable.

Plutarch, in Wilamowitz's judgment, draws characters well, which is what *bios* as a genre, again *pace* the historians, should be about: the well-rounded account of life as a coherent attitude. Moreover, much as he draws from the Peripatetics and from Aristotle, his Plutarch never condescends to simple labelling. And yet, and this is a grave fault in Wilamowitz's eyes, 'it never even occurred to him to describe [the characters'] actual becoming (*Werden*)'.[18] As discussed above, this is Wilamowitz's issue with a great deal of Greek literature. Despite flashes of insight into and expression of individuality in archaic poetry, and with the big exception of Greek tragedy and, despite himself, Plato, there is for him a clear lack of understanding individuality as personality in Greek writing.[19] In the Plutarch essay, Wilamowitz portrays Plato briefly as the philosopher who had the power and the talent of a poet to describe and to create the characters and individualities of men, but who sublimated them to the realm of forms (a point I will return to later).

Much as we probably think of Wilamowitz as an ardent defender of the Greekness and hence the special value of Greek writing, he presents us in the Plutarch essay with a genealogy of modern character description where a new freshness of character arrives only with the Macedonians (as a kind of overwhelming vital force), and with the rough (*knorrig*) nature of Roman personality.[20] He finishes his piece with a brief comparison between Plutarch and Tacitus as a portraitist of Roman character and closes what started as a piece ostensibly in defence of Plutarch as a biographical artist with the opinion that

> the outstanding artist will always maintain his superior status, but even historical scholarship will eventually change its judgment, and what it seeks in Plutarch is in any case only part of what can be found in him. Behind this remains the amiable citizen of Chaironeia, who continues to invite us into his hospitable home, where he will tell us many a thing about men and gods over some local Boeotian wine, and finally he will point to the lion, that faithful guardian over the earthly tomb of the old, immortal greatness of Greece.[21]

[18] Ibid., p. 274.
[19] Wilamowitz's review of Misch's *History*, with its discussion of ancient approaches to individuality, does not even mention Plutarch.
[20] Wilamowitz, 'Plutarch', p. 277. [21] Ibid., p. 278.

This is the familiar tag about Plutarch as a genial host and chatty raconteur, not without political and social savvy, but essentially a busy provincial writer of many different genres, with many fingers in many pies.[22] Wilamowitz suggests that the strict historicists might want to modify their extreme opinion, yet he places Plutarch firmly within a history of biography that relegates him, despite some initial promise, to the good, even though not the very or truly good.

Extending his map of biographical writing and Greek attitudes to individuality across time, Wilamowitz pinpoints the advent of real insight into individuality as inner development to the early Christian writers and especially Augustine. Wilamowitz's final point reveals the direction in which the essay had been tending all along, namely that traces of such modern, more inward-looking and developmental individuality may have existed in rudimentary form in the imperial period, even if they were not clearly articulated. The task of the modern scholar is to unearth those traces and make them explicit. This, as he says in his final, otherwise rather abrupt sentence, has been his own intention in a different publication altogether, one that featured a sketch of Aristides: 'In this field there remains much to be done, and to point this out was a main purpose of this sketch. In the meanwhile I have tried to develop this myself in the case of Aristides.'[23] And thus ends the piece.

The way Wilamowitz frames his essay, then, is by beginning with an indictment of historical criticism, or rather historicist zeal, and by finishing with a confident expression of belief that it is the discipline of philology itself that has the power to restore Plutarch to his proper place. As he puts it, while it was historical criticism that had done such damage to Plutarch as a historian, it is also *Wissenschaft* that 'heals the wounds which it has to inflict'.[24] Not least, though, it is Wilamowitz himself as the quasi-personification of *Wissenschaft* who sets about rescuing Plutarch, first by giving a biographical and coherent account of his (developing!) character as a biographer, and then by putting him within a larger genealogy of biographical writing. Wilamowitz puts himself centre-stage in such a way that at the end Plutarch is almost occluded in favour of Wilamowitz's own

---

[22] S. Goldhill, 'The Value of Greek. Why Save Plutarch?', in *Who Needs Greek? Contests in the Cultural History of Hellenism* (Cambridge 2002), pp. 246–93, treats the narrative of Plutarch's waning mostly in the British context. For the Victorian and Edwardian periods, he sees a similar ambivalence about the gentleman historian of an earlier period, expressed in disdain (from mild to strong) for Plutarch as the learned, though parochial country squire versus the urbane modern scientist and intellectual (representative quotations by Mahaffy and Barrow at p. 288).
[23] Wilamowitz, 'Plutarch', p. 279.   [24] Ibid., p. 249.

work on Aristides. To understand 'Plutarch as a Biographer', in fact, we hardly need Plutarch, but we certainly need Wilamowitz.

Wilamowitz's earlier short monograph *Antigonos von Karystos* (1881) is a good example of spelling out the demand for a modern biographer who still continues to grapple with integrating the templates of Alexandrian scholarly practice. Here, Wilamowitz takes the lead from Hermann Diels's edition and study of the *Doxographi Graeci* (1879) when he discusses programmatically some approaches to ancient biography and to the doxographical tradition, that is, the gathering of ancient authors' opinions (*doxae*), usually on philosophical or scientific topics. The compilations of biographical and of doxographical information often intersected. In his monograph, Wilamowitz uses the fourth-century BC compiler Antigonos as an example of such compilatory practice, but also as the justified object of biographical interest and of inquiry in his own right. Wilamowitz showcases his own programme that two approaches to ancient biographical and doxographical traditions are possible: either to take at random one ancient figure and follow the tradition of his or her 'legend', or to take one single source from the diverse primary materials and give as clear an image of that *persona* and figure as possible.

By choosing the latter approach, which in fact means directing the biographical-philological view towards the ancient biographer himself, Wilamowitz advocates greater historical realism as a goal to get closer to the figure of the ancient biographer. At the same time, Wilamowitz's ambiguity is palpable and it repeats the ambiguity vis-à-vis the Alexandrian scholars as 'coming after'. His Antigonos is an 'average' individual of his time (*typischer Durchschnittsmensch*), as he reflects retrospectively in an essay of 1913, unlike the 'true' individuality he sees emerge only rarely.[25] On the other hand, for Wilamowitz, the genre of *bioi* reflects a historical interest in leaders of spiritual and intellectual life more than in political leaders, and his Antigonos, likewise, is a researcher into past philosophers. Significantly, though, he emerges as both an artist and art writer in his own right, and a compiler much more interested in his philosopher's characters than their doctrines, in their humanity and their literary styles.[26] Wilamowitz's own scholarly attention to Antigonos displays the simultaneous resistance to ancient biographers as misapprehending

---

[25] U. von Wilamowitz-Moellendorff, *Sappho und Simonides: Untersuchungen über griechische Lyriker* (Berlin: Weidmannsche Buchhandlung, 1913) p. 7.

[26] Wilamowitz identifies his Antigonos, arguably, with a sculptor and with the author of a work *de arte sua* of the same name, mentioned in Pliny. For a detailed account of Wilamowitz's arguments, see R. Dorandi, 'Antigonos von Karystos (1881)', in W. M. Calder III, et al. (eds.), *Wilamowitz in*

individuality, and yet the almost self-lacerating engagement with their 'scientific' strategies and self-positioning as a genealogical template. He tries to unearth a drive for empathy and an instinctive longing for personal understanding that is sought out by proxy in the ancient authors.

'Platon der Mensch': Wilamowitz's *Platon* (1919)

The clearest reflection of this tension of art and science in the work of biography comes probably in Wilamowitz's biographical study of Plato. Here he puts Plato the individual centre stage, offers what is essentially a reflection of the identity of the modern scientist, and projects a Plato who is symptomatic of the tensions and expectations invested in biography as a tool of interpretation. Like Misch and others before him, Wilamowitz, too, attempts to establish Plato as the axis around which ancient biography can be made to fit a modern definition. Like Bruns's study of characterization and personality of 1895, the Plato book is dedicated to Hermann Diels in memory of their long scholarly friendship and to commemorate the creation of the Institute for *Altertumswissenschaft* in Berlin, which 'contains all the branches of science of antiquity in exemplary fashion' (vii). The book starts with an appeal to the unity of science, a belief that will be carried over into the biographical mode, too.

Wilamowitz's belief in Plato as a true and rare representative of individuality, the view he expressed in his review of Misch's *History*, was only intensified in his biography of the philosopher, the main aim of which was to show Plato 'the man' (*den Menschen*). The focus is explicitly not on philosophical content or the details and system of Plato's philosophy. It is on the 'thinker' (*Denker*), not the 'thought' (*Gedanken*), echoing the basic tenet of the hermeneutic task that understanding the author is prior to understanding the work. At the same time, the material we have at hand as scholars, the works and texts, are framed in analogy to the living being. There is a rhetorical sliding between Plato the man and his body of works as Wilamowitz extends his programme to reflect more generally on the task of the philologist:

> He is confronted, in the first instance, with the works, each of which is for him, as it is, something alive (*etwas Lebendiges*). This he aims to comprehend and to make comprehensible; from the literal meaning, of which each word is valuable, down to the letters and their sound, he wants to penetrate the

Greifswald: Akten der Tagung zum 150. Geburtstag Ulrich von Wilamowitz-Moellendorffs in Greifswald, 19.-22. Dezember 1998 (Hildesheim: Olms, 2000), pp. 586–604.

soul. For something that is alive has a soul. Behind the works stands the man who created them.[27]

Unlike the ancients' suggested aloofness, evident in what passes for their biographical writings, Wilamowitz's method is emphatically to 'see the poet, with whose soul I try to empathize' (*So sehe ich den Dichter, in dessen Seele ich mich einzufühlen versuche*).[28] Wilamowitz grudgingly acknowledges that Plato himself may still display a remarkable lack of belief in individuality (meaning in strongly individual psychological developments), though he then counters this insight by appeal to the 'strong feeling' that is evident in Plato's writings, 'because Plato himself had such a strongly individual soul' (*weil Platon selbst eine so stark individuelle Seele besass*).[29] In other words, and in spite of himself, Plato's own individuality cannot but break through, evidence for Wilamowitz that Plato's works are an expression of his life as someone continually growing and developing (*immer ein Werdender*). There emerges a Plato who is determined by the 'necessity to remain a teacher' (*Zwang, ein Lehrer zu bleiben*), while living in the hope 'to achieve more' (*mehr zu erreichen*), and who is continually returned to as a point of reflection on the contemporary scholar and his challenges.[30] In quite obvious ways, this is then also a Plato who fits a late nineteenth- and early twentieth-century scheme of developmental biography. Here, the hero is seen to move through a sequence of *Lehrjahre* and *Wanderjahre* in the Goethean tradition of the *Bildungsroman*, including schooling, military service, and professional commitments – in fact, a *curriculum vitae* not far from Wilamowitz's own.[31]

The thirteenth chapter, 'A Happy Summer's Day', can stand as representative of Wilamowitz's approach, a chapter that treats the genesis of Plato's *Phaedrus*. Wilamowitz is much less invested than Schleiermacher was in singling out this dialogue as the foundational piece of Platonic dialectic, nor does he accept his chronology. Instead, the *Phaedrus* signals a moment of affective reorientation in Plato's genesis as a philosopher. Wilamowitz evokes a Plato who remains tangled in his desire for the life of a dramatist. He is marked, after completion of the *Republic*, by a state of simultaneous mental exhaustion (*Ermattung*) and liberation (*Befreiung*),

---

[27] Wilamowitz, *Platon*, p. 3–4.   [28] Ibid., p. 454.   [29] Ibid., p. 470.   [30] Ibid., p. 6–7.
[31] Margherita Isnardi Parente charts well the obvious projections of Wilamowitz's own biographical cornerstones onto a Plato who looks noticeably different from the earlier priorities of the historiography of philosophy; 'Rileggendo il *Platon* di Ulrich von Wilamowitz-Moellendorff', *Annali della Scuola Normale Superiore di Pisa*. Classe di Lettere e Filosofia, serie III, 3.1 (1973), pp. 147–67.

which provokes the cathartic composition of a new dialogue: 'it was another of those fortunate moments when all that was contained in his soul rushed together as one, into a feeling as much as knowledge. He had to write so as to get it off his soul and in this way a new work came to be, right after the *Republic*', a work characterized by 'happiness, contentment, satisfaction'.[32] This Plato is a philosopher who has committed to scientific scholarship, *Wissenschaft*, and its pedagogy, but is not able yet to shed the experience of poetry, abandoning himself to its pleasure.

In a remarkable act of ventriloquism, Plato's writing of the *Phaedrus* for the sake of his own enjoyment is likened to the actions of the young Athenian girls who grow short-lived flowers for the festival of Adonis:

> Writing is the game that refreshes him. Even if it held only as much value and was as transient as the flowers girls grow in potsherds for the festival of Adonis, so that they stand in full bloom for the one day, only to wilt when Adonis is fated to die. He sows the fertile seed in the souls of his disciples; but the lovely bright little flowers of his poetry he grows only for his own pleasure. He cannot help himself; by denouncing poetry in the voice of the poet he admits to this.[33]

Wilamowitz deliberately takes up the imagery of seeds and of Adonis's festival used by Plato in the *Phaedrus*, but he turns the image in on Plato himself in order to give substance to a new narrative of seduction and renunciation of the creative impulse in the face of scientific duty and dedication. And yet, he does this in the same section in which he inserts reflections on the role of *eros*/Eros in the academy/Academy: 'Eros lives next to the Muses in the Academy, and the soul of the pupil will let itself be led towards the True and Good most happily when the soul of the teacher is compelled by Eros'.[34] Incidentally, the pull of poetry, as stimulated by *eros*, remains in focus when Wilamowitz right here uses the opportunity to mention the collection of poems that were in some ancient sources attributed to Plato and transmitted in Byzantine manuscripts. Wilamowitz exerts some text-critical energy to suggest emendations that, to his mind, reflect better the sublimated appreciation of beauty and youth expressed in those short pieces. He had already evoked *eros* in an earlier section on the *Symposium*, where it was folded back into an additional and personal little narrative of disappointment and inaccessibility: 'For the biographer it is bitter that he cannot discern the erotic experiences of [Plato's] youth even from a distance, given that they must have been of the most passionate and

---

[32] Wilamowitz, *Platon*, p. 454.   [33] Ibid., p. 448.   [34] Ibid., p. 457.

most consequential kind.'[35] Wilamowitz registers doubt about the philosophical validity of Diotima's speech in the *Symposium*, but the speech nonetheless reflects, and thus gains value from, Plato's own experiences: 'The ladder of erotics contains within itself one of deepest expressions of Plato's inner life' (*Nun steckt aber doch in der Stufenleiter der Erotik eine der tiefsten Äusserungen Platons über sein eigenes Innenleben*).[36] Plato's own supposed generative feelings and experiences (the Diltheyan term *Erlebnis* is used) are contrasted with the insufficiency of the biographer to discern them, a sleight of hand that recasts the scholar in the light of his rejected longing.

The chapter that follows is appropriately entitled 'A Teacher Only' (*Nur noch Lehrer*). If his Plato is the figure of the *Wissenschaftler* overcoming the desire to be an artist, then Wilamowitz is, like his contemporaries, also responding to a familiar anecdote found in Diogenes Laertius (III.5). Here, Plato's first encounter with Socrates is suggested as the prompt that leads the younger aspiring dramatist to burn his tragedies and follow the philosopher instead. This is not only, in Diogenes, a conscious reprise of the powers of Socratic-pedagogic *eros* and its life-changing qualities. It becomes, in Wilamowitz's narrative, transposed to the autoerotic moment of composing the *Phaedrus* as the culminating moment of a now more substantial, long-lasting, and character-determining process of first acknowledging and then, ostensibly, also of solving this tension.

The foundational tension between science and feeling at the heart of *Wissenschaft* remains part of the narrative and biographical approach that Wilamowitz advocates. To understand the *Phaedrus*, as much as any of Plato's other works, scientific philological knowledge and training are required, precisely in order to comprehend personality and the personal:

> The main value and the main attraction (*Hauptreiz*) of the *Phaedrus* lies in the personal that speaks to us loudest here; the work is written with the least calculation about a readership. One ought to have entered into Platonic dialectics already; and if one has, then *Phaedrus* will be the closest we have instead of the best that Plato's disciples received from him: namely contact with the living man (*die Berührung mit dem lebendigen Menschen*).[37]

This 'living man' is marked by his desire for knowledge and *Wissenschaft*, and the expression of Wilamowitz's *Wissenschaft* is, in turn, to understand Plato's *Wissenschaft* as inseparable from his biography: 'It is my task to show this Plato and this philosophy. The path he takes and prescribes is

---

[35] Ibid., p. 385.   [36] Wilamowitz, *Platon*, ii, p. 174.   [37] Wilamowitz, *Platon*, p. 483.

that of strict science' (*Der Weg, den er geht und den er weist, ist die strenge Wissenschaft*).[38] The 'highest and ultimate' (*Allerletztes und Höchstes*) cannot be scientifically proven (*ist wissenschaftlich nicht beweisbar*), but it can be intuited through inner experience (*angeschaut durch inneres Erleben*), in a language that is in part Platonizing and in part recalling Dilthey.[39]

At the same time, the Plato whose development Wilamowitz so painstakingly outlines is the young man torn between the personal aspiration to become a poet and the insight of his vocation as a teacher and thinker, which ultimately forces him to renounce the life of the poet. In a fundamental way, we are left again with the triad of *Wissenschaft – Erlebnis – Dichtung* popularized by Dilthey, simultaneously as method and object of study. The method discovers itself completely in the material it is applied to. *Wissenschaft*, experience, and poetry merge as method and object of knowledge, yet without losing their mooring within the sphere of academic scholarship:

> Nobody will invest a good part of his life and his energy into a task of this kind if he did not love the man and his work; [. . .] The philologist is an interpreter, a translator, though not merely of words: he will not understand them fully unless he also understands the soul from which they spring. He has to be the interpreter of this soul, too. For that reason, because it proves its art in interpretation, biography is the true work of the philologist, raised to a higher level (*Denn weil sie ihre ganze Kunst im Interpretieren bewährt, ist die Biographie recht eigentlich Philologenarbeit, nur in höherer Potenz*).[40]

Platonic philosophy, the scholar's work, and the modern scholar's identity are thus all interdependent. As Wilamowitz puts his imperative at the end of the opening chapter of the Plato biography: 'If a work of art is a piece of life, viewed through a temperament, or better through an individual human soul, then the correct interpretation of a whole work of art must be the same, and even more so the correct interpretation of a whole human life. However much we strive for scientific objectivity, nothing can change this.'[41] Paradigmatically, Wilamowitz insists on the particularity of *Wissenschaft* as sharing in both the accountability of scientific method and the necessity for artistic energy. Paradigmatically, this plea is prompted by the work of biography.

That is not to say that Wilamowitz is simply or straightforwardly a narrative biographer. His Plato biography, together with his other works that advocate a focus on capturing the life of the individual, are notable for their opposing tendencies of containment and sprawl; of a clear

---

[38] Ibid., p. 1.   [39] Ibid., p. 1.   [40] Ibid., p. 4.   [41] Ibid., p. 9.

narrative line and an excessive assemblage of philological, historical, and text-critical discussions; and of character portrayal and simultaneous display of self-involved, scholarly microdiscussion.[42] The arrangement of the Plato book into two separate volumes, 'Life and Works' and 'Appendices and Text Criticism' (*Beilagen und Textkritik*), might be the clearest acknowledgement of this. The second volume, at a solid 450 pages matching the first volume, mostly adds further reflections and continued discussions of specific Platonic texts, paraphrases, and additional information, with only a short section on text-critical points, which makes it in fact quite hard to distinguish between the two volumes. At the same time Wilamowitz sets out clearly that all those further explanations require (*voraussetzen*) a representation of Plato's life first (*Darstellung des Lebens*), making interpretation conditional on the comprehension of the trajectory of individual character.

The same is true for his *Pindaros*, published in 1922. Equally ambitious and comprehensive in scope (it runs to 700 pages), it singles out Pindar, too, as a poet of genuine individuality. This time Wilamowitz combines within one volume large and at times disordered amounts of archaeological and historical information, text-critical, metrical, and stylistic analysis, and recapitulations of existing scholarship, with speculation about the personal experiences and events shaping Pindaric poetry.[43] The point is that Wilamowitz, while presenting a large and unwieldy collection of material on Pindar's poetry, holds on to framing his work in terms of biographical cohesion and a narrative of wholeness, even if the tendencies of the material may suggest differently.[44] It takes him over one hundred pages of contextualizing sixth- and fifth-century BC Boeotia and its local geographical and cultural character in order to arrive at a summary of Pindar's career, even though he signposts it as the central parameter:

> With the explanation [of Pythian X] begins the presentation of his life and it moves on from poem to poem. It cannot be different, for in the poems lies

---

[42] One of Wilamowitz's critics in Stefan George's circle (on whom more later), Edgar Salin, called the work 'a painful book in its mixture of uncommon learnedness and uncommon banality'; E. Salin, *Platon und die griechische Utopie* (Munich, 1921), p. 280.

[43] It is archaeological evidence in particular that to him seems to promise a new kind of access to the aristocratic, archaic world of Pindar. The book is dedicated to the archaeologist Adolf Furtwängler and signals a change from Wilamowitz's earlier and often critical comments on archaeology (for example, with regard to reading Homer).

[44] For one of the few considerations of Wilamowitz's Pindar book as a reflection of contemporary biographical interests as well as in relation to his Plato, see L. E. Rossi, 'Rileggendo due opere di Wilamowitz: *Pindaros* e *Griechische Verskunst*', *Annali della Scuola Normale Superiore di Pisa*. Classe di Lettere e Filosofia, serie III, 3.1 (1973), pp. 119–45.

everything included. To understand the poet we need to tread the path of *Wissenschaft*, step by step. An interpreter will need to rely on any external evidence available, but he must also demand that to follow him we must experience the poems themselves anew.[45]

Wilamowitz oscillates in *Pindaros* uneasily between ekphrastic, novelistic scenes of Pindar's family homestead or his wide-eyed walks through Athens, and a juxtaposed, compulsive repertoire of highly varied and often technical source materials. He is equally and awkwardly invested in the evocation of subjective moments and in the insistence on objective methods, that is, in the recognized practices of scientific research. His introduction frames his method by way of a personal recollection: 'Ever since I attempted to explain some of his poems to students, the task has remained before my soul to make this person emerge as a whole from the large number of mostly datable works.'[46] The German term for 'emerge' or more literally 'work out', *herausarbeiten*, indicates the scholarly and also pedagogical labour as much as the artist's or artisan's skill to work a human figure out of the raw material. The echoes of Pygmalion thus reverberate in the closing statement of the introduction: 'I wished to do justice to this Boeotian with the philologist's true love (*mit der rechten Philologenliebe*).'[47]

   It is easy enough to treat both Wilamowitz's *Platon* and his *Pindaros* as atypical works and to classify them as 'late', as the products of the retired, tired former figurehead of classical scholarship, nationally and internationally, who was disappointed by war and personal loss. Germany had lost World War I, which Wilamowitz had at first prominently advocated, and his son Tycho, himself a classicist, had been killed in action towards the end of the war. Wilamowitz himself hints at the resonances created by his protagonists, sometimes explicitly so. His Plato book, he readily admits, breaks with the conventions or expectations of scholarship on ancient philosophy. Instead, he insists, he offers it as a deeply personal work that reflects a life-time of reading and growing with Plato, written during the upheavals of the war and seen by Wilamowitz as both a form of consolation, an appeal for humanistic learning, and in fact his own contribution to the war effort.[48] His Pindar is in large part an aristocrat wilfully cultivating a conservative aesthetic, and loyal to his place of origin despite his various

---

[45] U. von Wilamowitz-Moellendorff, *Pindaros* (Berlin: Weidmann, 1922), p. 114.
[46] Ibid., pp. 10–11.   [47] Ibid., p. 11.
[48] Wilamowitz, *Platon*, p. 9. Wilamowitz's own political conservatism, especially in the context of World War I, is well attested. For the context of Wilamowitz's attitude and his implication in both nationalist fervour and internationalist disappointment, see R. Norton, 'Wilamowitz at War', *International Journal of the Classical Tradition* 15.1 (2008), 74–97.

appointments to foreign courts and polities. He is conscious of and con-
versant with the impulses of fifth-century modernity and the intellectual
ferment represented by Athens, and yet he champions an ethos on the
verge of disappearance.[49] Incidentally, Wilamowitz repeatedly chooses the
vocabulary of *Berufung* and *berufen* for Pindar's commissions, expressions
that also designate a vocation or 'calling'. In addition, those are the
technical terms for the appointment process of German academic posts.

Classical scholars, for all their lasting admiration of Wilamowitz, do not
put much store by his Plato book these days (or, for that matter, the one on
Pindar). But Wilamowitz had early detractors as well, among them maybe
most prominently Friedrich Gundolf, the scholar and writer who was close
to the circle around the poet Stefan George. Gundolf is reported to have
called Wilamowitz's book a 'Plato for maids' (*Platon für Dienstmädchen*),[50]
and the hostility of George and his circle to Wilamowitz is well attested
(George is said to have called him 'Wilamops').[51] So is their hostility to
Wissenschaft, as a discredited and stale rival to poetic forms of knowing and
being, in the context of George's own Hellenic idealizations.[52] In fact, it
may actually have been Wilamowitz's reading of Plato as primarily
a devoted scholar which struck a dissonant chord with George and his
followers rather than simply the classicist's standing as a representative of
institutionalized science.

George and his circle were heavily invested in a language of Platonic
erotic sociability, based on their readings and translations of the *Symposium*
and the *Phaedrus* in particular, a language and programme that aimed for
an elite community in aesthetic, social, and political terms. Taking this
into account, it is not hard to see that the prickliness vis-à-vis someone like
Wilamowitz may be an indicator of structural similarities and continuities,

---

[49] On Wilamowitz's Pindar as a reflection of his own standing, see also John Hamilton's insightful
discussion in *Soliciting Darkness: Pindar, Obscurity and the Classical Tradition* (Harvard, 2003), pp.
23–35.

[50] Reported by Karl Hildebrandt in *Erinnerungen an Stefan George und seinen Kreis* (Bonn: Bouvier,
1965), p. 55, n. 11. Hildebrandt himself, who also translated Plato's *Symposium*, attacked Wilamowitz
in an earlier essay, 'Hellas und Wilamowitz (zum Ethos der Tragödie)', *Jahrbuch für die geistige
Bewegung* 1 (1910), 64–117.

[51] George's moniker is reported in another volume of reminiscences, E. Salin, *Um Stefan George*
(Godesberg: Küpper 1948), p. 251.

[52] For the hostility to *Wissenschaft* in general, see, among others, F. Jolles, 'Die Entwicklung der
wissenschaftlichen Grundsätze des George-Kreises', *Etudes Germaniques* 22.3 (1967), pp. 346–58;
with detailed reference to *Wissenschaft* in the context of Plato, M. S. Lane, 'The Platonic Politics of
the George Circle: A Reconsideration', in M. S. Lane and M. A. Ruehl (eds.), *A Poet's Reich: Politics
and Culture in the George Circle* (Rochester, NY: Camden House), pp. 133–63. The most comprehensive study of George and his circle in English is R. Norton, *Secret Germany: Stefan George and His
Circle* (Ithaca, NY: Cornell University Press, 2002).

a narcissism of small differences that indicated separate ways over the status of rational *Wissenschaft* rather than marking an absolute and insurmountable contrast.[53] The development of political readings of Plato in the early twentieth century is a separate topic and one that far exceeds my present argument about Wilamowitz.[54] But when Melissa Lane characterizes George's 'Platonic politics' as one of 'education, legislation, love, self-cultivation, and self-abnegation before a leader',[55] then this sounds not too far from a Platonic politics that rings familiar for the concerns of an institutional academic setting.

'Personality': *Sappho und Simonides* (1913)

However much one wants to allow special pleading for the shape of Wilamowitz's *Platon* and his *Pindaros* as rather embarrassing outliers, the fact that we tend to read Wilamowitz's late works through an apologetic lens of biographical expectation ourselves (still treating Wilamowitz as *de facto* exemplary) is significant and misleading. It diverts attention from his insistence that his method of interpretation be considered a highly reflective expression of science, and it deflects from the continuities with his earlier work, with the structural expectations of classical scholarship, and with the contemporary hermeneutic issues reflected in them.

One such example is Wilamowitz's pre-war volume *Sappho und Simonides* (published 1913), a collection of contributions on Greek lyric poetry that is prominently prefaced with an essay entitled 'Personality'.[56] Here, too, we find the biographical mode explicitly and insistently harnessed to the essential task of understanding. As with Plato and Pindar, the volume includes highly varied, technical, specialist discussions at the same time as it prioritizes statements about 'personality' as the key to interpretation. Again, it also links the hermeneutic task of understanding individuality with the erotic energy released in classical scenes of instruction and

---

[53] Melissa Lane in her reconsideration of George's approach to Plato traces carefully just how long-standing the engagement with Plato by George and members of his circle was; among other things, she shows that Gundolf was initially led to an interest in Plato precisely through Wilamowitz's lectures, which he speaks of in positive terms; Lane, 'Platonic Politics', p. 137, with notes.

[54] On this topic see, for example, Lane, *Plato's Progeny*; A. Follak, *Der 'Aufblick zur Idee': Eine vergleichende Studie zur Platonischen Pädagogik bei F. Schleiermacher, P. Natorp, and W. Jaeger* (Göttingen: Vandenhoeckh & Ruprecht, 2005); Isnardi Parente also makes a case for Wilamowitz's portrayal of Plato looking ahead to the typical twentieth-century trope of the 'political man', 'Rileggendo il *Platon*', pp. 166–7.

[55] Lane, 'Platonic Politics', p. 150.

[56] U. von Wilamowitz-Moellendorff, 'Persönlichkeit', *Sappho und Simonides*, pp. 3–16.

comprehension, and also with the articulation of longing, loss, and non-reciprocated striving.

The pull between inclination and duty, between feeling and philology, and between satisfaction and insufficiency shapes the frame Wilamowitz suggests for his reflections on Greek lyric poetry. While new archaeological and papyrological finds encourage the interest of his 'heart', he argues, namely to attempt an extensive study of the biographical traditions of lyric poets, the duty of attending to the corpus project of the *Inscriptiones Graecae* (which Wilamowitz had been directing at the Berlin-Brandenburg Academy of Science since 1902) allows him only a one-off debt payment in the form of the present volume.[57] From the outset, then, he situates the focus on 'personality', deepened in his opening essay, within a frame of self-conscious insufficiency and of striving towards a larger whole. This, in turn, replicates the structures of understanding modelled on biography.

The essay reads in the first instance like an advocacy of historicism as the practical and expedient methodological stick, yet it holds out as a carrot and true reward the promise of glimpses into extraordinary characters and their personality expressed in poetry. 'The people of a foreign country appear to us at first as members of a species (*Gattungswesen*) of which we notice the differences that distinguish them from what is familiar to us. This is not so dissimilar to the people of a previous generation', he states, and to discern this commonality in difference is already evidence of true and modern historical comprehension (evolved from an earlier universal humanism of the likes of Rousseau, Gibbon, and Lessing). 'We value the knowledge of a single person as representative of his time', Wilamowitz's argument continues, 'especially because they do not stand out' (*dass er uns als Typus seiner Zeit dienen kann, gerade weil er persönlich nichts besonderes ist*).[58] Individuality and personality in the full meaning of the term, 'in contradistinction to the herd of people (*Herdenvolke*)', are different, and he tendentiously enlists here the voices and exempla of Carlyle, Goethe, and the Stoics as proof of this sentiment. This assumption then leaves modern professional and historicist scholarship, for all its achievements and virtues, in the permanently secondary, hamstrung position that most nineteenth-century commentators on the task of philology had already worried

[57] For Wilamowitz and the *Inscriptiones Graecae*, see Rebenich, 'Berlin und die antike Epigraphik', pp. 22–34; for the rhetoric of duty fulfillment, M. Hose, '"... und Pflicht geht vor Neigung". Ulrich von Wilamowitz-Moellendorff und das Leiden am Grossbetrieb der Wissenschaft', in Baertschi and King (eds.), *Die modernen Väter*, pp. 445–80.
[58] Wilamowitz, 'Persönlichkeit', p. 3.

about.[59] Wilamowitz, too, indulges the topos of insufficiency as counter-point to the aspiration towards comprehensive mastery of material, and while he is willing to acknowledge the advances of historical and material research, he also mocks the category mistake he claims to detect: 'Human beings means souls, and pots do not have souls.'[60]

Wilamowitz noticeably differentiates himself from earlier Romantic approaches to the organicism of culture: communal spirit is no longer the locus where individuality and organic wholeness can be detected. Instead, it signals the avoidance and elusiveness of individual greatness: 'We make do with generalities, we talk of the *Volksseele* and *Volkspoesie*, etc.; which we only do because the individual eludes us (*weil uns der Einzelne entgeht*), and even then the people only echoed the tone which a great individual sounded first.'[61] Our failure, he claims, is partly an effect of historical distance. His guarantor and exemplar for mapping historical distance onto the general epistemic inadequacy of comprehending an other individual is, again, none other than Plato: 'Even if all conditions are in place, if the overwhelming force of an individuality can impact us imme-diately, the goal of comprehending it in and of itself must remain out of reach (*ist . . . das Ziel, diese in ihrem eigensten zu fassen, unerreichbar*), if this individuality has deliberately hidden itself; this is the case with Plato.'[62] Once more, Plato is the ultimately elusive figure in his own right, but one whose dialogues in turn model the epistemological striving for full comprehension.

Wilamowitz is in fact thinking not only about Plato as the elusive authorial voice, and about the difficulty of cutting through the accretions and conflicting, mediating layers of the biographical traditions of anti-quity, but also about the scenes of understanding envisaged in the dialo-gues themselves. This is clear when, merely a few paragraphs later, he

---

[59] He also, more uncomfortably, pits personality against the collective, assuming a conflictual relation-ship that allows for the affirmative emergence of authoritarian individuality.

[60] Wilamowitz, 'Persönlichkeit', p. 5.

[61] Ibid., pp. 5–6. He will express the same sentiment in strikingly similar terms and even more explicitly in *Die Ilias und Homer* (1916): 'Man is an individual, even if the masses appear to be only members of a species (*Gattungswesen*). Creative, artistic man is so even more eminently. The Romantic viewpoint had utterly forgotten the man and the artist, the defining power of indivi-duality, when they justifiably drew attention to the power of national individuality and the soul of the people'; U. von Wilamowitz-Moellendorff, *Die Ilias und Homer* (Berlin: Weidmann, 1916), p. 21. It is in line with this approach that Wilamowitz comes down firmly on the side of those who identify Homer as a single poet whose extraordinary talent can be located in time and space. His Homer as poet of the *Ilias* dates to before 700 BC and comes from Smyrna; Wilamowitz, *Ilias*, ch. 18: 'The Iliad and Homeros', pp. 356–76.

[62] Wilamowitz, 'Persönlichkeit', p. 6.

frames a reflection on Roman characters in the following way: 'We simply cannot come close to their souls. We first begin to do that with Cato, as the first of all Romans, who still speaks to us. And we can do so with Scipio the Younger, for here we hear the voice of Polybius, who speaks with intimate knowledge of a trusted friend; here, too, Eros affirms himself as mediator between souls (*da hören wir Polybios, der aus der vetrauten Kenntnis eines verständnisvollen Freundes redet; und Eros bewährt sich auch hier als der Mittler zwischen den Seelen*).'[63] If not quite a non sequitur, this is an odd argument. The topos of Eros as mediator between souls may here owe more to Apuleius's myth of Cupid and Psyche, even if Apuleius's text is strongly oriented towards Platonic language, epistemology, and imagery. To mention Scipio with and through his mentor Polybius, though, also invokes the pedagogical relationship, which turns the erotic mediation back towards the Platonic precedent.

Wilamowitz follows this with an historical overview, to adjudicate on significant personalities among the ancient poets. Among them he positively mentions Homer, Hesiod, Archilochos, Solon (*qua* poet, not statesman), and certainly Pindar, who is characterised as 'the first person whose inner development we can chart'.[64] Significantly, Wilamowitz insists again that it is only modern scholarship, as a token of progress, that has made those developments visible. He adds apropos Pindar: 'Nothing is clearer evidence of this than his poems, but it is only we who detected it (*aber erst wir entnehmen das seinen Gedichten*); the ancient grammarians were content if they could date his victory odes.'[65]

Wilamowitz makes further remarks characteristic of the contemporary approach that was taken to ancient biographical writing, and one that would have a long tail in the continued study of ancient biographical traditions. Crucially, two claims are suggested: one, that the aim of studying an ancient biographical tradition is to come as close as possible to the biographee; secondly, that such a study is analogous to the work of textual criticism and its search for the 'real' text. The right way for him is exactly the same which textual criticism takes to get to the real text of a work, namely charting every step of transmission and building up the

---

[63] Ibid., p. 6.
[64] Ibid., p. 13. The case of Homer is complicated, given the ostensible lack of individual information in Homeric epic, compared to, for example, Hesiod. Wilamowitz works around this by suggesting that Homeric personality, parts of his 'soul', strategically dissolved into the collectivity of the Homerids (*hat er doch, indem er die Individualität einbüsste, dem ganzen Geschlechte der Homeriden von seiner Seele etwas mitgeteilt*), p. 9.
[65] Ibid., p. 12.

biographical strata of a text (rather than the imaginative leaps of conjecture when it is not based on intimate knowledge of all intervening steps). The biographical impulse is thus perfectly aligned with one of the core practices of classical scholarship, though it cleaves to an ostensibly self-evident modern template of developmental, linear, consistent biographical narrative. In turn, success or failure to identify a correct text reflects on and shapes the individual integrity – and integrity as an individual – of the classical scholar.

Wilamowitz sees the task of *Wissenschaft* fulfilled when the scholar can specify exactly how closely scholarship can approximate the *Person* in and of antiquity. What is left in order to cover the distance, what can serve as *Ersatz*, he leaves to 'the intuition of the historian, that is, to poetry' (*Mag dann die Intuition des Historikers, das ist die Poesie, versuchen Ersatz zu schaffen*).[66] This is a highly ambivalent conclusion, since the distance, if any, between the philological scholar and the *Historiker* is itself undecided, underlined by another appeal to Plato: 'Plato's science, too, fabricates myths where dialectic failed' (*Auch die Wissenschaft Platons dichtet Mythen, wo die Dialektik versagt*).[67] That he adds an exhortation to keep the boundary stones of the two realms as firm and clear as the philosopher may be drawing attention to the acknowledgment of proximity rather than to the successful policing of difference.

Sappho is the central exemplar of Wilamowitz, and her representative role for modelling comprehension of the individual is underlined by the dedication of the book to the memory of Friedrich Gottlob Welcker, who had taught at Göttingen and, for many decades, at Bonn, where Wilamowitz was a student. The way in which Wilamowitz articulates his memory, in the final lines of the essay on personality, bears out how integral the topos is of the pedagogical scene with its asymmetric relationship and its combination of admiration with unavailability: 'I did not meet him face to face in life; but he was already my teacher, pointing the way towards the soul of the Hellenes, when I walked behind his coffin.'[68] Welcker's *Sappho liberated from a ruling prejudice* (*Sappho von einem herrschenden Vorurtheil befreit*), published in 1816, had tried to defuse a perception of Sappho as sexually and morally tainted, and Wilamowitz, likewise, objects to this characterization. Unlike Welcker, though, he turns Sappho into a paradigmatic figure for the sublimation of erotic longing, reconfiguring all talk of *eros* and *philia* in Sappho's work as an expression of

---

[66] Ibid., p. 8.   [67] Ibid., p. 8.
[68] Ibid., p. 16. Welcker died in 1868, when Wilamowitz was twenty years old.

comprehending the soul of a fellow human being, and thus bringing her poetry and the study of her poetry in alignment with the task of classical scholarship itself.

Two examples show Wilamowitz's reading of Sappho as herself paradigmatic of the objectives, needs, and desires of scholarship as the attempt, threatened by one-sidedness and lack of reciprocity, to approach the person. One is his analysis of Sappho fr. 1, Ποικιλόθρον' ἀθάνατ' Ἀφρόδιτα, the prayer that begins 'Dapple-throned, immortal Aphrodite'; here the articulation of Sappho's *philotēs* (the term's meaning includes longing, affection, and sexual desire) and the imagined divine promise of a reciprocity of *philia* on the part of a girl becomes the quintessential expression of a communication of souls that he had just earlier described as the objective of understanding personality. This foregrounds a rather more chaste communion instead of relief from the damaging effects of *eros*: 'neatly and clearly, in the most explicit words, this expresses the content of Sappho's passionate, longing desire: the girl should be favourable to her, trust her teacher intimately, unlock her soul to her: *philia* should be between them (*das Mädchen soll ihr gut sein, der Lehrerin zutulich werden, ihr ihre Seele erschliessen: φιλία soll zwischen ihnen sein*).[69] That this is ostensibly the meaning of Sappho's desire is expanded on in the long discussion Wilamowitz offers about the ancient biographical and literary topos of Sappho's love for Phaon. Stripping the Phaon legend down to its bare bones, Wilamowitz seeks to identify its narrative core as one about idealizing, unrequited, and pure striving and desire, a desire that characterizes Sappho's erotic poetry and was therefore projected onto the Phaon story. He goes on to link Phaon structurally with related mythemes and figures such as those of Adonis, Phaeton, and Hippolytus: 'Phaeton, Phaon, and I even want to include Hippolytos here, may well help us to come close to the feelings of unrequited, unsatisfied love (*mögen uns wohl dazu verhelfen, den Gefühlen unbefriedigter Liebe nahezukommen*), out of which Sappho wrote her songs for girls. We need hardly say more: those who said that Sappho loved Phaeton felt in her poetry the expression of an always unsatisfied longing (*den Ausdruck ewig unbefriedigten Sehnens*).'[70] The comparison is to help the reader himself to 'come close' to the poet's desire of coming close, which characterizes her personality. Wilamowitz adds in a related piece that it is this paradigmatic expression of unfulfilled erotic longing that, in turn, earned her the title of the 'tenth Muse' in a short poem attributed to Plato (and which Wilamowitz seems to consider authentic).[71]

---

[69] Wilamowitz, *Sappho und Simonides*, p. 47.   [70] Ibid., pp. 39–40.   [71] Ibid., p. 75.

The inclusion of Hippolytus as a figure of comparison resonates with the recurrent fascination which he exerted on Wilamowitz and which is reflected in his work. It is a figure in whom the themes and structures of desirability, erotic longing, renunciation, rejection, and one-sidedness combine. The attention to Hippolytus as the proud, idealistic youth renouncing Aphrodite, whom Wilamowitz revisited consistently in his translations of and introductions to Euripides, his repeat teaching of the play, and in his memoir, has been read as a sign of Wilamowitz's 'profound affinity', a self-mirroring of his own 'loyalty' to the ideals of *Wissenschaft*, perseverance, and renunciation of aristocratic status.[72] Such psychologically (and to an extent hagiographically) oriented readings of Wilamowitz have a rather more difficult time accommodating the erotic aspects of the Hippolytus figure.[73] Just as importantly, they divert from the way in which the topos of erotic, sublimated desire for knowledge that reappears throughout Wilamowitz's scholarly works activates, and reaffirms, what are already available and well-rehearsed structural models for the complexities and challenges of a discipline of knowing antiquity. This is particularly clear when we see how the Hippolytus topos is pulled sideways or, literally, downwards into a long, extended footnote in the essay that opens Wilamowitz's well-known edition of and commentary on Euripides's *Herakles*. Both the initial publication of 1869 and the structurally refocused second edition of 1889 open with an introductory section on 'The Life of Euripides'. Here, for one thing, Wilamowitz explicitly reflects on the traditions, potential, and limitations of biographical writing. For lack of evidence, a developmental biography of an ancient Greek figure that could offer the same depth as, for comparison, that of Justi's *Winckelmann*, is in his view simply beyond reach. A more 'discursive' reflection, though, when compared, for example, to the achievement of Goethe's own Winckelmann essay, should be possible for Euripides, who for Wilamowitz is the second most suitable character for such treatment after Pindar.[74] And while Wilamowitz ostensibly defers any such Goethe-style account of Euripides, he returns to this thought experiment when he compares the growth and apex of creative and intellectual development in

---

[72] W. M. Calder III, 'Ulrich von Wilamowitz-Moellendorff: *Sospitator Euripidis*', *Greek, Roman, and Byzantine Studies* 27.4 (1986), 409–30, here p. 418, also quoting Friedrich Solmsen for the attraction and identification.

[73] W. M. Calder III, 'The Riddle of Wilamowitz's *Phaidrabild*', *Greek, Roman, and Byzantine Studies* 20.3 (1979), pp. 219–36.

[74] Wilamowitz, 'Das Leben des Euripides', in *Herakles*, vol. 1, pp. 1–2.

Euripides at the age of forty with, again, Goethe and, significantly, with Plato.[75]

Part of Wilamowitz's character portrayal of Euripides is the comparison and contrast between Socrates and Euripides as two, albeit different, 'new' Athenian thinkers. One is the sociable philosopher, proudly and provocatively valuing lack of knowledge, the other the more withdrawn defender of *Bildung* and detractor of *amathia*, even though both share, as a token of being at the height of their time, a preoccupation with understanding 'the human heart'. This, of course, reabsorbs them smoothly into the program and historiography of modern scholarly hermeneutics.[76] In this context, Wilamowitz triangulates both of them with Plato, which leads him to make the following claim: 'when we find in the Socratics, or rather in Plato, reflections on *eros* which sound strangely like Euripides, then it is plausible that Plato received from him insights that overlap with Socrates only in their shared objection to raw sensuality'.[77] The long footnote that accompanies this argument pins this influence down on the *Hippolytus*, of which Wilamowitz sees traces in the *Symposium* and the *Republic*, especially in its acknowledgement and development of the topos of Eros as tyrant.[78]

Wilamowitz's Plato thus effectively becomes Euripides's admiring student, re-enacting in Wilamowitz's description the core erotic and epistemological act of planting seeds in one's beloved, familiar from the *Phaedrus*. Plato understands fully what remained latent in the choral ode to Eros in the *Hippolytus*, regarding the deadly and pleasurable power of Eros: 'Plato gives us the explanation, because the seed flourished in his soul' (*Platon liefert die erklärung, weil der same in seiner seele aufgegangen ist*).[79]

Platonic *Wissenschaft* is, on this reading, taking an important lead not only from Socrates but also from Euripides, the stalwart of inner-directed *Bildung* and an authoritative voice on the powers of *eros*. It is fitting that Wilamowitz should point out twice, and both times apropos Hippolytus's description of Eros as tyrant, that there existed a cult altar to Eros in the Academy: in the long footnote just mentioned, and also, much later, in his Plato biography.[80] There, the theme deliberately echoes the beginning of chapter 2 of the biography, on Plato's Athens, that puts as an epigraph a quotation from the choral ode to Athens in Euripides's *Medea* (Med. 844–45). It is worth putting some pressure on

---

[75] Ibid., p. 18. Wilamowitz, in a gesture of assertive yet disingenuous modesty, calls his own contribution another biographical *genos*, little different from the Alexandrian type.
[76] Ibid., p. 24.   [77] Ibid.   [78] Euripides, *Hipp.*, 360–1.
[79] Wilamowitz, 'Das Leben des Euripides', p. 25, n. 44. The (lack of) capitalization is his.
[80] Ibid.; Wilamowitz, *Platon*, p. 361.

Wilamowitz's tendentious translation here: he suggests '*und der Wissenschaft schickt zum Geleiter sie Kunst/ und Anmut und Streben und Sehnen: da lernt/ das Höchste zu leisten der Mensch*' for the much more compressed Greek lines τᾷ Σοφίᾳ παρέδρους πέμπειν Ἔρωτας/ παντοίας ἀρετᾶς ξυνεργούς ('she sends the Erotes to Wisdom as her companions, co-workers for all kind of excellence').[81] The erotes sent by Aphrodite to Athens become 'art, grace, striving and longing', joined not to 'wisdom' (*sophia* here echoing in a more sinister way with Medea's own knowledge for which she is renowned) but to *Wissenschaft* and to the end of learning.

The erotic epistemological structure of knowing antiquity in analogy to knowing an individual, attractive personality remains intact in Wilamowitz's thought and writing. The ambiguity of someone like Alcibiades, though, attractive and attracted, rejecting and rejected, gives way in Wilamowitz's implicit and explicit reflections on such knowledge to the uncompromising and hostile renunciation of one kind of desire in the name of an idealized other. Wilamowitz may be invoking the biography and exemplarity of Winckelmann in an attempt to capture Euripides, but the emphasis has shifted to a new form of sublimation that foregrounds renunciation. Given the ambivalent attitudes towards Winckelmann as a scholar around 1900, this may, incidentally, suggest a renunciation of Winckelmann as a figure as much as it invokes, once more, renunciation as a precondition of disciplined scholarship.[82] The gesture of renunciation is an appropriate and necessary response that helps to calibrate the balance between academic duty and the raw pull towards 'feeling' and experiencing the personality and individuality of ancient authors. One of the most frequently quoted phrases of Wilamowitz, at least in the English-speaking world, is that of 'blood for the ghosts', from a lecture he gave in Oxford, in English, in 1908: 'The tradition is dead; our task is to revivify life that has passed away. We know that ghosts cannot speak until they have drunk blood; and the spirits which we invoke demand the blood of our hearts. We give it to them gladly; but if they then abide our question, something from us has entered into them; something alien, that must be cast out in the name of truth!'[83] Wilamowitz's *Herzblut* emphasizes the

[81] Wilamowitz, *Platon*, p. 13.

[82] For the lack of appreciation of Winckelmann as a scholar around 1900, see Sünderhauf, *Griechensehnsucht*.

[83] U. von Wilamowitz-Moellendorff, *Greek Historical Writing and Apollo, Two Lectures Delivered before the University of Oxford, June 3 and 4, 1908*, transl. Gilbert Murray (Oxford University Press, 1908), p. 25. Murray had Wilamowitz's aspirations pegged quite accurately when he speaks of his

heart's desire for proximity. It is usually only this first half of the statement that is widely quoted; but it equally and instantly provokes exhortation and the reactive need to pull back in the name of science.

'This Strange Centaur': Biography, Philology, and Nietzsche

For Wilamowitz, biography promised to be a key instrument of comprehending the individuality of antiquity as much as of integrating and justifying the practice of modern scholarship and its affective components. The 'life' in biography signifies both the quality of being alive and bringing to life, with all the affective implications of capturing that energy and of knowing a living whole; it also indexes the historicist imperative of capturing a life and all the traditions accruing around it, in all its details.

In the preface to the second edition of *Herakles*, in 1889, Wilamowitz speaks of 'the Hellenes, with whom and for whom I live' and of the goal of re-experiencing (*nachempfinden*) their sentiments and understanding of the gods. For him, 'religion' is again nothing other than an experiential form of both self-knowledge and knowing life.[84] Likewise, the opening affirmation of his *Geschichte der Philologie* (1921) is that the object of philological study is *Leben*: 'Greek and Roman culture in its essence and all expressions of its life' (*die griechisch-römische Kultur in ihrem Wesen und allen Äusserungen ihres Lebens*).[85] The task of philology, by extension, is

> to make this past life come alive again through the power of science (*jenes vergangene Leben durch die Kraft der Wissenschaft wieder lebendig zu machen*) . . . Here, as in all science, or to put it in Greek, in all philosophy, the beginning lies in wonder at that which is not understood (*das Verwundern über das Unverstandene*); the goal is the pure, enthusiastic intuition of understanding in its truth and beauty. And since the life whose comprehension we grapple with is a unity, our science too is a unity (*Weil das Leben, um dessen Verständnis wir ringen, eine Einheit ist, ist unsere Wissenschaft eine Einheit*).[86]

This praise of life and of biography as its narrative and methodological tool defaulted often enough to a philological and historicist manifestation of it, a thorn in the eye of Friedrich Nietzsche, who railed against 'our time habituated to the plague of biography' (*unsere an die biographische Seuche*

---

combination of 'historical insight and singular gift of imaginative sympathy with ancient Greece', *History of Ancient Greek Literature* (London: Heinemann, 1897), p. ix.
[84] Wilamowitz, *Herakles*, i, p. xvi.
[85] U. von Wilamowitz-Moellendorff, *Geschichte der Philologie*, p. 1.   [86] Ibid.

gewöhnte Zeit).[87] If one person more than anyone else had provoked Wilamowitz's outrage over the collapsing boundaries of science and art and of the inside and outside of the academy, it was his almost-contemporary Nietzsche.[88] And if there was someone blunter than anyone else about the risks of scholarly one-sidedness to lead to the un-lifelike life of 'narrow-hearted, frog-blooded micrologists' (*engherzige, froschblütige Mikrologen*), it was also Nietzsche.[89] But the ostensible contrast is instructive, and not self-evident, because it points to the underlying similarity of the challenges for the practice of philology, which both of them perceived. Both wrote at a time when the primacy of classical philology came under (some) strain through educational reform and, connected with it, through the rise and status of the natural sciences.[90] But the common ground goes beyond those contextual, external pressures, right to the core of how to translate into words and into scholarly practice the relationship between reasoning and experience when it comes to knowing an increasingly available yet equally elusive object.

The bulk of Nietzsche's own philological, disciplinary scholarship, before the publication of the *Birth of Tragedy* and before his decision to abandon the institutional world of studying antiquity altogether, was on ancient biographical materials, of just the kind that Wilamowitz had found

---

[87] F. Nietzsche, 'Die Philosophie im tragischen Zeitalter der Griechen', in G. Colli and M. Montinari (eds.), *Werke, Kritische Gesamtausgabe* III.2: Nachgelassene Schriften 1870–1873 (Berlin: de Gruyter, 1973), p. 312.

[88] For the controversy of the two philologists, especially apropos of Nietzsche's publication of *The Birth of Tragedy* and the ambiguous understanding of philology in the dispute, see L. Danneberg, 'Dissens, *ad-personam*-Invektiven und wissenschaftliches Ethos in der Philologie des 19. Jahrhunderts: Wilamowitz-Moellendorff *contra* Nietzsche', in R. Klausnitzer and C. Spoerhase (eds.), *Kontroversen in der Literaturtheorie / Literaturtheorie in der Kontroverse*, Bern, 2007, pp. 93–147; he makes a good case that the firm final distinction between 'art' (*Kunst*) and 'science' (*Wissenschaft*) was in place only by about 1900. The sources of the Nietzsche–Wilamowitz quarrel are collected in K. Gründer (ed.), *Der Streit um Nietzsches "Geburt der Tragödie": die Schriften von E. Rohde, R. Wagner, U. von Wilamowitz-Moellendorff*, Hildersheim, 1969. G. Ugolini, '"Philologus inter Philologos". Friedrich Nietzsche, die Klassische Philologie und die griechische Tragödie', *Philologus* 147 (2003), 316–42, makes a detailed argument for Nietzsche's thorough philological knowledge brought to the *Birth of Tragedy* even if not signposted in expected ways. On Nietzsche as a philologist, generally, C. Benne, *Nietzsche und die historisch-kritische Philologie*; J. I. Porter, *Nietzsche and the Philology of the Future* (Palo Alto, CA: Stanford University Press, 2000).

[89] From 'Autobiographisches aus den Jahren 1868/69', quoted in K. Westphalen, *Professor Unrat und seine Kollegen. Literarische Porträts des Philologen* (Bamberg: C. C. Buchner, 1986), p. 151. Of course, these philological invectives have in and of themselves a longer history. See P. Hummel, *Moeurs érudites: étude sur la micrologie littéraire (Allemagne, XVIe-XVIIIe siècles)* (Geneva: Droz, 2002).

[90] For the shifting demands on classical knowledge in the late nineteenth century and the pressures coming both from a top-down state level and the court of public and academic judgement, see, for example, Marchand, *Down from Olympus*; and the compressed but insightful editors' introduction to F. Nietzsche, *Anti-Education*, transl. D. Searls, ed. P. Reitter and C. Wellmon (New York: nyrb, 2016), pp. ivv–xxv.

so disappointingly lacking in a real sense of individuality (though he studied them regardless).[91] Nietzsche produced, in 1869 and 1870, three substantial publications on the sources of Diogenes Laertius, which together make up half of all his published philological writings. This is evidence that the concerns that arose from making the individual life a meaningful and representative category for the interpretation of antiquity could, when retrojected onto ancient materials, lay bare tensions that reached across the whole spectrum of classical scholarship. This spectrum included Nietzsche as much as Wilamowitz, who, following in good measure their own lead, we tend to cast as opposites rather than see as part of a shared scholarly world.[92]

Nietzsche's scholarship on Diogenes Laertius was built around a basic hypothesis: that Diogenes, writing his *Lives of the Philosophers* at the end of the third century CE, relied on the work of Diocles of Magnesia (whom Nietzsche dates to the late first century CE), of whose work he offered largely an *epitome*, supplemented with a few other sources as well as with Diogenes's own epigrams. Importantly, the hypothesis also included the notion that Diogenes's agenda was that of a *poet* who felt the need to construct a scholarly frame in which to embed his real focus, namely his poetic epigrams on a range of philosophers. It was this poetic agenda, in Nietzsche's opinion, that could be unpeeled as the true motivation for the narrative and analytical frame of the *Lives*. This recasting of the ancient biographer as someone motivated by the concerns of a poet and artist is not so far from Wilamowitz's own strategies in characterizing Antigonus of Karystos. Much as the ancient biographers in those two accounts are imagined to set different priorities, Nietzsche's early scholarship is a good reminder that there is a shared preoccupation with the biographical. At this point, where the ostensible extremes of classical work exemplified by Nietzsche and Wilamowitz intersect, the biographical serves a function in determining and reflecting on what classical scholars are meant to do, who they are, and what they are not.

If Socrates and Plato were held up as early paragons of individuality and, by extension, an (auto-)biographical account of the self, it is just as easy to

---

[91] For much of the following see J. Barnes, 'Nietzsche and Diogenes Laertius', *Nietzsche-Studien* 15 (1986), 16–40, with further references.

[92] Nietzsche's work on Diogenes Laertius, 'De Laertii Diogenis fontibus', 'Analecta Laertiana', and 'Beiträge zur Quellenkunde und Kritik des Laertius Diogenes', fill almost two hundred pages of his published philological work (the rest concerns his inaugural lecture on Homer; studies on Theognis and Greek lyric; and a textual study of the *certamen*, a text about the poetic competition between Homer and Hesiod); they are collected in Nietzsche, *Werke*, II.1: Philologische Schriften (1867–1873) (Berlin: de Gruyter, 1982).

draw attention to Nietzsche's extremely critical comments on both philosophers as forerunners not only of mock-enlightened modernity but also of a desiccated academy. Adam Lecznar has argued persuasively that Nietzsche in fact had a much more undecided early relationship with Plato and the Platonic account of striving for understanding, a relationship that was expressed most clearly in Nietzsche's immense admiration of the *Symposium* as 'an especially favoured piece of writing from antiquity' (*ein mir besonders liebes Werk des Alterthums*).[93] There is an argument, too, for Nietzsche's perceptive attention given to the figure of Alcibiades.[94] Alcibiades is an analogue to his imagination of a youthful Plato who, as reported by Diogenes Laertius, burns his tragedies as a passionate response to encountering Socrates. He is also the philosophical disciple who represents the sensual, passion-rooted follower who wilfully remains at a distance from the precepts of rational sublimation. Both Nietzsche, in the *Birth of Tragedy*, and Wilamowitz, in his Plato biography, evoke Plato's passionate book burning, both aware of the momentousness of a scene that signals passion as much as renunciation and sublimation.

In the *Birth of Tragedy*, Nietzsche is explicit about the importance of Plato's Alcibiades-like passion and the topical link with the *Symposium* to capture Socrates' elusive, non-affected erotic nature:

> The fact that he was condemned, not just to banishment but to death, is something that Socrates himself, with complete clarity and without the natural dread of death, seems to have accomplished; he went to his death with the same calm as he had shown when, according to Plato's account, he left the symposium as the last drinker in the grey of the dawn to begin a new day, while his sleeping companions remained behind, on the benches and on the ground, to dream of Socrates, the true eroticist. The dying Socrates became the new, hitherto unknown ideal of noble Greek youth; more than any of them, it was the typical Hellenic youth, Plato, who threw himself down before this image with all the passionate devotion of his enthusiastic soul.[95]

The allusion links the calm and imperturbability of the dying Socrates with the asymmetry of Socrates as *agalma*, which I suggest shows Nietzsche's

[93] A. Lecznar, 'Alcibiades in Love: Nietzsche, Plato and the Philosophy of Modernity', *Classical Receptions Journal* 9.4 (2017), pp. 447–69, here pp. 455–6; the reference is to Nietzsche's letters, *Briefwechsel*. I.4: Nachbericht zur ersten Abteilung: Briefe von und an Friedrich Nietzsche Oktober 1849–April 1869, eds. N. Miller and J. Salaquarda (Berlin: de Gruyter, 1993), p. 15.

[94] Nietzsche wrote an early essay, while still at school, entitled 'The relation between Alcibiades' speech and the other speeches of Plato's *Symposium*' (1863–64); Lecznar, 'Alcibiades in Love', pp. 455–8.

[95] F. Nietzsche, *The Birth of Tragedy and Other Writings*, ed. R. Geuss and R. Speirs (Cambridge University Press, 1999), p. 67; with Lecznar's commentary, pp. 464–5.

clear-sightedness about the link between the erotic longing of the Alcibiades figure and the epistemic *eros* directed at a dead and in this way also unavailable, non-reciprocating other. Lecznar is right to argue for Nietzsche's attachment to the *Symposium* as a dialogue that explores 'a form of desire that has become disconnected from (or that has perhaps never been able to connect with) a reciprocal human relationship', and for his attachment to Alcibiades as a key to addressing philosophy's treatment of reality, a turn modelled by Alcibiades's incursion into the orderly progress of the symposium, and his articulation of 'a desire that is not otherwise recoverable by rationalist philosophy'.[96]

Lecznar sees this, with clear evidence from Nietzsche, as a philosophical tension, but I submit that this is, just as pressingly, an expression of the tension that underpinned the practice, objectives, and self-perception of philology, which had, since the late eighteenth century, grappled with those paradoxes in strikingly similar terms. In fact, Nietzsche himself appears to suggest that the tension between ideal sublimation and the acknowledgement and difficult integration of reality is fundamental to philology. In his inaugural lecture at the University of Basel, on Homer and the Homeric Question, which leverages into a critical reflection on philology and the philologist, he calculatedly exposes the tradition of imagining the beautiful beloved humanity of antiquity by casting philology in the role of the part-human, part-animal centaur:

> The entire scientific-artistic movement of this strange Centaur (*die gesammte wissenschaftlich-künstlerische Bewegung dieses sonderbaren Centauren*) is directed, with incredible force but Cyclopean slowness, towards bridging the gulf between ideal antiquity – which may be nothing other than the most beautiful flower of Germanic love and longing for the South (*die schönste Blüthe germanischer Liebessehnsucht nach dem Süden*) – and real antiquity. In this way, classical philology strives for nothing other than the finite perfection of its true essence and character (*die endliche Vollendung ihres eigensten Wesens*), the true merging and becoming-one of its erstwhile hostile and violently brought together basic drives (*Grundtriebe*).[97]

The centaurs, in the mythographic tradition the descendants of Ixion, whose attempted, empty embrace of beautiful Hera Schlegel had invoked, make it impossible to forget the violence of erotic desire and the disavowals of sublimation. Philology as a centaur shows the incongruous, yet living and acting symbiosis of the drives of idealization and realism, aesthetics and historicism, *Bildung* and scientific drudgery, and the libidinal forces this composite, dangerous whole is formed by. With Chiron, tutor to many heroes, as one of the most famous centaurs, even pedagogy is implicated in this alternative vision. Winckelmann's beloved on the shore, Plato's disciples, Wilamowitz's Hippolytus, and Nietzsche's centaur: however subversive, they all affirm the expectation and the worry that what is desired is out of reach.

Epilogue
On Keeping a Distance

Scholarship creates its object. To give an account of scholarship is not just to produce a doxography or a successor narrative (*diadochē*), or to biographize. Instead, it is to show that the content and the aims of scholarship are permeable to the idiom in which it expresses itself, in which it enacts its possibilities, with which it interacts. The modelling of the self has been a part of the scholarly knowing of antiquity. In revisiting and analyzing how scholarship has confronted the distance from its object and attempted to imagine it, maybe the least we can do is to try to avoid some of its disavowals. This study has in effect turned a philological lens onto the philologist, engaging in the kind of double historicization that Sheldon Pollock has suggested *is* the task of philology.[1] Historicizing does not mean to remain in the past, though. What would it mean to nudge the idiomatic habits of classical scholarship, the 'metaphors we live by', onto slightly different terrain? If the persistent attachment to wholes has been keyed to the imagination of the human figure and to the affective comprehension of the individuality of an other being, out of reach yet furthering our own individuality, then there are several points where pressure could be put on those old familiar forms of relations and new forms of relations can be imagined: the human form, one-sidedness, distance, desire, and longing.

For Nietzsche the centaur in its grotesque appearance still exemplified the longing for the South. But the centaur also draws attention away from the human body, and the beautiful body at that, towards the less stable composite of human and animal. This is a reminder that the challenges of a post-human Classics, for example, are not merely about broadening the lens or changing the content of classical inquiry to include a more capacious understanding of nature or human–nature interactions. Instead,

---

[1] 'A double historicization is required, that of the philologist – and we philologists historicize ourselves as rarely as physicians heal themselves – no less than that of the text'; S. Pollock, 'Future Philology? The Fate of a Soft Science in a Hard World', *Critical Inquiry* 35 (2009), pp. 931–61, here p. 957.

those efforts are deeply entangled with structures of thought, disciplinary practices, and epistemological expectations within scholarly traditions with which a new focus on the post-human will have to contend. Likewise, Pygmalion is not evidently the only template for the trope of bringing an inanimate or lost figure back to life. What about automata, puppets, or machines? From the divine handmaidens and automata that are made to assist Hephaistos in the *Iliad*, to Pinocchio as the figure whose artifice and deceptiveness are an essential part of his liveliness, there is a wealth of figures made to come alive that could offer a new basis on which to consider the implications of the Pygmalion model and our imagination of the human form, as much as of the 'body' of antiquity.[2]

As for the scenes of instruction and the mechanisms of knowledge suggested by way of Plato's *Symposium*, are there ways to shift the balance and the imagination of one-sidedness? In the *Symposium*, and probably in the erotic social economy of pederastic love in classical Athens as well, a lingering sense of internal hierarchies and inequalities persists. Ostensible non-reciprocity is part of the role of the beloved, but the beloved also remains at a lower level of intensity than the active lover. The human figures that are part of the Platonic ladder may be indispensable, but they disappear from view for the philosopher at some stage. It is that same sublimation that made the Platonic imagery so suitable for the needs of a classical philology that operated with a contemporary vocabulary and with the twin discourses of science and sentimentalism. In bringing together those twin discourses, thinkers like Hamann and Schleiermacher had still kept an eye on the tragedy and comedy of Alcibiades as the lover tripped up by the misunderstanding of true *eros*, though with his own, autoerotic form of understanding. Fully institutionalized scholarship, however, may move closer and closer to aligning itself with the ideal, sublimating philosopher – though one caught in the position of self-distancing that characterizes the Platonic dialogue form.

Andrea Nightingale has argued that a good part of Plato's strategy within the dialogues is to create the impression that the speakers arrive at the practice of philosophy as an *a priori* concept, even though he actually invents

---

[2] On lifelike automata in Greek writing, see T. Power, 'Cyberchorus: Pindar's Κηληδόνες and the Aura of the Artificial', in L. Athanassaki and E. Bowie (eds), *Archaic and Classical Choral Song: Performance, Politics and Dissemination* (Berlin: de Gruyter, 2011), pp. 67–114. On the power of Pinocchio that derives precisely from creating a lifelike figure, the '"lie" of a secure design object' and the radical 'impossibility of knowing that what one makes will remain what one has made', see, for example, Gavin Steingo's discussion of the work of the contemporary Greek artist Kostas Velonis, 'Kostas Velonis' Pinocchio Effects', in E. Kountouri (ed.), *Kostis Velonis* (Athens: NEON/Skira, 2019), pp. 99–105.

philosophy as a genre *a posteriori*.[3] The reappropriation of a Platonic language
of *eros* by members of a discipline in the making may thus be a fitting
analogue to such an authority of the ostensibly self-evident. It may be
salutary, then, to resist the 'inevitability' of the Platonic model and instead
try to probe the paths offered, for example, in the figure of Alcibiades.
Victoria Wohl, discussing the two sympotic accounts of Xenophon and
Socrates, has contrasted what she calls the 'extromissive' logic of the
Platonic *eros* with the more 'intromissive' speculation suggested in
Xenophon. Where Platonic *eros* seeks to pull the subject towards
a transcendent goal to the point of solipsism, the reflections on *eros* articulated
in Xenophon essentially offer an account of mimesis. Here, the beloved as
a more active agent is not a stepping stone towards a higher abstraction but
instead forces us back towards engagement with a real other person. For
Wohl, the Alcibiades of Plato's *Symposium* actually exemplifies this intromissive logic, of granting greater agency to the beloved and of insisting on the
specificity of the other and our vulnerability to him or her. He also represents
the shifting emphasis from the upward and outward pull towards the inner
workings of what is present, not of what is absent. If nothing else, this is
a reminder of the tightrope walk between idealism and empiricism.[4] As we
saw, thinkers as different as Nietzsche and Nussbaum, for the aims of
philosophy, have already suggested such a readjustment of the figure of
Alcibiades. Given the efficacy of the Platonic scene of instruction for the self-
perception of a discipline, though, this is a matter for philological thinking as
much as for philosophy. Compared to Platonic accounts of knowledge and to
Platonic accounts of *eros*, authors like Xenophon or Plutarch seem to offer
a lesser frame, languishing in a 'secondary' category where they reflect the sun
by comparison. We could well ask, though, whether they do not also offer
new possibilities and tropes for reading, comprehending, and shaping the self.
Maybe it is time to read them again, with greater care for what they can say
constructively about knowing an other.

If the Platonic dialogues are marked by their self-distancing strategies, if
it is the point of Platonic philosophy that we do not hear Plato's 'voice', is
distance something that actually ought to be overcome? On the contrary.
The reflections that finish this study are intended to ask whether there are
ways instead to maintain distance without balancing it by a language of
longing for reunification, revitalization, or closeness.

[3] A. Nightingale, *Plato and the Construct of Philosophy* (Cambridge University Press, 1995).
[4] V. Wohl, 'The Eye of the Beloved: Opsis and Eros in Socratic Pedagogy', in Johnson and Tarrant,
Alcibiades and the Socratic Lover-Educator, pp. 45–60.

Forty years ago, the comparatist Peter Szondi in his *Introduction to Literary Hermeneutics* (which is still worth reading) highlighted a telling pattern. Trying to give an overview of the German hermeneutic tradition that was so closely connected with the development of philology as a discipline, he identifies two basic and never fully isolated tendencies of hermeneutics going back to antiquity. On the one hand there is what he calls the 'historical-grammatical', where we try to reconstruct a text or object as precisely as possible in its context; on the other hand there is the 'allegorical', where we dislodge part of it and extend and interrogate its meaning for the present time.[5] What Szondi does next is to invert our assumption about the relative distance those two approaches imply. For him, it is the historical-grammatical one that actually encourages a much more pronounced 'presencing' by trying to come as closely as possible to the 'original' in its most immediate state despite all the acknowledgements of the past's foreignness. The allegorical, by contrast, much more happily acknowledges and leaves in place a certain obscurity and an unresolved past, maintaining a sense of distance from the object as a whole.[6]

This is not to advocate a return to allegorical forms of readings above historical ones. Historicism as part of Classics is, one way or another, here to stay. Instead, it is about advocating for a form of reflection which is sensitive to history and recognizes that ostensibly 'distanced' reading strategies may have a greater tendency towards 'presencing' than strategies that seem *prima facie* less preoccupied with historical distance or historical context. But whatever kind of reading strategies are at stake, is it possible, finally, to rethink the affective charges those strategies carry in a move that unsettles the default position of desire and longing for a lost or even a newly found closeness? Can we not consider carefully calibrated forms of sustained suspension, a kind of detachment that is actually a no less active form of engaged attention?[7]

---

[5] P. Szondi, *Einführung in die literarische Hermeneutik* (Frankfurt am Main: Suhrkamp, 1975), pp. 21–3.

[6] In the advocacy of the 'powers of philology' and the 'acts of presencing' implied in it, one shouldn't overlook – or simply endorse – that the language of empathy (as a road to presence) has had a particularly functional place in Classics. For such an advocacy, see Gumbrecht, *The Powers of Philology*, and H. U. Gumbrecht, *The Production of Presence: What Meaning Cannot Convey* (Palo Alto, CA: Stanford University Press, 2004); for a critique, see I. Ziolkowski, 'Metaphilology', *The Journal of English and Germanic Philology* 104.2 (2005), pp. 239–72, and G. Harpham, 'Roots, Races and the Return to Philology', *Representations* 106 (2009), pp. 34–62.

[7] Amanda Anderson, in a punchy study on late nineteenth-century British writers and their ambiguous attitudes towards the cultivation of detachment in scientific, political, social, and cultural terms, has argued that such carefully scrutinized cultivation is quite the opposite of a more recent critique of detachment that equates it with a rather naïve belief in progress and critical distance, a form of

A good example might be found in the theoretical impulses of Roland Barthes. Classicists might read him most frequently for his work on the erotics of reading and the desire for the text. In a lecture course on 'the Neutral', Barthes approached the Neutral in the guise of twenty-three 'figures', not human figures but tropes and terms, many of them with affective meanings ranging from 'benevolence', 'weariness', and 'silence' to 'adjectives', 'anger', 'answer', 'retreat', or 'arrogance'.[8] All contain an element of the neutral in so far as they have a trace, a possibility of encounter with the neutral. Barthes describes the Neutral in and as a stance of shimmering, a fluctuation or 'twinkling' (*scintillations*), an oscillation that is not weakness, passivity, or indecision, but protestation. The Neutral is active, emphatic, and vivid, and in its lack of absoluteness it 'baffles' and 'outwits the paradigm', the need to choose one thing over and as defined against another. This is not indifference and certainly not a form of self-sovereign, bird's-eye aloofness. Instead, it is an intense form of suspension and attention. Above all, this is not distance as lack or distance as something that needs overcoming. It is the creation of a space in-between, an active engagement. If we think of the relation between the ancient and the here and now, it is not unlike the space in which the 'stranger', as the sociologist Georg Simmel described him a little more than a century ago, makes a habitat.[9] The distance that marks the stranger who has stopped wandering but maintains the potential to move again is one of meaningfulness, not passivity or lack of participation but a 'particular formation (*ein sonderbares Gebilde*) made from far-ness and closeness, *Gleichgültigkeit* and engagement'.[10] Simmel's German resists an easy, expected translation of *Gleichgültigkeit* as 'indifference', 'coolness', or 'dis-interestedness'; in its root meaning, it is the attaching of equal (*gleich*) value and validity (*gelten*; *Gültigkeit*) to things, an attitude in which opposing values can coincide. That they can do so without cancelling each other out may be the greatest challenge represented by the stranger. It is the challenge

---

critique she sees employed all too often and that she wants to overcome; A. Anderson, *The Powers of Distance. Cosmopolitanism and the Cultivation of Detachment* (Princeton University Press, 2001).

[8] R. Barthes, *The Neutral: Lecture Course at the Collège de France (1977–1978)*, edited and translated by R. Kraus and D. Hollier (New York: Columbia University Press, 2007). The book version is a collation of extant notes and notecards, complemented by recordings of Barthes' lectures.

[9] Originally published as 'Exkurs über den Fremden', in his *Soziologie: Untersuchungen über die Formen der Vergesellschaftung* (Berlin: Duncker & Humblot, 1908), pp. 509–12. Simmel himself struggled with academic acceptance, not only as a Jew, but also in terms of disciplinary belonging.

[10] Simmel, 'Exkurs', p. 510. In this short text, Simmel invokes the (Greek) *barbaros* as a similar placeholder; in addition, he treats as a parallel example of alienation and strangeness the realization that the beloved is not *per se* exceptional and singular.

of cultivating a kind of 'negative capability' in the scholar, to borrow Keats's famous expression, a willingness to sustain opposites, contradictions, and strangeness without wanting or striving to reduce them.

To imagine philology as the precarious, exclusive longing for a singular, embodied antiquity is not self-evident. There is room for alternative voices that push us not to take those epistemological structures of longing for granted, and they do not even need to be recent twentieth-century and twenty-first-century voices. Herder was certainly no stranger to the fantasy of closeness and intimacy with the past and the appeal of Pygmalion's erotic, revivifying touch. But in his *Kalligone* (1800), an essay on aesthetic theory that doubles as a critique of Kant, he offers a pedagogical scene of *Bildung* marked by presence and absence that is now familiar, but that veers off to make a case for an alternative orientation. Of a youth infatuated with the lectures of his philosophical (Kantian) teacher, he writes in his preface:

> Soon the youth discovered that, if he left himself to the gracefulness of the lecture, he would be surrounded by a fine, dialectical net in which he would stop thinking for himself. And thus he exhorted himself after each lesson to translate what he had heard into his own language and not to gaze after a favourite word (*Lieblingswort*) or turn of phrase of his teacher, but instead try even to avoid them. To this end he added to hearing the lectures the reading of acknowledged authors of old and recent times, with the same amount of care, and in this way he acquired, as he thought, the ability to live in the soul of each of these writers for some time as if in a house, and to use its furniture comfortably and usefully; which is also the ability to live in all periods and in the most diverse of mentalities, but at the same time to be able to move out and live on one's own. He was confirmed in this exercise especially by *Plato, Baco, Shaftesburi, Leibnitz* [sic]. And he never felt more free and more remote from his teacher's system than when he modestly honoured his wit and sharpness of mind. Young gives similar advice, namely to imitate the ancients following their own intention (*in ihrem Sinne nachzuahmen*) by distancing oneself from them.[11]

The capacity for empathy, 'to live in the soul of each of these writers for some time as if in a house', is as crucial as the ability 'to move out and live on one's own'. It is also a form of empathy that appears to be less hierarchical than the dialectic of closeness and of distance built on a notion of exclusivity, of focus on one other being only. The result may offer a form of commitment that does not conflate attentiveness with an absolute order of value.

---

[11] Herder, *Kalligone*, in *Werke, vol 8: Schriften zu Literatur und Philosophie 1792–1800*, ed. H. D. Irmscher (Frankfurt am Main: Deutscher Klassiker Verlag, 1998), pp. 641–964, here pp. 651–2.

Almost eighty years later, with classical philology firmly inscribed as the lead discipline for understanding the human, the classicist Jacob Bernays offered a refreshingly modified description of the philologist in a lecture series on the history of classical philology he gave at the University of Bonn in 1878. Under the heading 'The real definition of the word philology' he suggests, laconically, 'The word ph.[ilologist] means someone who enjoys matters of the mind (*einen Menschen, der an geistigen Dingen Freude hat*).'[12] Bernays was himself no stranger to forced and voluntary movement in and out of houses real and of the mind. As a Jewish scholar whose confessional identity excluded him from obtaining a regular chair, he moved professionally between teaching at a Jewish theological seminary, being a university librarian, and serving as a non-ordinary professor. His comment that the philologist's affect is and has been an experience not directed at a specific human object is a fitting reminder that enjoyment, in all its provisionality, has as much depth as desire. *Freude* requires our care and attention, no less so than *eros*.

---

[12] J. Bernays, *Geschichte der Klassischen Philologie: Vorlesungsnachschrift von Robert Münzel* (Hildesheim: Olms, 2008), p. 31.

Bibliography

Amigoni, D., *Victorian Biography: Intellectuals and the Ordering of Discourse* (London: Routledge, 1993)

Anderson, A., *The Powers of Distance: Cosmopolitanism and the Cultivation of Detachment* (Princeton University Press, 2001)

Armstrong, C., *Romantic Organicism: From Idealist Origins to Ambivalent Afterlife* (New York: Palgrave Macmillan, 2003)

A Compulsion for Antiquity: Freud and the Ancient World (Ithaca, NY and London: Cornell University Press, 2005)

Arndt, A., 'Schleiermacher und Platon', in F. D. E. Schleiermacher, *Über die Philosophie Platons*, pp. vii–xxii

'"Ueber den Werth des Sokrates als Philosophen". Schleiermacher und Sokrates', in H. Dierkes, et al. (eds.), *Schleiermacher, Romanticism, and the Critical Arts: A Festschrift in Honor of Herrmann Patsch* (Lewiston, NY: Edwin Mellen Press, 2007), pp. 293–302

Arnoldt, J., *Friedrich August Wolf in seinem Verhältnis zum Schulwesen* (Braunschweig: Schwetschke, 1861)

Ast, F., *Grundriss der Philologie* (Landshut: Krüll, 1808)

Auerochs, B., 'Platon um 1800. Zu seinem Bild bei Stolberg, Wieland, Schlegel und Schleiermacher', in K. Manger (ed.), *Wieland-Studien III* 1996 (Biberach: Wieland-Archiv), pp. 161–93

Baertschi, A. M. and King, C. G. (eds.), *Die modernen Väter der Antike: die Entwicklung der Altertumswissenschaften an Akademie und Universität im Berlin des 19. Jahrhunderts* (Berlin: de Gruyter, 2009)

Barker, W., *The Adages of Erasmus* (Toronto: Toronto University Press, 2001)

Barnes, J., 'Nietzsche and Diogenes Laertius', *Nietzsche-Studien* 15 (1986), 16–40

Barthes, R., *The Neutral: Lecture Course at the Collège de France (1977–1978)*. Edited and translated by R. Kraus and D. Hollier (New York: Columbia University Press, 2007)

Bayley, R., 'Herder's Sculptural Thinking', *Parallax* 17.2 (2011), pp. 71–83

Beard, M., 'Nil nisi bonum' (review of R. B. Todd (ed.), Dictionary of British Classicists), *Times Literary Supplement*, April 15, 2005, 3–4

Beiser, F., *The German Historicist Tradition* (Oxford University Press, 2011)

Belfiore, E., *Socrates' Daimonic Art: Love for Wisdom in Four Platonic Dialogues* (Cambridge University Press, 2012)

Benne, C., *Nietzsche und die historisch-kritische Philologie* (Berlin: de Gruyter, 2005)

Berg, S., *Eros and the Intoxications of Enlightenment: On Plato's Symposium* (Albany, NY: State University of New York Press, 2010)

Bernays, J., *Geschichte der Klassischen Philologie: Vorlesungsnachschrift von Robert Münzel* (Hildesheim: Olms, 2008)

Bersani L., and Phillips, A., *Intimacies* (University of Chicago Press, 2008)

Bettini, M., *The Portrait of the Lover* (Berkeley: University of California Press, 1999)

Billings, J., 'The Sigh of Philhellenism', in S. Butler (ed.), *Deep Classics: Rethinking Classical Reception* (London: Bloomsbury Academic, 2016), pp. 49–65

Birus, H., 'Hermeneutische Wende? Anmerkungen zur Schleiermacher-Interpretation', *Euphorion* 74.2 (1980), pp. 213–22

Blanshard, A., 'Hellenic Fantasies: Aesthetics and Desire in John Addington Symond's *A Problem in Greek Ethics*', *Dialogos* 7 (2000), pp. 99–123

Blok, J., 'Quests for a Scientific Mythology: F. Creuzer and K. O. Müller on History and Myth', *History and Theory* 33.4 (1994), pp. 26–52

Boeckh, A., 'Kritik der Übersetzung des Platon von Schleiermacher' (1804/5), in *Gesammelte Kleine Schriften*, ed. F. Ascherson and P. Eichholtz, vol. vii (Leipzig: Teubner, 1872), pp. 1–38
Encyklopädie und Methodologie der Philologischen Wissenschaften, ed. E. Bratuschek (Leipzig: Teubner, 1877)

Boehm, B., *Sokrates im achtzehnten Jahrhundert: Studien zum Werdegang des modernen Persönlichkeitsbewusstseins* (Leipzig: Quelle & Meyer, 1929)

Brandwood, L., *The Chronology of Plato's Dialogues* (Cambridge University Press, 1990)

Breuer, U., Bunia R., and Erlinghagen A. (eds.), *Schlegel und die Philologie* (Paderborn: Schoeningh, 2013)

Broughton, T. L., *Men of Letters, Writing Lives: Masculinity and Literary Autobiography in the Late Victorian Period* (London: Routledge, 1999)

Burnyeat, M. and Frede, M., *The Pseudo-Platonic Seventh Letter*, edited by D. Scott (Oxford University Press, 2015)

Butler, 'The youth of antiquity: reception, homosexuality, alterity', *Classical Receptions Journal*, 11.4 (2019), 373–406

Butler, S. (ed.), *Deep Classics. Rethinking Classical Reception* (London: Bloomsbury Academic, 2016)

Calder, W. M. III, 'Ulrich von Wilamowitz-Moellendorff: *Sospitator Euripidis*, *Greek, Roman, and Byzantine Studies* 27.4 (1986), pp. 409–30
'The Riddle of Wilamowitz's *Phaidrabild*', *Greek, Roman, and Byzantine Studies* 20.3 (1979), pp. 219–36

Calder, W. M. III and Rugullis, S., 'Ulrich von Wilamowitz-Moellendorff on Wilhelm Dilthey: His letters to Georg Misch (1914–1928)', *Illinois Classical Studies*, 17/2 (1992), pp. 337–45

Camp, E., 'Metaphor in the Mind: The Cognition of Metaphor', *Philosophy Compass* 1.2 (2006), pp. 154–70.

Chae, Y.-I., 'A Myth on Campus: No, Education Is Not Erotic', *Eidolon* 22 October 2018 [https://eidolon.pub/a-myth-on-campus-21b1ecdcd2c8]

Clark, W., *Academic Charisma and the Origins of the Research University* (University of Chicago Press, 2006)

Clay, D., 'The Hangover of Plato's Symposium in the Italian Renaissance from Bruni (1435) to Castiglione (1528)', in J. Lesher, D. Nails, and F. Sheffield (eds.), *Plato's Symposium*, pp. 341–60

Creuzer, F., *Das Akademische Studium des Alterthums* (Heidelberg: Winter, 1807)
Symbolik und Mythologie der alten Völker, besonders der Griechen (Leipzig and Darmstadt: Leske, 1810–12)

Crouter, R., *Friedrich Schleiermacher: Between Enlightenment and Romanticism* (Cambridge University Press, 2005)

Curtius, E., 'Das Mittleramt der Philologie' (1857), in *Göttinger Festreden* (Berlin: Hertz, 1964), pp. 23–51

Dainat, H., 'Überbietung der Philologie', in C. König and E. Lämmert (eds.), *Literaturwissenschaft und Geistesgeschichte 1910–1925* (Frankfurt am Main: Suhrkamp, 1993), pp. 232–9
'Ein Fach in der "Krise": Die "Methodendiskussion" in der Neueren deutschen Literaturwissenschaft', in O. G. Oexle (ed.), *Krise des Historismus*, pp. 247–72

Danneberg, L., 'Ganzheitsvorstellungen und Zerstückelungsphantasien. Zum Hintergrund und zur Entwicklung der Wahrnehmungen ästhetischer Eigenschaften in der zweiten Hälfte des 18. und zu Beginn des 19. Jahrhunderts', in J. Schönert and U. Zeuch (eds.), *Mimesis – Repräsentation – Imagination: Literaturtheoretische Positionen von Aristoteles bis zum Ende des 18. Jahrhunderts* (Berlin: de Gruyter, 2004), pp. 241–82
'Dissens, *ad-personam*-Invektiven und wissenschaftliches Ethos in der Philologie des 19. Jahrhunderts: Wilamowitz-Moellendorff *contra* Nietzsche', in R. Klausnitzer and C. Spoerhase (eds.), *Kontroversen in der Literaturtheorie / Literaturtheorie in der Kontroverse* (Bern: Peter Lang, 2007), pp. 93–147
'Schleiermacher und die Hermeneutik', in A. M. Baertschi and C. G. King (eds.), *Die modernen Väter der Antike*, pp. 211–76

Daston, L. and Galison, P., *Objectivity* (Cambridge, MA: Massachussetts Institute of Technology Press, 2007)

Daston, L. and Most, G., 'History of Science and History of Philologies', *Isis* 106.2 (2015), pp. 378–90.

Daston, L. and Park, K., *Wonders and the Order of Nature, 1150–1750* (Cambridge, MA: Massachussetts Institute of Technology Press, 1998)

Davis, W., 'Winckelmann Divided: Mourning the Death of Art History', in W. Davis (ed.), *Gay and Lesbian Studies in Art History* (Binghamton, NY: State University of New York Press, 1994), pp. 141–59

'Winckelmann's "Homosexual" Teleologies', in N. B. Kampen (ed.), *Sexuality in Ancient Art* (Cambridge University Press, 1996), pp. 262–76

Décultot, E., *Johann Joachim Winckelmann. Enquête sur la genèse de l'histoire de l'art* (Paris: Presses Universitaires Françaises, 2000)

Dehrmann, M.-G., *Studierte Dichter: zum Spannungsverhältnis von Dichtung und philologisch-historischen Wissenschaften im 19. Jahrhundert* (Berlin: de Gruyter, 2015)

Derks, P., *Die Heilige Schande der Päderastie. Homosexualität und Öffentlichkeit in der deutschen Literatur, 1750–1850* (Berlin: Rosa Winkel, 1990)

Dilthey, W., *Das Leben Schleiermachers* (Berlin: Reimer, 1870)

'Über das Studium der Geschichte der Wissenschaft vom Menschen, der Gesellschaft, und dem Staat' (1875); *Gesammelte Schriften*, vol. v, 'Die Geistige Welt: Einleitung in die Philosophie des Lebens', ed. G. Misch (Göttingen: Vandenhoeck & Ruprecht, 1924), pp. 31–73

Der Aufbau der geschichtlichen Welt in den Geisteswissenschaften (Berlin, 1910)

Dorandi, R., 'Antigonos von Karystos (1881)', in W. M. Calder III, et al. (ed.), *Wilamowitz in Greifswald: Akten der Tagung zum 150. Geburtstag Ulrich von Wilamowitz-Moellendorffs in Greifswald, 19.-22. Dezember 1998* (Hildesheim: Olms, 2000), pp. 586–604

Douglas, M., *Purity and Danger: An Analysis of Concepts of Pollution and Taboo* (London, New York: Routledge, 2002 [1966])

Eckel, J., *Geist der Zeit: Deutsche Geisteswissenschaften seit 1870* (Göttingen: Vandenhoeck und Ruprecht, 2008)

Eckermann, J. P., *Gespräche mit Goethe, in den letzten Jahren seines Lebens*, ed. G. Moldenhauer, vol. I: 1823–7 (Leipzig: Reclam, 1884)

Eden, K., *The Renaissance Rediscovery of Intimacy* (University of Chicago Press, 2012)

Elsner, J., 'Paideia: Ancient Concept and Modern Perception', *International Journal of the Classical Tradition* 20.4 (2013), pp. 136–52

'Introduction', in J. Elsner and M. Meyer (eds.), *Art and Rhetoric in Roman Culture* (Cambridge University Press, 2014), pp. 1–34

Endres, N., 'Diderot, Hogarth, and the Aesthetics of Depilation', *Eighteenth-Century Studies* 38.1 (2004), pp. 17–38

Espagne, M., 'De Heyne à Lachmann. Biographies héroïques de philologues allemands', in C. König and D. Thouard (eds.), *La philologie au present: pour Jean Bollack* (Villeneuve d'Ascq: Septentrion, 2010), pp. 127–39

Espagne, M. and Rabault-Feuerhahn, P. (eds.), *Hermann Usener und die Metamorphosen der Philologie* (Wiesbaden: Harrassowitz, 2011)

Fabian, J., *Time and the Other: How Anthropology Makes Its Object* (New York, Columbia University Press, 1983)

Fichte, J. G., 'Einige Vorlesungen über die Bestimmung des Gelehrten', *Gesamtausgabe der Bayerischen Akademie der Wissenschaften*, ed. R. Lauth and H. Jacob, vol. I.3: Werke 1794–1796 (Stuttgart-Bad Cannstatt: Frommann, 1966), pp. 23–68

'Deduzierter Plan zu einer zu Berlin zu errichtenden höhern Lehranstalt, die in gehöriger Verbindung mit einer Akademie der Wissenschaften stehe', in W. Weischedel (ed.), *Idee und Wirklichkeit einer Universität: Dokumente zur Geschichte der Friedrich-Wilhelms-Universität zu Berlin* (Berlin: de Gruyter, 1960), pp. 30–105 = 'A Plan, Deduced from First Principles, for an Institution of Higher Learning to Be Established in Berlin, Connected to and Subordinate to an Academy of Sciences', in L. Menand, P. Reitter, and C. Wellmon (eds.), *The Rise of the Research University: A Sourcebook* (University of Chicago Press, 2017), pp. 67–83

Flashar, H., Gründer, K. and Horstmann, A. (eds.), *Philologie und Hermeneutik im 19. Jahrhundert: Zur Geschichte und Methodologie der Geisteswissenschaften* (Göttingen: Vandenhoeckh & Ruprecht, 1979)

Follak, A., *Der 'Aufblick zur Idee': Eine vergleichende Studie zur Platonischen Pädagogik bei F. Schleiermacher, P. Natorp, and W. Jaeger* (Göttingen: Vandenhoeckh & Ruprecht, 2005)

Forster, M. N., 'Schleiermacher's Hermeneutics: Some Problems and Solutions', *The Harvard Review of Philosophy* 13.1 (2005), pp. 100–22

Frevert, U., 'Gefühle definieren: Begriffe und Debatten aus drei Jahrhunderten', in U. Frevert (ed.), *Gefühlswissen: eine lexikalische Spurensuche der Moderne* (Frankfurt am Main: Campus, 2011), pp. 9–39; republished as 'Defining Emotions: Concepts and Debates over Three Centuries', in U. Frevert (ed.), *Emotional Lexicons: Continuity and Change in the Vocabulary of Feeling* (Oxford University Press 2014), pp. 1–31

Gildenhard, I., 'Philologia Perennis? Classical Scholarship and Functional Differentiation', in I. Gildenhard and M. Ruehl (eds.), *Out of Arcadia. Classics and Politics in Germany in the Age of Burckhardt, Nietzsche and Wilamowitz*, Bulletin of the Institute of Classical Studies Supplement 79 (London: Institute of Classical Studies, 2003), pp. 161–203.

Gildersleeve, B., 'The Spiritual Rights of Minute Research [1895]', in W. W. Briggs Jr. (ed.), *Selected Classical Papers of Basil Lanneau Gildersleeve* (Atlanta: Scholars Press, 1992), pp. 93–105

Gjesdal, K., 'Imagination, Divination, and Understanding: Schleiermacher and the Hermeneutics of the Second Person', in G. Gentry and K. Pollok (eds.), *The Imagination in German Idealism and Romanticism* (Cambridge University Press, 2019), pp. 190–207

Herder's Hermeneutics: History, Poetry, Enlightenment (Cambridge University Press, 2017)

Goldhill, S., *Who Needs Greek? Contests in the Cultural History of Hellenism* (Cambridge University Press, 2002)

A Very Queer Family Indeed: Sex, Religion, and the Bensons in Victorian Britain (University of Chicago Press, 2016)

Grafton, A., 'Polyhistor into Philolog', *History of Universities* 3 (1983), pp. 159–92

'Juden und Griechen bei Friedrich August Wolf', in R. Markner and G. Veltri (eds.), *Friedrich August Wolf*, pp. 9–31

'Humanist Philologies: Texts, Antiquities, and their Scholarly Transformations in the Early Modern West', in S. Pollock, et al. (eds.), *World Philology*, pp. 154–77

Grote, S., 'Vom geistlichen zum guten Geschmack? Reflexionen zur Suche nach den pietistischen Wurzeln der Ästhetik', in A. Allerkamp and D. Mirbach (eds.), *Schönes Denken – Baumgartens Epoche (1714/2014)* (Hamburg: Meiner, 2016), pp. 365–80

'Theological Origins of Aesthetics', in M. Kelly (ed.), *Encyclopedia of Aesthetics*, 2nd ed., vol. 5 (Oxford University Press, 2014), pp. 51–4

Gründer K. (ed.), *Der Streit um Nietzsches "Geburt der Tragödie": die Schriften von E. Rohde, R. Wagner, U. von Wilamowitz-Moellendorff* (Hildersheim: Olms, 1969)

Güthenke, C., '"Enthusiasm dwells only in specialization". Classical Philology and Disciplinarity in Nineteenth-Century Germany', in B. Elman and S. Pollock (eds.), *World Philology* (Cambridge, MA: Harvard University Press, 2014), pp. 304–38

'Warum Boeckhs Encyklopädie lesen?', *Geschichte der Germanistik: Historische Zeitschrift für die Philologien* 51.52 (2017), pp. 83–97

'Postclassicism, Disturbed Philology, and Kleist's Fencing Bear', *Oxford German Studies* 47.2 (2018), pp. 184–200

'After Exemplarity. A Map of Plutarchan Scholarship', in P. Mack and J. North (eds.), *The Afterlife of Plutarch*, Bulletin of the Institute of Classical Studies Supplement 137 (2018), pp. 191–203

'"The Alexandrian Scholar Poets Are Our Ancestors": Ancient Scholarship and Modern Self-Perception', in W. Beck, A. Kelly, and T. Phillips (eds.), *The Ancient Scholia to Homer's Iliad: Exegesis and Interpretation.* Bulletin of the Institute of Classical Studies Supplements (London, forthcoming)

Gumbrecht, H. U., *The Powers of Philology: Dynamics of Textual Scholarship* (Urbana: University of Illinois Press, 2003)

The Production of Presence: What Meaning Cannot Convey (Palo Alto, CA: Stanford University Press, 2004)

Habicht, C., *Pausanias' Guide to Ancient Greece* (Berkeley: University of California Press, 1985)

Hackel, C., 'Philologische Fachenzyklopädien. Zu Charakter und Funktion eines wenig beachteten Genres', in C. Hackel and S. Seifert (eds.), *August Boeckh*, pp. 243–72

Hackel, C. und Seifert, S. (eds.), *August Boeckh: Philologie, Hermeneutik und Wissenschaftspolitik* (Berlin: BVW, 2013)

Hackforth, R., *The Authorship of the Platonic Epistles* (Manchester University Press, 1913)

Hägg, T., *The Art of Biography in Antiquity* (Cambridge University Press, 2012)

Hamann, J. G., *Sokratische Denkwürdigkeiten*, ed. F. Blanke (Gütersloh: Mohn, 1959)

Hamilton, J., *Soliciting Darkness: Pindar, Obscurity and the Classical Tradition* (Cambridge, MA: Harvard University Press, 2003)

Hammerstein, N. and Herrmann, U. (eds.), *Handbuch der deutschen Bildungsgeschichte, Band II: 18. Jahrhundert. Vom späten 17. Jahrhundert bis zur Neuordnung Deutschlands um 1800* (Munich: Beck, 2005)

Hanhart, R., *Erinnerungen an Friedrich August Wolf* (Basle, 1825)

Harloe, K., 'Allusion and Ekphrasis in Winckelmann's Paris Description of the Apollo Belvedere', *The Cambridge Classical Journal* 53 (2007), pp. 229–52

'Pausanias as Historian in Winckelmann's *History*', *Classical Receptions Journal* 2.2 (2010), pp. 174–96

Winckelmann and the Invention of Antiquity: History and Aesthetics in the Age of Altertumswissenschaft (Oxford University Press, 2013)

Harloe, K. and Russell, L., 'Life and (Love) Letters: Looking in on Winckelmann's Correspondence', *Proceedings of the English Goethe Society* 88.1 (2019), pp. 1–20

Harpham, G., 'Roots, Races and the Return to Philology', *Representations* 106 (2009), 34–62

Hartung, G., King, C. G. and Rapp, C. (eds.), *Aristotelian Studies in the 19th Century* (Berlin, New York: de Gruyter 2018)

Herder, J. G., 'Über Thomas Abbts Schriften' (1768), *Sämmtliche Werke* [*SWS*], ed. Bernhard Suphan, 33 vols. (Berlin: Weidmann, 1877–1913), ii, pp. 249–94

Philosophical Writings, ed. M. N. Forster (Cambridge University Press, 2002)

Kalligone, in *Werke vol 8: Schriften zu Literatur und Philosophie 1792–1800*, ed. H. D. Irmscher (Frankfurt am Main: Deutscher Klassiker Verlag, 1998), pp. 641–964

Hermann, K. F., *Geschichte und System der Platonischen Philosophie* (Heidelberg: Winter, 1839)

Herzog, R., 'On the relation of disciplinary development and historical self-presentation – the case of Classical Philology since the end of the Eighteenth Century', in L. Graham, W. Lepenies, and P. Weingart (eds.), *Functions and Uses of Disciplinary Histories* (1983), pp. 281–90

van Heusde, P. W., *Initia philosophiae Platonicae*, vols. i–iii (Utrecht: Altheer, 1827–36)

Hildebrandt, K., 'Hellas und Wilamowitz (zum Ethos der Tragödie)', *Jahrbuch für die geistige Bewegung* 1 (1910), pp. 64–117

Erinnerungen an Stefan George und seinen Kreis (Bonn: Bouvier, 1965)

Hinderer, W., 'Introduction', in W. Hinderer (ed.), *Codierungen von Liebe in der Kunstperiode* (Würzburg: Königshausen und Neumann, 1997), pp. 7–33

Hirzel, R., *Plutarch* (Leipzig: Dieterich, 1912)

Hoffmann, V., *Johann Georg Hamanns Philologie: Hamanns Philologie zwischen enzyklopädischer Mikrologie und Hermeneutik* (Stuttgart: Kohlhammer, 1972)

Holzer, A., *Rehabilitationen Roms: Die römische Antike in der deutschen Kultur zwischen Winckelmann und Niebuhr* (Heidelberg: Winter, 2013)

Horstmann, A., *Antike Theoria und moderne Wissenschaft. August Boeckhs Konzeption der Philologie* (Frankfurt am Main: Peter Lang, 1992)

Hose, M., '" ... und Pflicht geht vor Neigung". Ulrich von Wilamowitz-Moellendorff und das Leiden am Grossbetrieb der Wissenschaft', in A. M. Baertschi and C. G. King (eds.), *Die modernen Väter*, pp. 445–80

von Humboldt, W., 'Über das Studium des Alterthums, und des Griechischen insbesondre', in *Gesammelte Schriften*, ed. A. Leitzmann (Berlin: de Gruyter, 1968), vol. I, pp. 255–81

Hummel, P., *Moeurs érudites: étude sur la micrologie littéraire (Allemagne, XVIe-XVIIIe siècles)* (Geneva: Droz, 2002)

Humphreys, S. C., 'Classics and Colonialism: towards an erotics of the discipline', in G. Most (ed.), *Disciplining Classics – Altertumswissenschaft als Beruf* (Göttingen: Vandenhoeck & Ruprecht, 2002), pp. 207–51

Isnardi Parente, M. 'Rileggendo il Platon di Ulrich von Wilamowitz-Moellendorff', *Annali della Scuola Normale Superiore di Pisa*. Classe di Lettere e Filosofia, serie III, 3.1 (1973), pp. 147–67

Jackson-Ravenscroft, R. *The Veiled God: Friedrich Schleiermacher's Theology of Finitude* (Leiden: Brill, 2019), esp. part 2: 'Human Formation and Literary Form in Schleiermacher's Soliloquies (1800)', pp. 95–168

Jannidis, F., '"Individuum est ineffabile". Zur Veränderung der Individualitätssemantik im 18. Jahrhundert und ihrer Auswirkung auf die Figurenkonzeption im Roman', *Aufklärung* 9.2 (1996), pp. 77–110

Janz, R.-P., 'Ansichten der Juno Ludovisi. Winckelmann – Schiller – Goethe', in P.-A. Alt, et al. (ed.), *Prägnanter Moment. Studien zur Deutschen Literatur der Aufklärung und Klassik* (Würzburg: Königshausen & Neumann, 2002), pp. 357–72

Jefferson, A., *Biography and the Question of Literature in France* (Oxford University Press, 2007)

Johnson, M. and Tarrant, H. (eds.), *Alcibiades and the Socratic Lover-Educator* (London: Bloomsbury Academic, 2012)

Jolles, F., 'Die Entwicklung der wissenschaftlichen Grundsätze des George-Kreises', *Etudes Germaniques* 22.3 (1967), pp. 346–58

Joyce, R. A., *The Languages of Archaeology: Dialogue, Narrative, and Writing* (Oxford: Blackwell, 2002).

Jung, M., *Dilthey zur Einführung* (Hamburg: Junius, 1996)

Justi, C., *Winckelmann, sein Leben, seine Werke und seine Zeitgenossen: mit Skizzen zur Kunst- und Gelehrtengeschichte des 18. Jahrhunderts* (Leipzig: Vogel) I: Winckelmann in Deutschland (1866); II: Winckelmann in Italien (1872)

Die aesthetischen Elemente in der platonischen Philosophie, ein historisch-philosophischer Versuch (Marburg: Elwert, 1860)

Kapl-Blume, E., 'Liebe im Lexikon. Zum Bedeutungswandel des Begriffes "Liebe" in ausgewählten Lexika des 18. und 19. Jahrhunderts. Ein Forschungsbericht', in L. Jäger (ed.), *Zur Historischen Semantik des Deutschen Gefühlswortschatzes*.

Aspekte, Probleme und Beispiele seiner lexikographischen Erfassung (Aachen: Alano, 1988), pp. 215–46

King, S., 'Amelia Opie's "Maid of Corinth" and the Origins of Art', *Eighteenth-Century Studies* 37.4 (2004), pp. 629–51

Kipf, S., 'Von Arrian bis Xenophon. Der griechische Lektüreplan der Berliner Gymnasien unter dem Einfluss des Neuhumanismus', in B. Seidensticker and F. Mundt (eds.), *Altertumswissenschaft in Berlin um 1800 an Akademie, Schule und Universität* (Hannover: Wehrhahn, 2006) pp. 167–87

Kirchner, H.-M., *Friedrich Thiersch: ein liberaler Kulturpolitiker und Philhellene in Bayern* (Munich: Hieronymus, 1996)

Körte, W., *Leben und Studien Friedrich August Wolfs, des Philologen* (Essen: Bädeker, 1833)

Konaris, M., *The Greek Gods in Modern Scholarship: Interpretation and Belief in Nineteenth and Early Twentieth Century Germany and Britain* (Oxford University Press, 2015)

Kopp, D. and Wegmann, N., '"Die deutsche Philologie, die Schule und die Klassische Philologie". Zur Karriere einer Wissenschaft um 1800', in J. Fohrmann and W. Voßkamp (eds.), *Sonderheft der deutschen Vierteljahrsschrift für Literaturwissenschaft und Geistesgeschichte zur Wissenschaftsgeschichte der deutschen Literaturwissenschaft* 61 (1987), pp. 123–51

Koselleck, R., '*Historia Magistra Vitae*: Über die Auflösung des Topos im Horizont neuzeitlich bewegter Geschichte', in H. Braun and M. Riedel (eds.), *Natur und Geschichte: Karl Löwith zum 70. Geburtstag* (Stuttgart: Metzler, 1967), pp. 196–219

'Zur anthropologischen und semantischen Struktur der Bildung', in R. Koselleck (ed.), *Bildungsbürgertum im 19. Jahrhundert*, 4 vols. (Stuttgart: Klett-Cotta, 1985–92), vol. ii, pp. 11–46

'Einleitung', in O. Brunner, W. Kunze, and R. Koselleck (eds.), *Geschichtliche Grundbegriffe: Historisches Lexikon zur politisch-sozialen Sprache in Deutschland* (Stuttgart: Klett, 1972), pp. xiii–xxvii

Kruckis, H.-M., 'Biographie als literaturwissenschaftliche Darstellungsform im 19. Jahrhundert', in J. Fohrmann and W. Vosskamp (eds.), *Wissenschaftsgeschichte der Germanistik im 19. Jahrhundert* (Stuttgart: Metzler, 1994), pp. 550–75

Kuhlmann, P. and Schneider, H. (eds.), *Geschichte der Altertumswissenschaften. Biographisches Lexikon*. Der neue Pauly. Supplemente 6 (Stuttgart: Metzler, 2013)

Kurbjuhn, C., *Kontur. Geschichte einer ästhetischen Denkfigur* (Berlin: de Gruyter, 2014)

Lakoff, G. and Johnson, M., *Metaphors We Live By* (University of Chicago Press, 1980)

Laks, A., 'Schleiermacher on Plato: From Form (*Introduction to Plato's Works*) to Content (*Outlines of a Critique of Previous Ethical Theory*)', in A. Kim (ed.), *Brill's Companion to German Platonism* (Brill: Leiden, 2019), pp. 146–64.

Lamm, J., 'Schleiermacher as Plato Scholar', *Journal of Religion* 80.2 (2000), 206–39

'Reading Plato's Dialectics: Schleiermacher's Insistence on Dialectics as Dialogical', *Zeitschrift für Neuere Theologiegeschichte/ Journal for the History of Modern Theology* 10.1 (2003), pp. 1–25

'The Art of Interpreting Plato', in J. Marina (ed.), *The Cambridge Companion to Schleiermacher* (Cambridge University Press, 2005), pp. 91–108

'Schleiermacher's "Christmas Dialogue" as Platonic Dialogue', *Journal of Religion* 92.3 (2012), pp. 392–420

Landfester, M., 'Ulrich von Wilamowitz-Moellendorff und die hermeneutische Tradition des 19. Jahrhunderts', in H. Flashar, et al., *Philologie und Hermeneutik*, pp. 156–80

Lane, M. S., *Plato's Progeny: How Plato and Socrates still Captivate the Modern Mind* (London: Duckworth, 2001)

'The Platonic Politics of the George Circle: A Reconsideration', in M. S. Lane and M. A. Ruehl (eds.), *A Poet's Reich: Politics and Culture in the George Circle* (Rochester, NY: Camden House), pp. 133–63

Langen, A., *Wortschatz des Deutschen Pietismus*, 2nd ed. (Tübingen: Niemeyer, 1968)

La Vopa, A. J., 'Specialists against Specialization: Hellenism as a Professional Ideology in German Classical Studies', in G. Cocks and K. Jarausch (eds.), *German Professions: 1800–1950* (Oxford University Press, 1990), pp. 27–45

Lecznar, A., 'Alcibiades in Love: Nietzsche, Plato and the Philosophy of Modernity', *Classical Receptions Journal* 9.4 (2017), pp. 447–69

Leo, F., *Die griechisch-römische Biographie nach ihrer literarischen Form* (Leipzig: Teubner, 1901)

Leonard, M., *Socrates and the Jews: Hellenism and Hebraism from Moses Mendelssohn to Sigmund Freud* (University of Chicago Press, 2012)

Lerer, S., *Error and the Academic Self: The Scholarly Imagination, Medieval to Modern* (New York University Press, 2002)

Lesher, J., Nails, D., and Sheffield, F. (eds.), *Plato's Symposium: Issues in Interpretation and Reception* (Washington, DC: Centre for Hellenic Studies, 2007)

Lessing, H.-U., 'Dilthey als Historiker', in N. Hammerstein (ed.), *Deutsche Geschichtswissenschaft um 1900* (Wiesbaden: Harrassowitz, 1988), pp. 113–30

Leventhal, R. S., *The Disciplines of Interpretation: Lessing, Herder, Schlegel and Hermeneutics in Germany, 1750–1800* (Berlin: de Gruyter, 1994)

'The Emergence of Philological Discourse in the German States, 1770–1810', *Isis* 77 (1986), pp. 243–60

Lin, Y.-J., *The Erotic Life of Manuscripts: New Testament Textual Criticism and the Biological Sciences* (Oxford University Press, 2016)

Luhmann, N., *Liebe als Passion: Zur Codierung von Intimität* (Frankfurt am Main: Suhrkamp, 1982) = *Love as Passion: The Codification of Intimacy*, tr. J. Gaines (Cambridge, MA: Harvard University Press, 1987)

Lynch, D., *Loving Literature: a Cultural History* (Cambridge, MA: Harvard University Press, 2015)

Makkreel, R. A., *Dilthey: Philosopher of the Human Studies*, 3rd ed. (Princeton University Press, 1992 [1975])

Marchand, S. L., *Down from Olympus: Archaeology and Philhellenism in Germany, 1750–1970* (Princeton University Press, 1996)

  German Orientalism in the Age of Empire: Religion, Race, and Scholarship (Cambridge University Press, 2009)

Marcus, L., *Auto/biographical Discourses: Theory, Criticism, Practice* (Manchester University Press, 1994)

Markner, R., and Veltri, G. (eds.), *Friedrich August Wolf: Studien, Dokumente, Bibliographie* (Stuttgart: Franz Steiner, 1999)

Matuschek, S., 'Die Macht des Gastmahls. Schlegels *Gespräch über die Poesie* und Platons *Symposion*', in S. Matuschek (ed.), *Wo das philosophische Gespräch ganz in Dichtung übergeht. Platons Symposion und seine Wirkung in der Renaissance, Romantik und Moderne* (Heidelberg: Winter, 2002), pp. 81–96

Matzner, S., 'Queer Unhistoricism: Scholars, Metalepsis, and Interventions of the Unruly Past', in S. Butler, *Deep Classics*, pp. 179–201

Meckenstock, G., 'Die Wandlung der "Monologen" Schleiermachers', in G. Meckenstock and J. Ringleben (eds.), *Schleiermacher und die wissenschaftliche Kultur des Christentums* (Berlin: de Gruyter, 1991), pp. 403–18

Meisner, H. (ed.), *Briefwechsel Friedrich Schleiermachers mit August Boeckh und Immanuel Bekker, 1806–1820* (Berlin: Litteraturarchiv-Gesellschaft, 1916)

Mendelssohn, M., 'Ueber die kleine Schrift "Sokratische Denkwürdigkeiten für die lange Weile des Publikums", für deren Verfasser jetzt Joh. Georg Hamann gilt', in *Gesammelte Schriften*, ed. G. B. Mendelssohn, vol. iv.2 (Leipzig: Brockhaus, 1844), pp. 99–105

Mergenthaler, M., *Zwischen Eros und Mitteilung: Die Frühromantik im Symposion der "Athenäums-Fragmente"* (Paderborn: Schöningh, 2012)

Mezzanzanica, M., 'Die Lebenskategorien, das Problem der Individualität und die Logik des historischen Geschehens in der Geschichte der Autobiographie von Georg Misch', in *Dilthey-Jahrbuch für Philosophie und Geschichte der Geisteswissenschaften* 12 (1999–2000), pp. 107–19

Miller, J. H., *Versions of Pygmalion* (Cambridge, MA: Harvard University Press, 1990)

Misch, G., *Geschichte der Autobiographie. Erster Band: Das Altertum* (Leipzig: Teubner, 1907)

Misch, G., *Geschichte der Autobiographie. Erster Band: Das Altertum*, 3rd rev. ed. (Frankfurt am Main: Schulte-Bulmke, 1949)

Momigliano, A., *The Classical Foundations of Modern Historiography* (Berkeley: University of California Press, 1990)

  The Development of Greek Biography (Cambridge, MA: Harvard University Press, 1993)

Mommsen, T., 'Rede bei Antritt des Rektorates 1874: Über das Geschichtsstudium', *Reden und Aufsätze von Theodor Mommsen* (Berlin: Weidmann, 1905), pp. 3–12

Morat, D., 'Verstehen als Gefühlsmethode. Zu Wilhelm Diltheys hermeneutischer Grundlegung der Geisteswissenschaften', in U. Jensen and
D. Morat (eds.), *Rationalisierungen des Gefühls. Zum Verhältnis von
Wissenschaft und Emotionen 1880–1930* (Munich: Fink, 2008),
pp. 101–18

Moser, C., *Buchgestützte Subjektivität: Literarische Formen der Selbstsorge und der
Selbsthermeneutik von Platon bis Montaigne* (Tübingen: Narr, 2006)

Most, G., 'Classicism, Modernism, Postclassicism', in A. Leonard and L. Norman
(eds.), *Classicisms* (Chicago: Smart Museum of Art, 2017), pp. 129–35

Muecke, F., '"Taught by Love": The Origin of Painting Again', *The Art Bulletin*
81.2 (June 1999), pp. 297–302

von Mücke, D., 'Pygmalion's Dream in Herder's Aesthetics, or Male Narcissism
as the Model for *Bildung*', *Studies in Eighteenth-Century Culture* 19 (1989),
pp. 349–65

Mülder-Bach, I., 'Eine "neue Logik für den Liebhaber". Herders Theorie der
Plastik', in H.-J. Schings (ed.), *Der Ganze Mensch. Anthropologie und
Literatur im 18. Jahrhundert. DFG-Symposium 1992* (Stuttgart: Metzler,
1994), pp. 341–70

*Im Zeichen Pygmalions: Das Modell der Statue und die Entdeckung der
"Darstellung" im 18. Jahrhundert* (Munich: Fink, 1998)

'Ferngefühle. Poesie und Plastik in Herder's Ästhetik', in T. Borsche (ed.),
*Herder im Spiegel der Zeiten. Verwerfungen der Rezeptionsgeschichte und
Chancen einer Relektüre* (Munich: Fink, 2006), pp. 264–77

Müller, P., 'Ranke in the Lobby of the Archive: Metaphors and Conditions of
Historical Research', in S. Jobs and A. Lüdtke (eds.), *Unsettling History:
Archiving and Narrating in Historiography* (Frankfurt am Main: Campus,
2010), pp. 109–25

Murray, G., 'German Scholarship', *Quarterly Review* 223 (1915), pp. 330–9

History of Ancient Greek Literature (London: Heinemann, 1897)

Nemoianu, V., *The Triumph of Imperfection: The Silver Age of Sociocultural
Moderation in Europe, 1815–1848* (Columbia: University of South Carolina
Press, 2006)

Neumann, G., 'Lektüren der Liebe', in H. Meier and G. Neumann (eds.), *Über die
Liebe: Ein Symposion* (Munich: Fink, 2001), pp. 9–79

'"Ich bin gebildet genug, um zu lieben und zu trauern." Die Erziehung zur
Liebe in Goethe's Wilhelm Meister', in T. Heydenreich (ed.), *Liebesroman –
Liebe im Roman. Eine Erlanger Ringvorlesung* (Erlangen: Universitätsbund
Erlangen-Nürnberg, 1987), pp. 41–82

Nietzsche, F., 'Die Philosophie im tragischen Zeitalter der Griechen', *Werke,
Kritische Gesamtausgabe* III.2: Nachgelassene Schriften 1870–1873, ed.
G. Colli and M. Montinari (Berlin: de Gruyter, 1973)

'Homer und die klassische Philologie (1869)', in *Werke*, II.1 (1982), pp.
247–69

Werke, II.1: Philologische Schriften (1867–1873) (Berlin: de Gruyter,
1982)

Briefwechsel. I.4: Nachbericht zur ersten Abteilung: Briefe von und an Friedrich Nietzsche Oktober 1849–April 1869, eds. N. Miller and J. Salaquarda (Berlin: de Gruyter, 1993)

The Birth of Tragedy and Other Writings, tr. R. Speirs and eds. R. Geuss and R. Speirs (Cambridge University Press, 1999)

Anti-Education, transl. D. Searls, ed. P. Reitter and C. Wellmon (New York: nyrb, 2016)

Nightingale, A., *Plato and the Construct of Philosophy* (Cambridge University Press, 1995)

Norton, R., *Secret Germany: Stefan George and His Circle* (Ithaca, NY: Cornell University Press, 2002)

'Wilamowitz at War', *International Journal of the Classical Tradition* 15.1 (2008), pp. 74–97

Nussbaum, M., *The Fragility of Goodness* (Cambridge University Press, 1986)

O'Boyle, L., 'Klassische Bildung und soziale Struktur in Deutschland zwischen 1800 und 1848', *Historische Zeitschrift* 207 (1968), 584–608

Oehler, K., 'Dilthey und die Klassische Philologie', in H. Flashar, et al., *Philologie und Hermeneutik*, pp. 181–98

Oexle, O. G., '"Wissenschaft" und "Leben"', *Geschichte in Wissenschaft und Unterricht* 41 (1990), pp. 145–61

'Krise des Historismus – Krise der Wirklichkeit. Eine Problemgeschichte der Moderne', in O. G. Oexle (ed.), *Krise des Historismus – Krise der Wirklichkeit. Wissenschaft, Kunst und Literatur 1880–1932* (Göttingen: Vandenhoeck & Ruprecht, 2007), pp. 11–116

Orrells, D., *Classical Culture and Modern Masculinity* (Oxford University Press, 2011)

Parker, K., 'Winckelmann, Historical Difference, and the Problem of the Boy', *Eighteenth Century Studies* 25.4 (1992), pp. 523–44

Patsch, H., 'Friedrich Asts "Euthyphron"-Übersetzung im Nachlass Friedrich Schlegels. Ein Beitrag zur Platon-Rezeption in der Frühromantik', *Jahrbuch des Freien Deutschen Hochstifts* (1988), pp. 112–27

Paulsen, F., *Geschichte des Gelehrten Unterrichts auf den Deutschen Schulen und Universitäten vom Ausgang des Mittelalters bis zur Gegenwart. Mit besonderer Rücksichtnahme auf den klassischen Unterricht* (Leipzig: Veit, 1885).

Petraschka, T., 'Takt als heuristische Kategorie in Erkenntnis- und Interpretationsprozessen', in A. Arndt, et al. (eds.), *Theorien, Methoden und Praktiken des Interpretierens* (Berlin: de Gruyter, 2015), pp. 591–608

Pfau, T., *Romantic Moods: Paranoia, Trauma, and Melancholy, 1790–1840* (Baltimore: Johns Hopkins University Press, 2005)

Pfeiffer, R., *History of Classical Scholarship: from the Beginnings to the End of the Hellenistic Age* (Oxford: Clarendon, 1968)

Phillips, M. S., 'Distance and Historical Representation', *History Workshop Journal* 57.1 (2004), pp. 123–41

On Historical Distance (New Haven: Yale University Press, 2015)

Pinch, A., *Strange Fits of Passion: Epistemologies of Emotion, Hume to Austen* (Palo Alto, CA: Stanford University Press, 1996)

Plamper, J., *The History of Emotions: An Introduction* (Oxford University Press, 2015)

Poiss, T., 'Die unendliche Aufgabe. August Boeckh als Begründer des Philologischen Seminars', in A. M. Baertschi and C. G. King, *Die modernen Väter*, pp. 45–72

Pollock, S., 'Future Philology? The Fate of a Soft Science in a Hard World', *Critical Inquiry* 35 (2009), pp. 931–61

Popkin, J., *History, Historians and Autobiography* (University of Chicago Press, 2005)

Porter, J. I., *Nietzsche and the Philology of the Future* (Palo Alto, CA: Stanford University Press, 2000)

Potts, A., *Flesh and the Ideal: Winckelmann and the Origins of Art History* (New Haven, CT: Yale University Press, 2000)

Power, T., 'Cyberchorus: Pindar's Κηληδόνες and the aura of the artificial', in L. Athanassaki and E. Bowie (eds.), *Archaic and Classical Choral Song: Performance, Politics and Dissemination* (Berlin: de Gruyter, 2011), pp. 67–114

von Ranke, L., *Sämtliche Werke*, 54 vols., ed. A. Dove (Berlin: Duncker & Humblot, 1867–90)

Das Briefwerk, ed. W. P. Fuchs (Hamburg: Hoffman und Campe, 1949)

Rebenich, S., 'Berlin und die antike Epigraphik', in W. Eck, et al. (eds.), *XIV Congressus Internationalis Epigraphiae Graecae et Latinae* (Berlin: de Gruyter, 2014), pp. 7–75

Reddy, W., *The Navigation of Feeling: a Framework for the Study of Emotion* (Cambridge University Press, 2001)

Reeve, C. D. C., 'A Study in Violets. Alcibiades in the Symposium', in J. Lesher, D. Nails, and F. Sheffield (eds.), *Plato's Symposium*, pp. 124–46

Renaud, F. and Tarrant, H., *The Platonic Alcibiades I: the Dialogue and Its Ancient Reception* (Cambridge University Press, 2015)

Renner, K., '"Kreuzzüge des Philologen": Polemics and Philology in Johann Georg Hermann', in H. Bajohr, et al. (eds.), *The Future of Philology* (Newcastle: Cambridge Scholars Publishing, 2014), pp. 120–45

Richter, S., 'Winckelmann's Progeny: Homosocial Networking in the Eighteenth Century', in A. Kuzniar (ed.), *Outing Goethe & His Age* (Palo Alto, CA: Stanford University Press, 1996), pp. 44–6

Ritschl, F. W., *Kleine philologische Schriften*, 5 vols., ed. C. Wachsmuth (Leipzig: Teubner, 1866)

Rohls, J., 'Schleiermachers Platon', in N. J. Cappelørn, et al. (eds.), *Schleiermacher und Kierkegaard: Subjektivität und Wahrheit* (Berlin: de Gruyter, 2008), pp. 709–32

Rosenblum, R., 'The Origin of Painting: A Problem in the Iconography of Romantic Classicism', *Art Bulletin* 39 (1957), pp. 279–90

Rossi, L. E., 'Rileggendo due opere di Wilamowitz: *Pindaros* e *Griechische Verskunst*', *Annali della Scuola Normale Superiore di Pisa*. Classe di Lettere e Filosofia, serie III, 3.1 (1973), pp. 119–45

Salin, E., *Platon und die griechische Utopie* (Munich: Duncker & Humblot, 1921)
  Um Stefan George (Godesberg: Küpper, 1948)
Saunders, M., *Life-Writing, Autobiografiction, and the Forms of Modern Literature*
  (Oxford University Press, 2010)
Schlegel, F., 'Über das Studium der Griechischen Poesie' (1795–7), *KA*, vol.i,
  pp. 203–367
  'Über die Diotima', *Kritische Friedrich-Schlegel-Ausgabe*, ed. E. Behler, vol. 1
  (Paderborn: Schoeningh, 1979), pp. 70–115
  On the Study of Greek Poetry (Albany, NY: State University of New York Press,
  2001)
Schleiermacher, F. D. E., 'Monologen', in *Friedrich Schleiermacher. Kritische
  Gesamtausgabe*, I.12, ed. G. Meckenstock (Berlin: de Gruyter, 1995), pp.
  323–93
  'Über den Werth des Sokrates als Philosophen', *Abhandlungen der Königlich
  Preussischen Akademie der Wissenschaften zu Berlin 1814/15, Philosophische
  Klasse* (Berlin 1818), pp. 50–68
  'Gelegentliche Gedanken über Universitäten im deutschen Sinn. Nebst
  einem Anhang über eine neu zu errichtende' (1808), in E. Aurich (ed.),
  *Die Idee der deutschen Universität: die fünf Grundschriften aus der Zeit ihrer
  Neugründung durch klassischen Idealismus und romantischen Realismus*
  (Darmstadt: Wissenschaftliche Buchgesellschaft 1956), pp. 219–308
  Über die Philosophie Platons, ed. P. Steiner (Hamburg: Meiner, 1996)
Schlüter, H., *Das Pygmalion-Symbol bei Rousseau, Hamann, Schiller: Drei Studien
  zur Geistesgeschichte der Goethezeit* (Zurich: Juris, 1968)
Schmidt, P. L., 'Zwischen Anpassungsdruck und Autonomiestreben: die
  deutsche Latinistik vom Beginn bis in die 20er Jahre des 20.
  Jahrhunderts', in H. Flashar (ed.), *Altertumswissenschaft in den 20er
  Jahren. Neue Fragen und Impulse* (Stuttgart: Franz Steiner Verlag, 1995),
  pp. 115–82
Schmidt-Linsenhoff, V., 'Dibutadis. Die weibliche Kindheit der Zeichenkunst',
  Kritische Berichte 4 (1996), pp. 7–20
Schnicke, F., *Die Männliche Disziplin: zur Vergeschlechtlichung der Deutschen
  Geschichtswissenschaft 1780–1900* (Göttingen: Wallstein, 2015)
Scholtz, G., 'Schleiermacher im Kontext der neuzeitlichen Hermeneutik-
  Entwicklung', in A. Arndt and J. Dierken (eds.), *Schleiermachers
  Hermeneutik: Interpretationen und Perspektiven*, Berlin: de Gruyter, 2016,
  pp. 1–26
Schott, A. H., *Über das Studium des Homers in niederen und höheren Schulen*
  (Leipzig: Crusius, 1783)
Schrader, J., 'Die Sprache Canaan: Pietistische Sonderterminologie und
  Spezialsemantik als Auftrag der Forschung', in H. Lehmann (ed.),
  Geschichte des Pietismus (Göttingen: Vandenhoeck und Ruprecht, 2004),
  vol. iv, pp. 404–27
Schultze, F., 'Griechische Grammatik', *Jahrbücher für Philologie und Pädagogik* 1.1
  (Leipzig: Teubner, 1826), 381–94

Sheffield, F. C. C., *Plato's Symposium: The Ethics of Desire* (Oxford University Press, 2006)

Simmel, G., 'Exkurs über den Fremden', in his *Soziologie: Untersuchungen über die Formen der Vergesellschaftung* (Berlin: Duncker & Humblot, 1908), pp. 509–12

Smith, B. G., *The Gender of History: Men, Women, and Historical Practice* (Cambridge, MA: Harvard University Press, 1998)

Smith, J. H., 'Dialogic Midwifery in Kleist's *Marquise von O* and the Hermeneutics of Telling the Untold in Kant and Plato', *Proceedings of the Modern Language Association* 100.2 (1985), pp. 203–19

Spoerhase, C. and Dehrmann, M.-G., 'Die Idee der Universität. Friedrich August Wolf und die Praxis des Seminars', *Zeitschrift für Ideengeschichte* 5.1 (2011), pp. 105–17

Stafford, B. M., 'Beauty of the Invisible: Winckelmann and the Aesthetics of Imperceptibility', *Zeitschrift für Kunstgeschichte* 43.1 (1980), 65–78

Steiner, D., 'For Love of a Statue: a Reading of Plato's Symposium 215A-B', *Ramus* 25.2 (1996), 89–111

Steiner, G., *Lessons of the Masters* (Cambridge, MA: Harvard University Press, 2003)

Steingo, G. 'Kostas Velonis' Pinocchio Effects', in *Kostis Velonis*, ed. E. Kountouri (Athens: NEON/Skira, 2019), pp. 99–105

Stoichita, V. I., *A Brief History of the Shadow* (London: Reaktion, 1997)
   The Pygmalion Effect: From Ovid to Hitchcock (University of Chicago Press, 2008)

Strawson, G., 'Against Narrativity', *Ratio* 17(4) (2004), pp. 428–52

Sünderhauf, E. S., *Griechensehnsucht und Kulturkritik: Die deutsche Rezeption von Winckelmanns Antikenideal 1840–1945* (Berlin: Akademie Verlag, 2004)

Szlezak, T. A., 'Schleiermacher's "Einleitungen" zur Platon-Übersetzung von 1804. Ein Vergleich mit Tiedemann und Tennemann', *Antike und Abendland* 43 (1997), pp. 46–62

Szondi, P., *Einführung in die Literarische Hermeneutik*, ed. J. Bollack and H. Stierlin (Frankfurt am Main: Suhrkamp, 1975)

Tarrant, H., 'Improvement by Love: From Aeschines to the Old Academy', in M. Johnson and H. Tarrant, *Alcibiades*, pp. 147–63

Tennemann, W. G., *System der Platonischen Philosophie* (Leipzig: Barth, 1792)

Thesleff, H., *Studies in Platonic Chronology* (Helsinki: Societas Scientiarum Fennica, 1982)

Thiersch, F. W., *Specimen editionis Symposii Platonis. Inest et quaestio qua Alcaeo carmen vindicatur quod vulgo Theocriti putaverunt* (Göttingen: Dieterich, 1808)
   Griechische Grammatik, vorzüglich des homerischen Dialekts (Leipzig: Fleischer, 1812)

Thiersch, H. W. J., *Friedrich Thiersch's Leben*, 2 vols. (Heidelberg: Winter, 1866)

Thouard, D. (ed.), *Aristote au XIXe Siècle* (Villeneuve d'Ascq: Septentrion, 2004)
   'Hamann and the History of Philosophy', in C. R. Ligota and J.-L. Quantin (eds.), *History of Scholarship* (London: Warburg Institute, 2006), pp. 413–31

'Von Schleiermacher zu Trendelenburg. Die Voraussetzungen der Renaissance des Aristoteles im 19. Jahrhundert', in A. M. Baertschi and C. G. King, *Die modernen Väter*, pp. 303–28

Tiedemann, D., *Dialogorum Platonis Argumenta exposita et illustrata* (Biponti [Zweibrücken]: ex typographia societatis, 1786)

Tigerstedt, E. N., *Interpreting Plato* (Stockholm: Almqvist and Wiksell International, 1977)

The Decline and Fall of the Neoplatonic Interpretation of Plato: An Outline and Some Observations (Helsinki: Societas Scientariarum Fennica, 1974)

Tilley, C. Y., *Metaphor and Material Culture* (Oxford: Blackwell, 1999)

Trabant, J., 'Humboldt, eine Fussnote? Wilhelm von Humboldt als Gründergestalt der modernen Altertumswissenschaft', in A. M. Baertschi and C. G. King, *Die modernen Väter*, pp. 25–43

Trapp, M. (ed.), *Socrates from Antiquity to the Enlightenment* (Aldershot: Ashgate, 2007)

Tresch, J., 'Even the Tools Will Be Free: Humboldt's Romantic Technologies', in D. Aubin, C. Bigg, and O. H. Sibum (eds.), *The Heavens on Earth: Observatories and Astronomy in Nineteenth-Century Science and Culture* (Durham, NC: Duke University Press, 2010), pp. 253–85

Turner, F., 'The Homeric Question', in B. Powell and I. Morris (eds.), *A New Companion to Homer* (Leiden: Brill, 1999), pp. 123–45

Turner, J., *Philology: The Forgotten Origins of the Modern Research University* (Princeton University Press, 2014)

Turner, R. S., 'Historicism, Kritik, and the Prussian Professorate, 1790–1840', in M. Bollack, T. Lindken, and H. Wisman (eds.), *Philologie und Hermeneutik im 19. Jahrhundert II* (Göttingen, Vandenhoeck & Ruprecht, 1983), pp. 450–77

Ugolini, G., '"Philologus inter Philologos". Friedrich Nietzsche, die Klassische Philologie und die griechische Tragödie', *Philologus* 147 (2003), pp. 316–42

Usener, H., 'Organisation der wissenschaftlichen Arbeit. Bilder aus der Geschichte der Wissenschaft' (1884), in *Vorträge und Aufsätze* (Leipzig/Berlin: Teubner, 1907), pp. 67–102

'Philologie und Geschichtswissenschaft' (1882), in *Vorträge und Aufsätze*, pp. 1–36

Vick, B., 'Greek Origins and Organic Metaphors: Ideals of Cultural Autonomy in Neohumanist Germany from Winckelmann to Curtius', *Journal of the History of Ideas* 63.3 (2002), pp. 483–500

Vierhaus, R., 'Bildung', in O. Brunner, et al. (eds.), *Geschichtliche Grundbegriffe: historisches Lexikon zur politisch-sozialen Sprache in Deutschland* (Stuttgart: Metzler, 1972–1997), vol. i, pp. 508–51

Waetzoldt, W., 'Carl Justi', in W. Waetzold, *Deutsche Kunsthistoriker. Zweiter Band: von Passavant bis Justi* (Leipzig: Seemann, 1921), pp. 239–78

Ware, O., 'Love Speech', *Critical Inquiry* 34.3 (2008), pp. 491–508

Warren, J., 'Diogenes Laërtius, Biographer of Philosophy', in J. König and T. Whitmarsh (eds.), *Ordering Knowledge in the Roman Empire* (Cambridge University Press, 2007), pp. 133–49

Wegmann, N., *Diskurse der Empfindsamkeit: Zur Geschichte eines Gefühls in der Literatur des 18. Jahrhunderts* (Stuttgart: Metzler, 1988)

Weingarten, H., (ed.), *Eine "andere" Hermeneutik. Georg Misch zum 70. Geburtstag. Festschrift aus dem Jahr 1948* (Bielefeld: transcript, 2005)

Wellmon, C., *Organizing Enlightenment: Information Overload and the Invention of the Modern Research University* (Baltimore: Johns Hopkins University Press, 2015)

Wessels, A., *Ursprungszauber: zur Rezeption von Hermann Useners Lehre zur religiösen Begriffsbildung* (Berlin: de Gruyter, 2003)

Westphalen, K., *Professor Unrat und seine Kollegen: Literarische Porträts des Philologen* (Bamberg: C. C. Buchner, 1986)

White, P., 'Introduction', special issue The Emotional Economy of Science, *Isis* 100.4 (2009), pp. 792–7

von Wilamowitz-Moellendorff, U., *Euripides Herakles*, 2nd ed. (Berlin: Weidmann, 1889 [1868])

'Die Thukydideslegende', *Hermes* 12 (1877), 326–67

Greek Historical Writing and Apollo, Two Lectures Delivered before the University of Oxford, June 3 and 4, 1908, translation by Gilbert Murray (Oxford University Press, 1908)

Sappho und Simonides: Untersuchungen über griechische Lyriker (Berlin: Weidmannsche Buchhandlung, 1913)

Die Ilias und Homer (Berlin: Weidmann, 1916)

Platon (Berlin: Weidmann, 1919)

Geschichte der Philologie (1921), ed. A. Henrichs (Wiesbaden: Springer, 1998)

Pindaros (Berlin: Weidmann, 1922)

'Plutarch als Biograph' (1922), in *Reden und Vorträge*, vol. ii (Berlin 1926), pp. 247–79

Wilson, E., *The Death of Socrates* (Cambridge, MA: Harvard University Press, 2007)

Winckelmann, J. J., *Geschichte der Kunst des Alterthums*, Schriften und Nachlaß, vol. 4, ed. Max Kunze (Mainz: von Zabern, 2002)

Wohl, V., *Love among the Ruins: The Erotics of Democracy in Classical Athens* (Princeton University Press, 2002)

'The Eye of the Beloved: Opsis and Eros in Socratic Pedagogy', in M. Johnson and H. Tarrant, *Alcibiades and the Socratic Lover-Educator*, pp. 45–60

Wolf, F. A., *ΠΛΑΤΩΝΟΣ ΣΥΜΠΟΣΙΟΝ. Platons Gastmahl: ein Dialog* (Leipzig: Schwickert, 1782)

'Darstellung der Alterthumswissenschaft', in *Kleine Schriften in lateinischer und deutscher Sprache*, ed. G. Bernhardy (Leipzig: Waisenhaus, 1869), vol. ii, pp. 808–95

Prolegomena to Homer, ed. A. Grafton, G. Most, and J. Zetzel (Princeton University Press, 1986)

Wundt, M., 'Die Wiederentdeckung Platons im 18. Jahrhundert', *Blätter für deutsche Philosophie* 15 (1941–42), pp. 149–58

Yovel, Y., *Kant and the Philosophy of History* (Cambridge, MA: Harvard University Press, 1980)

Zemon Davis, N., 'History's Two Bodies', *American Historical Review* 93 (1988), pp. 1–30.

Ziolkowski, I., 'Metaphilology', *The Journal of English and Germanic Philology* 104.2 (2005), pp. 239–72

Ziolkowski, T., *German Romanticism and Its Institutions* (Princeton University Press, 1990)

Index